Reading Mastery Plus

Teacher's Guide

Level 1

Siegfried Engelmann
Elaine C. Bruner
Jean Osborn
Karen Lou Seitz Davis

A Division of *The McGraw·Hill Companies*

Columbus, Ohio

NOTE TO THE TEACHER

Your hard work in practicing these *Reading Mastery Plus* exercises will provide you with a valuable set of skills for working with children of all abilities. You will learn how to present and how to correct so that children can master critical skills. You may be surprised to find the correction techniques you learn are often important in working with higher-performing children. If you have mastered the techniques, no child in your beginning reading classroom will fail to learn to read. By achieving this goal, you will provide a valuable service both to your community and to the children.

www.sra4kids.com

SRA/McGraw-Hill

A Division of The McGraw-Hill Companies

Send all inquiries to:
SRA/McGraw-Hill
8787 Orion Place
Columbus, OH 43240-4027

Printed in the United States of America.

ISBN 0-07-569024-1

7 8 9 POH 06

Table of Contents

Table of Contents

Overview of *Reading Mastery Plus*, Level 1

Reading Mastery Plus, Level 1 is a 160-lesson program that provides children with a solid foundation in language concepts and beginning reading skills that build on the *Reading Mastery Plus,* Level K reading program.

Note: The *Reading Mastery Plus,* Level 1 Reading sequence is not a beginning-reading program. It assumes that children have learned basic phonological skills, sound-identification skills, beginning word-reading procedures—for sounding out and identifying words—and a basic reading vocabulary consisting of 50 regularly-spelled words. First-grade children who have not had *Reading Mastery Plus,* Level K need to complete *Fast Start,* a 25-lesson *Reading Mastery Plus*

fast-track supplement that teaches the basic skills children need to begin *Reading Mastery Plus,* Level 1.

Program Components

Reading Mastery Plus, Level 1 includes the following materials:

Teacher Materials

- **Four Teacher Presentation Books** provide the teacher with exercises for directing all the Reading and Language lessons. There is 1 presentation book for Language, and there are 3 presentation books for Reading. The

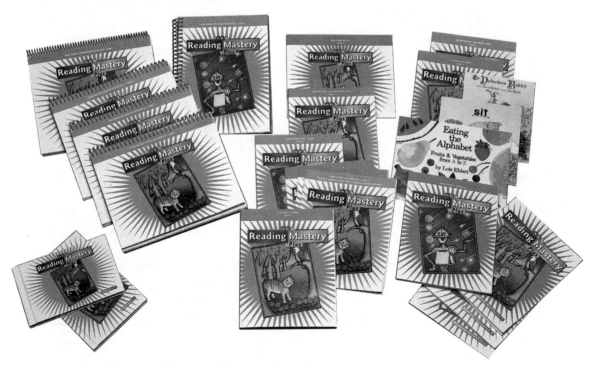

script indicates the teacher wording and the correct student responses for each activity. The script also includes directions for firming correct responses.

- **The Teacher's Guide** provides complete explanations of the program and how to teach it. The guide is divided into several parts, including Reading tracks and Language tracks. Blackline masters for two family letters are also available in the appendices.

  For Reading, the guide contains rationale for the various conventions, details of the Reading skill sequences children learn, placement-test information, lists of all new reading vocabulary words, a sound pronunciation guide, and reproducible material.

  For Language, the guide summarizes the content of the program and describes useful teaching techniques and specific correction procedures for various exercises. The guide also has grouping information and reproducible calendar material.

- **The Literature Guide** supplies lessons, blackline masters, and suggestions for additional materials to be used with the accompanying 15 trade books.

- **The Literature Collection** of fifteen trade books is used in conjunction with teacher-led Literature lessons to reinforce the skills children are learning in the Reading program and to enrich their experiences with literature.

- **The Answer Key** contains answers for the Reading worksheet activities.

- **The Audiocassette Tape** gives instruction on presenting key exercises and demonstrates how to pronounce the sounds for letters and letter combinations.

- **The Acetate Page Protector** enables you to write on the pages of the Reading Presentation Books, when necessary.

- **The Spelling Book** contains 160 Spelling lessons, which begin at lesson 1 and continue through the remainder of the program.

- **A Behavioral Objectives Book** provides specific objectives for each skill taught in the program.

- **A Skills Profile Folder** summarizes the skills taught in the program and provides a space for indicating when a child has mastered each skill. One folder is needed for each child.

- **A Set of Group Progress Indicators** enables you to keep track of the place each group has reached in the program.

- **The Seatwork Book** provides blackline masters that are correlated with the skills taught in the Reading lessons. These worksheets can be completed independently while the teacher works with other students.

- **The Language Arts Guide** contains 50 additional scripted lessons and blackline masters that support the Reading lessons and supply additional writing, editing, listening, viewing, and speaking activities.

- **The Independent Readers Guide** provides blackline masters to accompany the eight Independent Readers. Each blackline master can be completed independently after the student reads the corresponding Independent Reader book.

Student Materials

- **The Storybook** (hardbound) contains illustrated Stories 37–105 and Read-the-item exercises that children read during daily reading lessons.

- **The Textbook** (hardbound) contains word lists, illustrated Stories 106–160, and Read-the-item exercises that children read during daily reading lessons.

- **Four Workbooks** (1 Language, 3 Reading) contain consumable student worksheets for Reading and Language lessons. The early stories (lessons 1–36) appear in the first Reading Workbook (Workbook A).

- **Eight Independent Readers** correlate with reading stories in orthography and vocabulary.

Reading Mastery Plus, Level 1

Program Summary

READING

Total number of Reading lessons:	160
Number of Mastery Tests (Reading lessons 6–100):	20
Number of rate and accuracy Reading Checkouts (Reading lessons 54–160):	23
Number of special take-home stories (Reading lessons 41–105):	16
Reading lesson length: Group reading: 25–30 minutes daily	
Independent activity: 15–20 minutes daily	

LANGUAGE

Total number of Language lessons:	145
Language lesson length: Group lesson: 15 minutes daily	
Independent activity: 5–10 minutes daily	

OTHER

Number of Literature lessons:	15
10th-lesson Literature selections:	30 minutes
Spelling lesson length:	5-10 minutes daily

READING MATERIALS

- **Number of Storybooks** (hardbound): **1** (lessons 1–105)
- **Number of Textbooks** (hardbound): **1** (lessons 106–160)
- **Number of Workbooks: 3** (consumable worksheets)
- **Number of Teacher Presentation Books: 3** (All components are coordinated. The first book for the three components present lessons 1–50; the next, 51–105; and the last, 106–160.)
- **Answer Key**

- **Spelling Book Component:** 1 Teacher Presentation Book.

- **Seatwork Book** (blackline masters)

- **Independent Readers Guide: 1** **Independent Readers: 8**

LANGUAGE MATERIALS

- **Number of Workbooks: 1** (consumable worksheets)
- **Number of Teacher Presentation Books: 1**

- **Teacher's Guide**

- **Literature Collection:** 15 trade books and 1 **Literature Guide** containing instructions and blackline masters.

- **Language Arts Guide**

Side B for Level 1
- **Audiocassette Tape**
Side A for Fast Start

MATERIALS

- **Total number of hardbound student readers: 2** (1 Storybook and 1 Textbook)
- **Total number of workbooks: 4** (1 Language workbook, 3 Reading workbooks)
- **Total number of Teacher Presentation Books: 4** (1 Language book. 3 Reading books having all components coordinated; the first book presents lessons 1–50; the next, 51–105; and the last, 106–160.)

- **Teacher's Guide**
- **Literature Component:** 15 trade books and a Literature Guide containing instructions and blackline masters
- **Spelling Book**
- **Answer Key**
- **Audiocassette Tape**
- **Acetate Page Protector**
- **Behavioral Objectives Book**
- **Skills Profile Folder**
- **Set of Group Progress Indicators**
- **Seatwork Book**
- **Language Arts Guide**
- **Independent Readers:** 8 independent readers and a guide containing instructions and blackline masters

About This Teacher's Guide

This Teacher's Guide gives the teacher an overview of the *Reading Mastery Plus,* Level 1 program. The guide provides information about the use of each component and gives information about teaching the 160 lessons, about appropriately placing students in the program, and about responding to specific student-performance problems.

Reading Mastery Plus, Level 1 is research-based and has been completely field-tested. By carefully reading and studying this guide before teaching *Reading Mastery Plus,* Level 1, you will be well prepared to guide children successfully through the program.

Scope and Content

Reading Mastery Plus, **Level 1 provides children with over 145 lessons of Language concepts and applications and with 160 Reading lessons.**

The program is designed for first-grade children who have completed *Reading Mastery Plus,* Level K and who need careful instruction. These children are not highly familiar with the language of instruction and may not be well practiced in learning from adults. Statistically, they tend to fail to learn to read in a timely manner and often lag well behind grade-level norms for reading, writing, and spelling. These children need the kind of careful attention to detail that *Reading Mastery Plus,* Level 1 provides. The program is designed to start where the children are, to present all the skills they will need to decode well and understand what they read, to teach basic spelling skills, and to lay a solid foundation for writing and oral-language expression.

The **Language lessons** teach children basic language conventions and various problem-solving strategies. Children learn basic information, facts such as calendar facts, and concepts, ranging from the most elementary statement concepts to problem-solving and sophisticated concepts.

The Reading and Language activities may be scheduled during the same period, or the Reading may be presented at a separate time. **Language lessons** require 15 minutes per day, and the **Reading lessons** require about 25–30 minutes per day. The daily **Spelling lessons** component takes 5 to 10 minutes.

Why Language?

Children who have gone through *Reading Mastery Plus,* Level K have learned many basic language conventions and concepts that they have later applied to their reading. They have learned to follow a variety of instructions involving words like **first, next, before, under, touch, move, draw,** and so on. These children have also learned to produce a wide variety of verbal responses. They have learned to say complete sentences, to use basic pronouns and plural endings appropriately, and to communicate to tell how things are the same or how they are different.

A goal of instruction in the early primary grades is to make sure that the children's language skills always remain ahead of their reading skills. **Children should never read a story that they would not thoroughly understand if it were presented as an oral story.** Unlike sophisticated learners who have well developed reading skills that permit them to learn extensively from what they read, the early reader is not well prepared to read material that presents ideas or descriptions the learner would not understand if the material were presented orally.

For at-risk children to meet the challenge of beginning reading, they need continuing language instruction. They need facts and information about people and places. They need practice in following a variety of directions and in comparing things. They also need a certain level of "cultural literacy" if they are to have the background knowledge needed to understand the setting of some stories and what motivates the characters.

The *Reading Mastery Plus,* Level 1 Language lessons build this foundation. They start with a review of the simpler concepts and language skills introduced in *Reading Mastery Plus,* Level K and introduce increasingly sophisticated applications. In Level 1, children learn about absurdities, how to draw conclusions from facts, how to make intelligent predictions about what may occur next, and how to formulate analogies. They learn about common classification labels for both things and words. They learn to apply synonyms, opposites, homonyms, comparatives and superlatives. They learn about maps, directions, and calendar facts. They learn about materials things are made of and parts things have. Most important of all, the children learn to apply what they learn to figure out the answers to problems.

The following section details the design strategies of the Reading component, which is the major part of *Reading Mastery Plus,* Level 1.

Level 1 Reading Design Strategies

At the end of *Reading Mastery Plus,* Level K, children read simple one-sentence stories in their workbook and answer simple comprehension questions.

Here's an example of a story from *Reading Mastery Plus,* Level K Lesson 144 (Fast Start lesson 21).

All reading words and story words appear in the special *Reading Mastery* orthography, or print. The system is designed to point out the regularities in words. This special *Reading Mastery* orthography has joined letters (such as **th**) and long lines over long vowels (such as **ē**, which is pronounced as the ending sound in the word **me**).

Introduction

Like many other Reading programs, *Reading Mastery Plus,* Level 1 includes reading skill exercises, activities associated with beginning decoding, work with symbol identification, rhyming, comprehension activities, and so forth. Unlike many other programs, however, *Reading Mastery Plus,* Level 1 presents each of these activities in a carefully programmed sequence.

1. The exercises are structured as simply as possible. The vocabulary used by the teacher is reduced. The procedures that are followed with one exercise are followed with a similar exercise so that the children can see how the exercises are the same.

2. The practice the children receive is carefully controlled and realistic. For example, symbols like **b, o,** and **p** are introduced at the rate of one every three or four days, so that the children receive enough practice to master each of the symbols. The practice for every other skill the children are taught is controlled in a similar way.

3. The sequence of skills is structured so that the children master all the skills

they need for later, more complicated exercises.

4. A final aspect of the Reading (and Language) program design has to do with the teacher's behavior. What the teacher does and says is specified. The teacher is not given general instructions; rather, the teacher is provided with the exact words that are to be used when presenting each of the exercises. Other behaviors—pointing, signaling the group to respond, and the like—are specified precisely. The program indicates where the children are likely to make mistakes and precisely what the teacher should do to correct each mistake.

The reason for the attention to detail in the design of the program is that details make a difference. Well-intentioned teachers frequently confuse children, particularly lower-performing children, with explanations that are beyond the children's understanding. General teaching suggestions don't give the teacher enough direction and frequently lead to activities that don't reach every child. Poorly sequenced exercises may further confuse the children, delay their learning, and perhaps result in their losing interest in reading.

The *Reading Mastery Plus,* Level 1 programs prevent these problems from developing. A teacher who follows the program carefully will be able to teach children who would be likely to fail if less care were used.

Does it follow that the Reading program is appropriate only for low performers? Not at all. It is appropriate for any child—

regardless of age—who has not mastered the basic decoding and comprehension skills. It is designed for the bright and curious child, as well as for the slower-learning child. (The child who speaks no English should be taught language skills before starting *Reading Mastery Plus.*)

Children can proceed through the program as fast as they are capable of moving. The extremely low performers will probably not complete the entire program by the end of the school year, although they should complete at least 130 of the 160 lessons.

Decoding Skills

Reading Mastery Plus, Levels K and 1, introduce children to a sounding-out analysis of words. Teaching the children to sound out words has these advantages:

1. Children learn more words from a given amount of teaching. If children are taught ten words as sight words, the children are capable of reading only ten words. If children learn ten symbols introduced in *Reading Mastery Plus* as sounds, they are capable of reading hundreds of regularly-spelled words composed of those sounds.

2. The emphasis on sounds assures that children attend to the details of words, or how the words are spelled. This information becomes very important when children are confronted with words that are similar in "shape," such as: **when, then, where,** and **there.**

3. Although the sounding-out procedure is replaced with a procedure for reading the fast way, beginning with Lesson 21

the sounding-out procedure serves as an important backup, particularly when children read independently. By using the sounding-out procedure, the children can verify the pronunciation of words that they may not be able to identify by sight.

4. All reading words and story words appear in the special *Reading Mastery* orthography, or print. The system is designed to point out the regularities in words. The special *Reading Mastery* orthography has joined letters (such as **th** and **sh**), long lines over long vowels (such as **ē**, which is pronounced as the ending sound in the word **me**), and small letters that are not to be pronounced (such as the **a** in the word **ēₐt**.)

Before children begin sounding out words, they work on *pre-skills.* These are the oral skills and the symbol-identification skills that are needed when children sound out a word by identifying each symbol in a word as a "sound" and saying the word fast. By the end of Level K (or Fast Start), children have learned 13 sounds in isolation. They have practiced saying words slowly and saying them fast. They have also practiced rhyming by starting with different beginning sounds and saying a specified word ending. They have practiced sequencing symbol–action events so that they develop a general skill of combining the "first event" with the "next event."

Throughout the program children continue to practice the Level K skills. For instance, children continue to practice rhyming and symbol identification of earlier-taught sounds. Also, after Level 1

lesson 21, children continue to read some words by sounding them out.

Note that as part of the word-reading practice, children learn words that are "irregular" as well as regularly-spelled words. The word **was** is irregular because it is pronounced in a way that is not predicted by the sounds of the individual letters. (The word **was** does not rhyme with **gas,** which is what it would do if it were regular.)

Comprehension Skills

Just as the decoding skills are sequenced so that the children work first on easy examples and then on more difficult applications, the comprehension skills are also sequenced. Comprehension skills include picture comprehension and sequencing events.

After children are introduced to story reading, they answer questions while reading the story. When the story is completed, the students predict what the story picture will show. They then answer questions about the story picture. Children are introduced to written reading comprehension items starting with Lesson 66. These items become increasingly complex as the children become more skilled. Written story comprehension items start with Lesson 77.

Finally, games that require the students to follow instructions are introduced at Lesson 96. To play these games, the children must read carefully and must understand what they read.

For activities that relate to decoding and comprehension, see the following charts.

Program Activities That Relate to Word Decoding

FAST START/LEVEL K	LEVEL 1		
Pre-skills	**Sounding out words (Lessons 1–20)**	**Reading words the fast way (Lessons 21–105)**	**Word analysis (Lessons 106–160)**

Sound pronunciation
Symbol action
  sequencing
Oral blending:
  Saying words slowly
  Saying words fast
Rhyming
Symbol identification
  (as sounds)
	Sound pronunciation
	
	Rhyming
	Symbol identification
	
	Reading vocabulary
	  (word lists)
	
	Story reading
	  (workbook)
		Symbol identification
		
		Reading vocabulary
		  (word parts)
		
		Story reading
		  (storybook)
		Individual checkouts
		  for rate and accuracy
			Symbol identification
			  (sound combinations)
			Reading vocabulary:
			  Word parts
			  Final-e words
			  Lists in textbook
			Story reading
			  (textbook)

Independent workbook practice	Independent workbook practice	Independent workbook practice	Independent workbook practice

Program Activities That Relate to Comprehension

FAST START/LEVEL K	LEVEL 1	
Pre-skills	**Lessons**	**Comprehension activities**

Sequencing events
  (symbol action)
 	
Picture comprehension
  (oral)
	1–160
	21–160
	77–160
	66–160
	1–160
	
	96–142
	
	113–160
	156–160
		Comprehension of vocabulary words
		Story comprehension—oral
		Story comprehension—written
		Reading comprehension—written
		Picture comprehension
		  (oral and words for pictures)
		Comprehension games
		  (read the items)
		Following instructions
		Story-picture items

Written Work

The children begin their work on Reading worksheets (perforated sheets bound in workbook form) on the first day of the program. The worksheets provide up to 20 minutes a day of independent work that relates to the skills the children are learning in the program. The program leads the children through each new kind of exercise for a few days; then the children do the exercises independently. Worksheet activities include story sentence copying, sound-writing practice on the new and review sounds, work with pattern recognition, and matching exercises. Reading comprehension and picture comprehension exercises relate to the stories the children are reading. Many of the activities prepare the children for taking standardized tests.

The written work also provides a means of teaching the children to work independently. After new skills are introduced, the children complete their worksheets by themselves. This allows you time to work with the other groups.

Scheduling and Grouping for Reading Lessons

Time Requirements for Reading

Lessons should be scheduled on every available school day. The children are divided into small, homogeneous groups for instruction. The teacher and student times required each day for all of the reading activities are as follows:

Activity	Teacher Time	Student Time
Group Instruction	25–30 minutes for each group	25–30 minutes for each group
Independent Work	——	15–20 minutes for each group
Work Check	5 minutes for each group	——

Scheduling the Daily Reading Lessons

Schedule reading for the same time each day.

- Allow thirty minutes for teacher-directed work with each reading group.

- Allow another fifteen to twenty minutes each day for the children to work independently at their desks on the Reading worksheet activities.

- Allow twenty minutes each day to check the independent work of the children and to remedy problems. Note that you are not merely to mark papers and hand them back to the children. If a child makes an error, you are to diagnose the problem and actually correct the source of the error by firming the weak skill.

Grouping

Here is a guide for grouping children according to their performance on the placement test and in-program tests.

1. Divide the class into no more than three groups.

2. Make the lowest-performing group the smallest. Ideally, there should be no more than five or six children in this group.

3. The highest-performing group should be the largest.

4. Regrouping should occur periodically.

Testing Throughout the Year

In-Program Mastery Tests		
Individual Rate-and-Accuracy Checkouts		54-56 61 66 71 76 81 86 91 95 100 105 110 115 120 125 130 135 140 145 150 155 160
Individual Mastery Tests	6 11 16 21 26 31 36 41 46 51 56 61 66 71 76 81 86 91 95 100	
Group Accuracy Tests		115 121 131

Throughout the program, children are given in-program mastery tests and checkouts. The tests are short, generally test only one skill, and are given after specified lessons in the program. They are administered separately from the regular reading lesson.

There are 20 individual Mastery Tests, three Group Accuracy Tests, and over 20 rate-and-accuracy Reading Checkouts. These tests appear in the Presentation Books at the points at which they are to be presented.

The first mastery test is to be given after lesson 6; after that, a test is scheduled after every five lessons. There is a note at the end of each lesson that is to be followed by a test.

The mastery tests give you feedback on the effectiveness of your teaching, they serve as a backup for your daily evaluation of the children's performance, and they provide information for regrouping the children at later points in the program.

Regrouping

Any child who repeatedly fails items on the in-program mastery tests should be placed in a lower reading group. Repeated failure indicates that the child cannot maintain the pace set by other members of the group. If a child is already in the lowest-performing group, try to work with the child individually. If there are several teachers using *Reading Mastery Plus,* Level 1 in your school, consider forming a group of these low performers and assigning them to one teacher. This will permit the children to receive the individual attention they need. It will also allow the groups from which they have been removed to progress at a faster rate.

On the other hand, a child who entered the program with few skills may learn quickly. If a child consistently performs better than most of the other children in the group, the child should be moved to a higher group.

Suggested points for regrouping are after individual Mastery Test 4 (lesson 21), after Mastery Test 8 (lesson 41), after Mastery Test 14 (lesson 71), and after Group Accuracy Test 1 (lesson 115), Test 2 (lesson 121), and Test 3 (lesson 131).

Plan to regroup the children several times during the year. Here are the steps to follow for identifying the children who should be placed in another group:

1. A child who passes nearly every test and who performs well in the group should be considered for placement in a higher group.

2. A child who passes most of the tests is appropriately grouped.

3. A child who continually fails tests should be considered for placement in a lower-performing group.

4. A child who continually fails tests and who is in the bottom group should receive additional help on critical skills.

Group Performance

It is important to complete a lesson each day with each group, even with the lowest performers. With the highest performers, it is possible to complete five lessons in four days. When some new skills are introduced, however, you may find that if you firm the skill so that all children can perform, you will not be able to complete the entire lesson. When the choice is between firming all the children and completing the lesson, choose the firming. The best procedure is to firm the children when new skills are first introduced; however, the number of lessons that cannot be completed during the allotted time should be small compared to those that can be successfully completed (with all children firm on every exercise), particularly if you make sure that the children are firm early in the program.

There are 160 lessons in *Reading Mastery Plus*, Level 1. Below are reasonable expectations for the performance of different groups of children. These expectations are based on a school year of 170 available teaching days.

Highest-performing groups	210 lessons
Middle-performing groups	170 lessons
Lowest-performing groups	120–130 lessons

Note that the highest-performing groups and the middle-performing groups should complete *Reading Mastery Plus*, Level 1 in less than a school year. Upon completion of the Level 1 program, they should continue into *Reading Mastery Plus*, Level 2 until the end of the school year.

Teaching the Program

How to Use the Presentation Scripts

All four Presentation Books provide the teacher with directions for presenting each exercise. The three Reading Presentation Books, Books A, B, and C, also provide display material—the symbols and words—to be shown to the children.

The Language component and the Reading component are organized into tracks (such as Actions or Sounds), formats, and exercises. Each *track* extends through several lessons. A *format* is one segment of a track—one step in the programming of a skill. It is a pattern of teaching steps repeated in a number of successive lessons.

The Presentation Books are divided into lessons. The number of the lesson appears at the bottom of every page. The first page of the lesson is indicated by the word *Lesson* at the top preceding the number; the last page of the lesson is indicated by the words *End of Lesson* followed by the number of the lesson.

In each lesson the track headings, such as *Sounds, Reading Vocabulary,* or *Story,* indicate the major skills to be developed in the tasks that follow. Track headings are printed in boldface capitals.

The exercises that you present are numbered, and the number of each exercise is followed by a brief description of that exercise's objectives.

Here are the exercise conventions:

- What you are to say appears in blue type.
  You say this.

- What you do appears in parentheses. (You do this.)

- The responses of the children appear in italics.
  Children say this.

- As you progress through the Reading lessons, you will notice that there are black lines above and below some of the exercise headings. These lines signal the introduction of a new Reading format. A new format presents a significant change in the method of presenting an exercise.

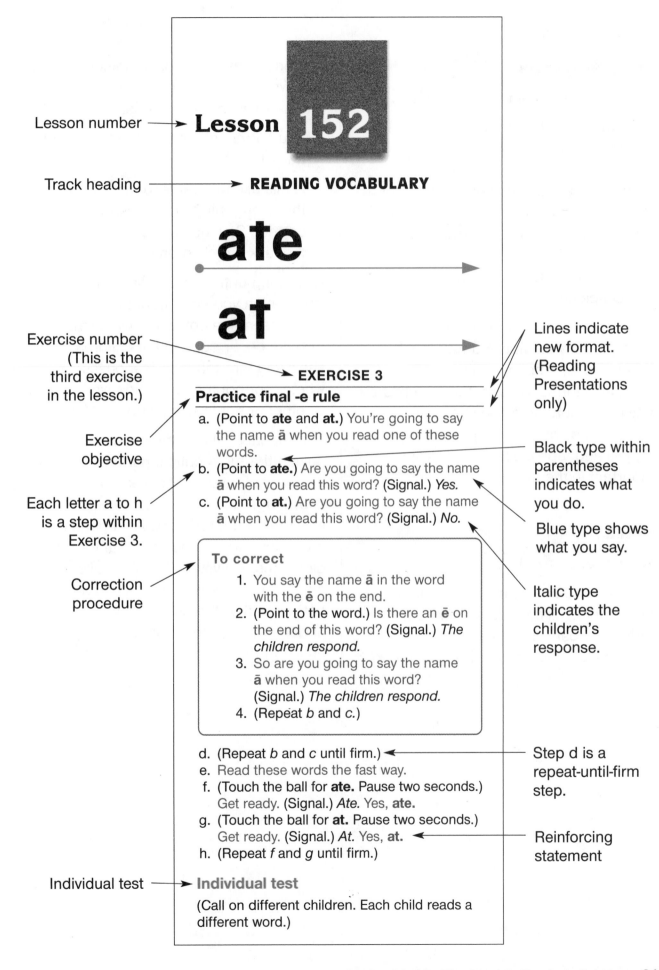

Lesson number →

Lesson 152

Track heading →

READING VOCABULARY

ate

at

Exercise number (This is the third exercise in the lesson.)

EXERCISE 3

Exercise objective

Practice final -e rule

Each letter a to h is a step within Exercise 3.

a. (Point to **ate** and **at**.) You're going to say the name ā when you read one of these words.

b. (Point to **ate**.) Are you going to say the name ā when you read this word? (Signal.) *Yes.*

c. (Point to **at**.) Are you going to say the name ā when you read this word? (Signal.) *No.*

Correction procedure

> **To correct**
> 1. You say the name ā in the word with the ē on the end.
> 2. (Point to the word.) Is there an ē on the end of this word? (Signal.) *The children respond.*
> 3. So are you going to say the name ā when you read this word? (Signal.) *The children respond.*
> 4. (Repeat *b* and *c*.)

d. (Repeat *b* and *c* until firm.)
e. Read these words the fast way.
f. (Touch the ball for **ate.** Pause two seconds.) Get ready. (Signal.) *Ate.* Yes, **ate.**
g. (Touch the ball for **at.** Pause two seconds.) Get ready. (Signal.) *At.* Yes, **at.**
h. (Repeat *f* and *g* until firm.)

Individual test →

Individual test

(Call on different children. Each child reads a different word.)

Lines indicate new format. (Reading Presentations only)

Black type within parentheses indicates what you do.

Blue type shows what you say.

Italic type indicates the children's response.

Step d is a repeat-until-firm step.

Reinforcing statement

Group Responses

(Signal.), (Tap.), and (Tap ___ times.)

Many tasks call for group responses. If children respond together with brisk unison responses, you receive good information about whether the children are performing correctly. The simplest way to direct children to respond together is to signal or tap in a predictable cadence—just like the cadence in a musical piece.

Think of signals this way: If you use them correctly, they provide you with much diagnostic information. A weak response provides information about which children may need more help and suggests whether you should repeat a task or not. Signals and taps are, therefore, very important in the program.

Firming

(Repeat until firm.)

When children make mistakes, you correct them. A correction may occur during any part of the teacher's presentation that calls for the children to respond. It may also occur in connection with what the children are writing. Here are the rules for corrections.

- You correct a mistake as soon as you hear it.

- A mistake on oral responses is saying the wrong thing or not responding. To correct: Say the correct answer. Repeat the task the children missed.

Repeating until firm is based on the information you need about the children. You present the context in which the mistake occurred, and the children can show you through their responses whether or not the correction worked and whether or not they are firm.

The repeat-until-firm direction appears only in the most critical parts of exercises. It usually focuses on knowledge and skills that are very important for later work. As a general procedure, follow the repeat-until-firm directions. However, if you're quite sure that the mistake was a "glitch" and does not mean that the children lack understanding, don't follow the repeat-until-firm directions.

Worksheet 124

EXERCISE 6

OPPOSITES

a. (Hold up worksheet. Point to top half.) Find the words in the box at the top of your worksheet. ✓
- I'll read those words. Touch and follow along: **rough, tall, old, pull.** ✓

b. Your turn. Touch the first word. ✓ ← *Check what the children are doing.*
  What word? (Signal.) *Rough.*
- Next word. ✓
  What word? (Signal.) *Tall.*
- Next word. ✓
  What word? (Signal.) *Old.*
- Last word. ✓
  What word? (Signal.) *Pull.*
- (Repeat step b until firm.) ← *Firming*

c. You're going to write words that tell the opposite.
- Touch number 1. ✓
- That word is **push.** What word? (Signal.) *Push.* ← *Group response*
- Everybody, what's the opposite of **push?** (Signal.) *Pull.*

d. The word **pull** is in the word box. Copy that word right after the word **push.** (Observe children and give feedback.) ← *Sample more children and give feedback.*

rough	tall	old	pull

1. push _____

2. young _____

3. smooth _____

4. short _____

Pacing Your Presentation

(Observe children and give feedback.) and ✔

You should pace your verbal presentation at a normal speaking rate—as if you were telling somebody something important.

Note: The presentation works much better and the inflections are far more appropriate if you pretend that you're talking to an adolescent, not a young child. Make your message sound important. The most typical mistakes teachers make are going too slowly or talking as if to preschoolers.

A ✔ is a note to check what the children are doing. It requires only a second or two. Monitor the responses of several "average-performing" children. If their responses are acceptable, proceed with the presentation.

The **(Observe children and give feedback.)** direction implies a more elaborate response. You sample more children and give feedback—not only to individual children, but also to the group.

Here are the basic rules for what to do and what not to do when you observe and give feedback.

- Make sure that you can see all the children's papers from where you are sitting.

- As soon as children start to work, start observing. As you observe, make comments to the whole group. Focus these comments on children who are following directions and working quickly and accurately. Wow, a couple of children are almost finished. I haven't seen one mistake so far.

- When children put their pencils down to indicate that they are finished, acknowledge them (for example, by nodding).

- If you observe mistakes, do **not** provide a great deal of individual help. Point out any mistakes. For instance, if a child misspells **hats,** say, You did not write the word **hats** correctly. If a child transposes a pair of letters say, You've written all of the letters for **hats,** but they aren't in the right order. Read what you wrote and get the letters in the right order. If a child writes some letters backwards, say, One of your letters is facing the wrong way. Fix it so it is facing the right way. If the child can't figure out which letter is facing the wrong way, write the word on the board and tell the child, Copy these letters.

- When higher-performing children do their independent activity, you may want to go over any parts of the lesson with the children who had trouble with the structured work (made mistakes or didn't finish). Make sure that you check all the independent work of lower performers and give them feedback. Show them what they did wrong. Keep your explanations simple. The more you talk, the more you'll probably confuse them.

If there are serious problems with the lesson, repeat it during the next period. Do not proceed with the program if children are making a high rate of errors.

General Teaching Strategies

Because *Reading Mastery Plus,* Level 1 is carefully designed, it is possible to teach all the children the desired behaviors of being self-reliant, following instructions, and working fast and accurately. If you follow the management rules for giving feedback, by the time the children have reached lesson 37, they should be able to find parts in the Storybook or on the Worksheet and navigate between the Storybook and Worksheets within a reasonable amount of time.

How to Set Up the Group

1. Seat the children in a semicircle in front of you. Sit so that you can observe every child in the group, as well as the other members of the class who are engaged in independent work. Children in the group should sit on chairs, not at desks.

2. **Reading group only** Test to see that all children can see the Reading Presentation Book. Do this by holding your head next to the book and looking to see whether you can see the eyes of all the children. If you have to look almost sideways from the book to see a child's eyes, that child won't be able to see what is on the page.

3. Keep all children within touching distance. There will be times during the lesson when you will want to hand the Reading Presentation Book to a child, or touch a child to reinforce him or her. This will be easier if they are all within arm's reach of you. Sit close to the children and group them close together.

4. Place the lowest performers directly in front of you (in the first row if there is more than one row). Seat the highest performers on the ends of the group (or in the second row). You will naturally look most frequently at the children seated directly in front of you. You want to teach until each child is firm. If you are constantly looking at the lower performers, you will be in a position to know when they are firm. When the lowest performers are firm, the rest of the group will be firm.

5. Seat the children so that cliques are broken. Assign the seats. The children should sit in their assigned seats each day. This will allow you to separate disruptive buddies, and allow you to learn which voices to listen to during the presentation.

Getting into the Lesson

1. Introduce the rules that the group is to follow on the first day that you begin a lesson. Tell the children what they are expected to do. Summarize the rules: "Sit tall, look at the book, and talk big." Note that these rules express precisely what the children are supposed to do. Reinforce the children for following the rules.

2. Get into the lesson *quickly.* If the group is shy or tends to present behavior problems, begin by telling the children "Stand up . . . touch your nose . . ." until all of them are responding without hesitation. This activity gets the children responding and establishes you as directing what they are to do. Then quickly present the first exercise. The

same technique can be used if the children's attention lags during the presentation. It will break the pace and again establish you as directing what the children are to do.

3. Present each exercise until the children are firm. If the first exercise is a Sounds task, do not move on to the second exercise in the lesson until all the children are firm. The best time to get them all responding together until firm is the first time the task is presented. This establishes what your criterion of performance is. Further information on teaching to criterion appears below.

4. Use clear signals. All signals have the same purpose: to trigger a simultaneous response from the group. All signals have the same rationale: if you can get the group to respond simultaneously (with no child leading the others) you will get information about the performance of all the children, not just those who happen to answer first.

Practice the specific signal for each new exercise before practicing the rest of the exercise. Practice the signals until they are natural and you can do them without concentrating on them. The execution of a clear, easy-to-follow signal will result in efficient teaching of all the exercises.

5. Pace exercises appropriately. Pacing is one of the more difficult presentational skills to master. Pacing is the rate at which different parts of the exercise are presented. All portions of an exercise should not be presented at the same rate.

Different pacing is specified throughout the guide. Many of the formats contain such instructions as "pause one second," or "pause three seconds." Note that all signals are paced with the same timing. The children learn that the signal will follow one second after you stop talking in an exercise. Keep this interval constant.

6. Reinforce the children's good performance. Make your praise specific. If the children are working hard on a difficult skill, tell them so. You are working hard and this is tough. Keep at it—you'll get it. If they just completed a Sounds page with no errors, reinforce them, Wow! You know every sound on the page. If they have just said the sounds in *am* correctly, say Yes, **am.** Repeating the children's correct response is very reinforcing.

Praise them for following the rules within the group. If they are all talking up, say, Good talking. I can hear everybody. Catch the children in the act of being good and reinforce them for responding correctly.

Early in the program, some of your lower-performing groups may not respond to verbal praise. These children may need more tangible rewards. Do not assume, however, that the children need tangible rewards. Reinforce them first with verbal praise and a handshake or a pat on the back. If they do not respond to this kind of praise, find something that works—stickers, raisins, or points accumulated toward a small reward. Remember, you have to find something that they like—something that they are willing to work for. If you have to use tangible rewards, always tell the children why they are receiving a star or a raisin. Say Good talking big, Mary, as you hand Mary a raisin.

Teaching to Criterion

At the conclusion of any exercise every child should be able to perform the exercise independently, without any need for corrections. Children are "at criterion" or "firm" on an exercise only when they can perform quickly and confidently with the correct response. Your goal is to teach so that every child is at criterion.

It is easier to bring the children to criterion on the first introduction of a format than it will be at a later time in the program, because they haven't performed the exercise incorrectly many times or heard others performing it incorrectly.

The initial formats in each track include a demonstration by you of the response that the children are to make. This allows the children to hear the correct response the first time that the exercise is presented.

Let the children know what your criterion is. Keep on an exercise until you can honestly say to them, Terrific. Everybody read every word correctly. The stricter your criterion, the fewer the exercises your group will have to repeat after taking the mastery tests.

Individual Turns

Individual turns are specified in the exercises or under the heading *Individual Test.* There are several rules to follow when administering individual turns:

1. Present individual turns only after the group is firm. If you go to individual turns too soon, many of the children will not be able to give a firm response. If you wait until the children are firm on group responses, the chances are much better that each will be able to give a firm response on an individual turn.

2. Give most of your individual turns to the lower-performing children in the group—those children seated directly in front of you. By watching these children during the group practice of the exercise, you can tell when they are ready to perform individually. When these children can perform the exercise without further need of correction, you can safely assume that the other children in the group will be able to perform the exercise.

3. Individual turns are not specified in all exercises. If you are in doubt about the performance of any children on these exercises, present quick individual turns. Always include the individual turns for exercises in which they are specified.

4. The following procedure is recommended for administering individual turns once the group responses on an exercise are firm. First you can state: Time for individual turns. Then <u>focus</u> on the exercise for the students to practice. Finally, call on an individual student to respond to the exercise. This procedure helps to keep the entire group alert to you and practicing the exercise until a specific student's name is called.

General Corrections

The major difference between the average *Reading Mastery Plus* teacher, who teaches <u>most</u> of the children, and the outstanding teacher, who teaches <u>all</u> of the children, is the ability to correct.

Information on general corrections appears below. Information on specific corrections is included with the discussions of individual exercises later in this guide. Study the procedures and practice them until you can execute them immediately, without hesitation. Corrections must be automatic. Failure to get each child to pay attention or allowing part of the group not to respond will result in some of the children not learning.

Unacceptable behavior that calls for correction includes nonattending, nonresponding, signal violations, and response errors.

1. *Nonattending.* This behavior occurs when a child is not looking where he or she should be looking during an exercise. For example, if a child is not attending to the sound to which you are pointing, correct by looking at the nonattender and saying:

   Watch my finger.
   Let's try it again.
   Return to the beginning of the exercise.

   Reinforce the children who are paying attention. Let them know you are watching all of them all the time. Always return to the beginning of the exercise to enforce your rule that everyone has to pay attention at all times.

2. *Nonresponding.* This behavior occurs when a child fails to answer when you signal a response. It is dangerous to overlook nonresponding. The children may learn to just listen the first time an exercise is presented and then join in later. They will learn dependence on other children and get the idea that they need not answer along with the rest of the group. If a child is not responding, correct the child by saying:

   I have to hear everybody.
   Return to the beginning of the exercise.

   Failure to return to the beginning of the exercise will teach the children that you really do not mean that you "have to hear everybody." It is very important to enforce this rule from the first day of instruction so that the children learn you are expecting everyone to perform on every exercise.

3. *Signal Violations.* A signal violation occurs when the child responds either before or too long after the signal, or during the portion of the exercise in which you are demonstrating. For example, a child might begin to say a sound after you have touched it and after the other children respond. The lower-performing children are most likely to violate the signal, because they will tend to wait for the higher-performing children in a group to respond first.

   If children respond either early or late, you will not get information from every child. Remember that the purpose of a signal is to trigger a simultaneous group response. If you fail to enforce the signal, you will have to resort to a great many individual turns to find out which children are firm and which children are weak.

Correct signal-violation mistakes in Sounds, for example, by telling the children what they did, repeating the signal, and then returning to the beginning of the exercise:

You're early, or You're late, or You didn't say it when I touched it, or I stopped touching it, but you kept saying it.
Watch my finger. Get ready. **Touch.**
Children respond as you touch.
Now, let's try it again.
Return to the beginning of the exercise.

Only if you consistently return to the beginning of the exercise after each signal-violation correction will the children learn to attend to your signal. Once they learn that you will repeat the exercise until they are all responding on signal, they will attend much more closely to the signal.

If you find that you are spending a lot of time correcting nonattending, nonresponding, and signal violations, your pacing is probably too slow, or your pacing of the signal inconsistent. The object of a signal is not to keep the children sitting on the edges of their seats, never knowing when they will have to respond next. The pacing of the signal should be perfectly predictable.

4. *Response Errors.* A response error is any response inconsistent with the one called for in the exercise. If you are teaching sounds, and the children say *mmm* when you touch under **a,** this is a response error. They may have followed your signal and said the sound just when you touched under it, but their response is inconsistent with the symbol you are pointing to.

Response errors are specific to the individual exercise. The correction for each response error, therefore, must be specific. The children's mistakes can be anticipated. Many of the corrections that will be most often required appear on the page with the appropriate format in the Presentation Book. The most common mistakes that children make are also identified, and the appropriate correction supplied, in the discussion of specific formats later in this guide. It is very important to practice these corrections. You must be able to present the correction without hesitation when the mistake occurs. By practicing the corrections, you will be well prepared for the common mistakes that the children will make.

The first formats in almost every track are written so that you first demonstrate, or *model*, the response the children are to make. Frequently the next step is a teacher *lead*, in which you respond with the children. Leading is a very powerful technique. It gives the children the benefit of responding with you until they are confident in the response they are to make. Many exercises require a number of teacher leads before the children are producing firm responses. The lead is a correction. Don't be afraid to continue leading until the children are producing the response with you. Following the teacher lead, present a *test* in which the children produce the response on their own. The final step in any correction is a *delayed* test. Go back to an earlier step in the *exercise* and present the steps in sequence. If the children respond correctly and firmly, the correction has been effective.

A useful way to think of all kinds of corrections is that they provide the child with the kind of practice needed to pass a test. The *exercise* that you present is a test. When the child makes a mistake, he or she fails the test. The child needs help. You can help by modeling, showing the child what to do. You may be able to help further by leading. When the child is firm, readminister the test. If the correction worked, the child will pass the test.

Mastering Signals

A signal shows each child when to respond, so that each will originate an independent response and yet all children will respond together. The signal or signals used in each track are described before specific formats are discussed, and should be learned through practice before you review the formats. If you learn these signals well, you will be prepared to execute the motor behaviors for any of the formats.

Summary

Above all, make the program seem like fun. The payoff for each lesson is the story the children read. The payoff is not free. Before children have the opportunity to read the story and look at the pictures, they have to perform on the word-attack portion of the lesson. Make it clear that the purpose of this work is so the children will be smooth in reading the story. Come on, let's get all these words right so we can go to the fun part and read the story.

When children are reading the story, model the kind of behavior you want them to follow. If there's a joke or something that is humorous in the story, respond as if it's funny. If you do it, they'll tend to do it, too. When they emulate your lead, reinforce them. We think that's funny—right, Jenny? . . . What's so funny about it?

The same general rule for modeling enjoyment applies to the significance of the stories. If you respond to the stories as if they are milestones for the children's learning, understanding, and enjoyment, the children will tend to respond to them in the same way. If you show that reading is fun—challenging, hard work, but fun—that's how your children will approach the program.

READING

Reading Scope and Sequence

SOUNDS	Sounds		1
		Sound Combinations	(1)th
READING VOCABULARY	Sounding Out Words Reading the Fast Way Word-Attack Skills		1
			6
		Regular Words	1
		Rhyming Words	1
		Words Beginning with Stop Sounds	
		Irregular Words	
		Word Build-Ups and Word Parts	
		Hard Words (Textbook)	
		Final-e Rule	
STORY READING	Sounding Out Story Words Reading the Fast Way Additional Skills		1
		Word Finding	3
		Period Finding	
		Sentence Saying	
		Quotation Finding	
		Question Mark Finding	
		Reading the Title	
	Comprehension	Picture Questions	1
		Story Comprehension—Oral	
		Story Comprehension—Written	
		Read the Items	
IN-PROGRAM TESTS	Stories	Individual Rate-and-Accuracy Checkouts	
	Stories/Vocabulary	Individual Mastery Tests	6
	Stories	Group Accuracy Tests	
	Vocabulary	Hard Words (Textbook)	
WORKSHEET ACTIVITIES	Writing	Sound Writing	1
		Story and Sentence Copying	1
	Pair Relations	Matching	1
		Cross-Out and Circle Games	1
		Pair Relations	1
	Reading Comprehension	Reading Comprehension Items	
		Story Items	
	Picture Comprehension	Words for Pictures	
		Story-Picture Items	
	Following Instructions		
	Additional Activities	Story Art	1
		Bonus Take-Home Story	

									134		
sh			ch	ing	er	oo	wh qu	(106)ar	(125)al	(140)ou	160

160

160

160

104 — 160

9

35 — 160

70 — 160

108 113 ■ ■ 127 ■ 142 ■

143 — 160

52

21 — 160

32

33 36

33 — 52

40 — 52

44 — 49

61 — 160

160

21 — 160

77 — 160

96 105 108 ■ 134 142 ■

54-56 61 66 71 76 81 86 91 95 100 105 110 115 120 125 130 135 140 145 150 155 160

11 16 21 26 31 36 41 46 51 56 61 66 71 76 81 86 91 95 100

115 121 131

108 113 127 142

120

143

65

76

89

66 — 160

77 — 160

90 — 120

156-160

113 — 160

65 (Plain paper activity 66–105) 105

41 46 51 56 61 66 71 76 81 86 91 100 105

Reading Tracks

The Scope and Sequence chart on pages 32 and 33 shows the major skills that are taught in *Reading Mastery Plus,* Level 1. Each Reading lesson is divided into four parts: **Sounds, Reading Vocabulary, Story Reading** and **Worksheet Activities.** Each of these parts is further divided into tracks.

Major skills are developed in tracks. Each lesson presents work from several different tracks. A particular track, such as **Sounds firm-up,** continues from lesson to lesson with new sounds introduced every few lessons. The track also provides reviews and firming of earlier-taught discriminations.

Development of Major Tracks or Skills

Children who enter the *Reading Mastery Plus,* Level 1 program should be able to sound out words that are presented in the unique *Reading Mastery* orthography.

thē fat man can ēₐt.

They should have had practice in handling simple picture comprehension exercises. The children should be able to read regular words by sounding out, and should be fairly proficient at decoding at least 13 symbols.

The *Reading Mastery Plus,* Level 1 program builds on these skills. The program teaches 27 more symbols, new skills for sound-letter analysis, for

attacking and analyzing words, for story reading, for comprehension, and for working independently.

Sounds

In *Reading Mastery Plus,* Level 1, which is continued from *Reading Mastery Plus,* Level K, children read a highly prompted orthography, one with joined letters and long lines over long vowels. These letters are identified as "sounds." These sounds allow children to read most words by identifying the sounds and joining them together. Included in the symbols for sounds are joined letters (**th, sh, ch, iñg, er, oo, wh, qu**), and letters with long lines over them (**ā, ē, ī, ō, ū**). Forty sounds are taught and reviewed in Level 1. All sounds, except **I**, appear as lowercase letters.

Three sound combinations are introduced in lessons 106, 125, and 140: **ar,** pronounced "are"; **al,** pronounced "all"; and **ou,** pronounced "ow" as in "out."

A complete pronunciation guide and list of sounds with corresponding lessons of introduction is on the inside back cover of this Teacher's Guide.

The list that follows illustrates the 40 symbols and 3 sound combinations covered in Level 1.

Sounds in order of introduction	
Review Sounds	**New Sounds Book A**
a as in **am**	**ā** as in **ate**
m as in **man**	**h** as in **hat**
s as in **sat**	**u** as in **under**
ē as in **eat**	**g** as in **tag**
r as in **ran**	**l** as in **pal**
d as in **mad**	**w** as in **wow**
f as in **fan**	**sh** as in **wish**
i as in **if**	**I** as in **I'll**
th as in **this**	**k** as in **tack**
t as in **tap**	**ō** as in **over**
n as in **nap**	**v** as in **love**
c as in **cat**	
o as in **ox**	

New Sounds Book B	
p as in **sap**	**x** as in **ox**
ch as in **touch**	**oo** as in **moon**
e as in **end**	**J** as in **judge**
b as in **grab**	**ȳ** as in **my**
ing as in **sing**	**wh** as in **why**
I as in **ice**	**qu** as in **quick**
y as in **yard**	**z** as in **buzz**
er as in **brother**	**ū** as in **use**

New Combinations Book C		
ar as in **car**	**al** as in **ball**	**ou** as in **out**

Reading Vocabulary

In every lesson, the children work on reading-vocabulary exercises. These exercises involve lists of words that are not presented in the context of a story or sentence. Following the reading-vocabulary exercises, the children read stories composed of words they have been taught. The reading vocabulary is designed to teach words at a relatively fast rate. By the end of *Reading Mastery Plus,* Level 1, children have learned nearly 900 new words.

The reading vocabulary is designed to achieve the following objectives:

1. To firm and reinforce the child's recognition of simple, regularly-spelled words that were introduced in *Reading Mastery Plus,* Level K: *man, sat, in, that,* and so on.

2. To introduce irregular words: *was, said, of, do, walk, talk,* and so on.

3. To introduce an analysis of words that have common sound combinations, such as *al* (always), *ar* (arm), *ou* (shout), and words that have initial consonant blends, such as *sw* (swam), and *cr* (creek).

4. To present an analysis of words that have two parts, such as *inside* or *himself,* or words that have endings such as *s, ed, ing,* or *er* so that children can appropriately attack these words.

5. To teach children to handle words that end in *e* and follow the long-vowel rule (*make, fine, those*). The analysis of these words is performed when the words are presented with no long line over the vowel and with a full-sized *e* on the end. Early in the program, the word *those* would be written this way:

thōse

When the analysis of long-vowel words begins, the word is written this way:

those

6. To expand the children's reading vocabulary so they have enough words by the end of *Reading Mastery Plus,* Level 1 to read material that is written at the beginning second-grade level. Basic words from vocabulary-frequency lists (including contractions) are taught.

The structure of the program ensures that the words, the attack skills, and the conventions are not merely presented to the children—they are taught to the children. In almost every lesson, ten or more words are presented. Some of these words are sounded out and then identified. Some are read the fast way without sounding out.

During the last half of the program, children sometimes identify part of a longer word, then identify the whole word. For some, the teacher covers part of the word and has the children read the entire word the fast way.

A given word appears an average of about five times in the reading vocabulary. Some words appear as many as 25 times. The same word will not always be presented the same way. Children may analyze the same word different ways in various lessons— sounding it out or analyzing it as a two-part word, or identifying the sound combination first, or identifying the word as a final-e word. This approach provides the children with a variety of strategies for attacking words.

Story Reading

Children read over 150 stories during the group story-reading part of the lessons. They respond to a wide range of oral comprehension questions presented by the teacher. In addition, they independently read comprehension passages during their independent-workbook-practice time. Children answer questions for each story (from lesson 77) and for each comprehension passage (from lesson 66) as they work independently.

The stories, written especially for the program, provide high interest for students from many backgrounds, and cumulatively review words and patterns that have been taught.

The stories are closely correlated with the reading vocabulary. (See the listing of vocabulary words in Appendix G of this guide.) New words or types of words are usually presented in reading vocabulary for two to four lessons before these words appear in stories. The lag time between the introduction of words in reading vocabulary and the appearance of the words in the stories is reduced in later lessons. By lesson 140 some words are introduced in the story in the same lesson in which they first appear in the reading vocabulary. This procedure is designed to let the children know that they will use the words that are introduced in the reading vocabulary and that they will be held accountable for identifying these words when they appear in stories.

In summary, by the end of the Level 1 program, the children have had a great deal of experience in reading a basic vocabulary of more than a thousand words. These words include words with the sound combinations *al, ou,* and *ar.* Children also discriminate words such as *pane-pan* and *kit-kite.*

Comprehension

The types of comprehension activities involved in the stories are carefully controlled. In early stories the story line is fairly simple and the sentences are straightforward. Later stories involve more sophisticated information.

By the end of the program

- The children have been introduced to a range of comprehension questions.

- They have practiced saying what a character in a story says (quotation saying).

- They have worked with serial stories in which information from one story is reviewed in the next.

Rate and Accuracy (Lessons 54–160)

Children are checked on their oral reading every fifth lesson. They read a specified selection from a story to the teacher. Procedures for improving children's reading fluency and accuracy are detailed later in this guide. (See pages 219–221.)

Supplemental Independent Reading

The Level 1 program includes Independent Readers. Each story is keyed to a particular part of the program and presents only words that children are able to read. In addition to reading the Independent Readers, children should be encouraged to supplement their classroom reading with their self-selected independent reading materials. An annotated list of suitable outside reading books appears in Appendix F of this guide. You might use the list to stock your own classroom library or ask your librarian to have the titles available for your students.

Worksheet Activities

The daily worksheets

- Reinforce reading and related skills that have been taught during the teacher-directed part of the reading lesson

- Provide practice in reading silently and working independently

- Introduce new skills, such as following instructions (lesson 113), that are required for future academic work, particularly work related to handling textbook instructions and information

- Give children practice in remembering information that was presented in the stories they read during any previous reading lessons

- Give children some practice in writing.

On a typical worksheet, four to eight activities appear. After lesson 77, they include story items, which are questions about the story that was read on that day or on preceding days. Other worksheet activities include reading comprehension, following instructions, pair relations, cross-out and circle games, matching, and sound and sentence copying.

Each activity is designed so that the items become increasingly difficult or more complex as the lessons progress. The first type of item in each track is quite simple and generally appears until the children are perfectly firm. More difficult items are then systematically introduced.

For example, in the Following-Instructions track, the items from lesson 114 are of this form:

1. māke __t__ in the box.

2. māke __c__ in the circle.

Worksheet 114

A later variation from lesson 127 is of this form:

1. māke a box ōver the circle.

2. māke __b__ in the box.

3. māke __c__ under the circle.

Worksheet 127

When the children have completed all the Worksheet activities, they are familiar with

- Independent paragraph reading

- Answering comprehension items by filling in the blanks, by circling the appropriate choices for the blanks, by making boxes under the answers, and so on

- Answering questions that involve such discriminations as *what, who, when, why, how many,* and *is*

- Referring to a picture and answering questions about what is illustrated

Comprehension Activities

The goal of the Reading component is not merely to teach children better decoding skills. The program contains a broad range of comprehension activities, and the program has provisions for actually teaching these skills, not merely exposing the children to them.

A summary of the various kinds of comprehension activities that are presented in the *Reading Mastery Plus,* Level 1 program follows.

Comprehension Activities Directed by the Teacher

1. *Stories,* lessons 1–160. Children read from their Workbooks (lessons 1–36), from their Storybooks (lessons 37–105) and from their Textbooks (lessons 106–160). You ask questions during the first or second reading of the story. The questions are specified in the Reading Presentation Books. Questions that relate to the story picture are presented after the reading of each story.

2. *Read the Item(s),* lessons 96–142. In their readers, children read one-sentence items such as, "When the teacher says 'go,' hold up your hands." After the children read the item, you do the action that the item specifies. The children then perform the action specified for them.

Comprehension Activities Performed Independently

1. *Story Items,* lessons 77–160. These are pencil-and-paper tasks in which children read questions about the story they read in the structured group presentation. The questions involve a variety of responses from the children, such as circling the correct answer, writing the answer in the blank, completing the sentence.

2. *Picture Comprehension,* lessons 90–120. These items involve a

worksheet picture and items that ask information about things illustrated in the picture. Children respond by writing in the word that is missing in each sentence that describes the picture.

3. *Story-Picture Items,* lessons 156–160. These items involve pictures that appear in the Textbook. Children read the items, refer to the details of the picture, and write the answers to the items.

4. *Worksheet Reading Comprehension,* lessons 66–160. One or two passages with comprehension items appear on each worksheet. Children read the passage and respond to the items. The vocabulary, length, and complexity of the passages parallel the presentation of skills that are taught during the structured reading lessons.

5. *Following Instructions Type 1,* lessons 113–155. These items involve figures (a circle or a box) and instructions that tell the children how to operate on the figures. Early instructions may involve making *s* over the circle and making *r* in the box. Later instructions involve writing words in the places specified by the instructions.

6. *Following Instructions Type 2,* lessons 142–160. These exercises present a sentence in a box. Below the box are items that direct the children to circle, underline, or make a line over a specified word or words in the sentence.

If the comprehension activities in Level 1 are presented adequately to the children, even those children who enter the program with low language skills will finish the program with the comprehension skills that are required for taking tests and for extracting new information from textbooks.

Sounds

The first sound symbol new to Level 1, **ā,** is introduced in lesson 4. The fortieth symbol, **ū,** is introduced in lesson 103. The Sounds firm-up track ends after lesson 134. A total of 11 sound combinations are introduced and reviewed throughout the program. The 13 sounds that are reviewed in Level 1 are shown on the Sound Review chart (see page 40). Children are expected to know sounds for the consonants: **c, d, f̄, m, n, r, s, t̄,** and the sound combination **th.**

Children also know the long sound for **ē.** They also know the short-vowel sounds for the letter **a** (as in **act**) and for the letter **o** (as in **ox**). The lesson numbers on the Sound Review Chart indicate when the sounds for each symbol are first reviewed in *Reading Mastery Plus,* Level 1.

Children read words composed of familiar sounds, starting with lesson 1. They follow procedures learned in *Reading Mastery Plus,* Level K. All words they read are composed entirely of "sounds" children have learned to identify.

Sounds (Lessons 1–134)

Here are a few suggestions for studying and practicing the sounds formats.

- Learn to execute the signal or signals smoothly and automatically.

- Read the format.

Sound Review Chart

Symbols	Sound Pronounced	As In	Sound First Reviewed in Lesson	Introduced in Fast Start Lesson
a	aaa	<u>a</u>nd	1	FS 1 (K)
m	mmm	ra<u>m</u>	1	FS 1 (K)
s	sss	bu<u>s</u>	2	FS 3 (K)
ē	ēēē	<u>ea</u>t	2	FS 4 (K)
r	rrr	ba<u>r</u>	2	FS 6 (K)
d	d	ma<u>d</u>	1	FS 9 (K)
f	fff	stu<u>ff</u>	1	FS 11 (K)
i	iii	<u>i</u>f	1	FS 13 (K)
th	ththth	<u>th</u>is and ba<u>th</u>e (not thing)	1	FS 15 (K)
t	t	ca<u>t</u>	1	FS 17 (K)
n	nnn	pa<u>n</u>	1	FS 19 (K)
c	c	ta<u>c</u>k	2	FS 21 (K)
o	ooo	<u>o</u>x	1	FS 23 (K)

- Review the teaching techniques.

- Rehearse the pacing of the key statements you are to make.

- Combine the script of the format with the signals.

- Practice the entire format, repeating it several times.

- Practice the format again, until you can perform it confidently.

After you are able to run the format smoothly, practice the format with corrections. Practice correcting mistakes the children are most likely to make. Anticipate that you will have to use each of these corrections. Facility in executing the corrections will make a great deal of difference in the performance of the children, especially those in your lowest-performing group.

Memorize the steps in the corrections. Continue to practice the corrections until you can respond automatically to any mistake with the appropriate correction. As soon as the error is made, go immediately into the correction, then return quickly to the appropriate step in the format.

In Level 1 students are initially taught to decode words by sounding them out. To sound out a word successfully students must be firm in sounds identification. Sounds activities, therefore, appear in almost every lesson through lesson 134. The two primary formats in the Sounds track are a *sound introduction* format, used to introduce and reinforce each new sound, and a *sound firming* format, in which several sounds are reviewed and firmed up. Other formats include game formats such as a cross-out game, a child-plays-teacher game, and a sounds game.

Letters are referred to as *sounds* in *Reading Mastery Plus,* Level 1. Alphabet names are taught in *Reading Mastery Plus,* Level K.

Throughout most of Level 1, each symbol stands for a single sound. The symbol **a** stands for the sound *aaa* (as in *and*). It does not stand for **a** as in **ate,** in **again,** or in **father.**

To allow the children to read more words as "regular words" four conventions are followed in the program:

1. Several sound combinations are represented by joined letters: **th, ch, sh, wh, qu, er, oo,** and **ing.**

2. Macrons (long lines over vowels) differentiate long vowels from short vowels. For example, the symbol **ā** makes the long vowel sound in *āte.*

3. Some symbols are altered to reduce some of the confusion children typically have between pairs of letters that appear very much alike in traditional orthography. For example:

   b d   h n   f t   j i

4. Capital letters are taught in Level K. Only lowercase letters are reviewed in *Reading Mastery Plus,* Level 1 so that the children will not have to learn two symbols for each sound. (Capital **I,** and **Ī** excepted.)

The children are taught 27 new sounds and review the 13 sounds taught in Level K. Initially only one value is taught for each sound. New sounds are introduced about every three to four lessons. A list of the lessons in which new sounds are introduced is included in the pronunciation chart on the inside back cover of this guide.

The first five review sounds are **a, m, s, ē** and **r.** Before teaching the program, practice pronouncing the sounds that appear on the pronunciation chart on the inside back cover of this guide. The cassette that accompanies this program models the correct pronunciation of all forty sounds.

Note that some sounds are continuous sounds and some are stop sounds. Continuous sounds can be held until you run out of breath. Continuous sounds include all vowels and such consonants and digraphs as **s, m, r, l, th,** and **sh.** Stop sounds are sounds that must be produced very quickly, like **d, b, c, g, h, p, t.**

Continuous sounds are easier for the children to pronounce.

Continuous Sound Signal

All signals follow the same basic rules:

- You talk first, then signal.

- You never signal when talking.

- You always pause the same length of time between the <u>end</u> of your talking and the signal for the children to respond, about one second.

Remember, talk first, then signal, and keep the timing the same for every signal.

You use signals to permit a group of children to respond together with every child in the group initiating the response, not merely imitating what others in the group do. Therefore, your signal must be very clear and easy to follow. Think of a signal as something like a dance step. If it's done right, and in time, your partner can follow. If the timing is off, somebody's going to stumble.

$$\bar{a}$$

To signal children to respond to a continuous sound, follow these steps:

- Point to the letter.

- Keep pointing as you say, Get ready.

- Pause for one second. Then quickly touch under $\bar{a}$ and hold on that $\bar{a}$ for two seconds. As soon as you touch that letter, all the children are to respond.

Practice pointing to the letter, saying, Get ready, pausing one second, then quickly touching the letter and holding your finger there for two seconds.

Continuous Sounds Teaching Techniques

Practice the following sounds-introduction format from lesson 5 after you are very consistent with your signal. Note that the last thing you say before signaling is always, Get ready. Timing is the same as it is for the simple signal that you practiced. Pause after saying Get ready and quickly touch the letter. Hold at the letter as either you or the children respond. The letters $\bar{a}\bar{a}\bar{a}$ in the teacher's script remind you to hold the sound.

Lesson 5

SOUNDS
EXERCISE 1
Teaching $\bar{a}$ as in $\bar{a}$te

a. (Point to $\bar{a}$.) My turn. (Pause. Touch $\bar{a}$ and say:) $\bar{a}\bar{a}\bar{a}$.
b. (Point to $\bar{a}$.) Your turn. When I touch it, you say it. (Pause.) Get ready. (Touch $\bar{a}$.) $\bar{a}\bar{a}\bar{a}$. (Lift your finger.)
c. Again. (Touch $\bar{a}$.) $\bar{a}\bar{a}\bar{a}$. (Lift your finger.)
d. (Repeat c until firm.)

- Step a models the behavior so the children know what they should respond and how they should respond in steps b and c.

- Step b is the first time the students are to respond.

- Step d directs you to repeat step c until firm. "Firm" means that all children are responding clearly as soon as you touch under the sound and that all children are saying the sound as long as you touch under it.

Corrections

- The correction below is to be used if the children respond incorrectly. Present the correction as soon as you hear or see any child responding incorrectly. The correction steps have been labeled to help you see the model-lead-test procedure.

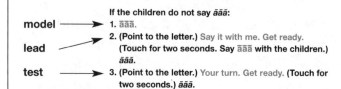

model → If the children do not say $\bar{a}\bar{a}\bar{a}$:
1. $\bar{a}\bar{a}\bar{a}$.
lead → 2. (Point to the letter.) Say it with me. Get ready. (Touch for two seconds. Say $\bar{a}\bar{a}\bar{a}$ with the children.) $\bar{a}\bar{a}\bar{a}$.
test → 3. (Point to the letter.) Your turn. Get ready. (Touch for two seconds.) $\bar{a}\bar{a}\bar{a}$.

Stop Sound Signal

g

The sound *g* above is a stop sound, a sound that cannot be held for more than an instant without distorting it.

The following procedures are used to signal for stop sounds:

- Point to the letter.

- Say Say it fast.

- Pause for one second.

- Quickly touch directly under the **g** for an instant; the children are to say the sound, *g* (not *guh* or *gih,* simply *g*).

Note that the signal for the stop sound involves the same timing as the signal for the continuous sound. The only difference is that you don't stop under the sound; you just tap briefly.

If you have trouble pronouncing a stop sound, say a word that ends in the sound. Say the sound in an exaggerated manner. That is the way you would pronounce it when teaching children to identify the symbol. For instance, say the word **sag,** exaggerating the **g.** Be careful not to say *saguh.*

Stop Sounds Teaching Techniques

In the teacher's script and on the pronunciation guide, stop sounds are represented by a single letter such as **d, t, h, g** or **c,** to help you remember to say the sound fast. This compares with the three letters **(āāā)** used to remind you to hold continuous sounds. After practicing the basic signal for stop sounds, practice the following sounds-introduction format.

Lesson 14

SOUNDS

EXERCISE 1

g Teaching g as in go

a. (Point to **g.**) Here's a new sound. It's a quick sound.
b. My turn to say the sound for this letter. (Pause. Touch **g** for an instant, saying:) g.
   (Do not say **guuh.**)
c. Again. (Touch **g** and say:) g.
d. (Point to **g.**) Your turn. When I touch the letter, you say the sound. (Pause.) Get ready. (Touch **g.**) g.
e. Again. (Touch **g.**) *g.*
f. (Repeat e until firm.)

In step *d,* pause after you say, When I touch the letter, you say the sound to give the children a moment to think.

Corrections

If students mispronounce the sound at step *d,* correct as follows:

model ⟶ **1.** (Say:) **g.**
test ⟶ **2.** (Point to the letter.) When I touch the letter, you say the sound. (Touch **g** for an instant.)

Sounds Firm-up Teaching Techniques

In sounds firm-up exercises children review and practice the sounds they have learned. Sounds firm-up tasks appear in almost every lesson through lesson 134. Firm-up tasks are the most important source of feedback about how well children have learned sounds. There are no new signals in the exercise. Use the signals for a continuous sound and for a stop sound that you have already practiced.

SOUNDS

EXERCISE 1

Sounds firm-up

a. (Point to first **a.**) When I touch the letter, you say the sound.

b. (Pause.) Get ready. (Touch **a.**) ăăă.

c. Again. (Repeat *b* until firm.)

d. Get ready to say the sounds for all these letters when I touch them.

e. (Alternate touching **d, n, t, a, f, th, m, o, i,** and **a** three or four times. Point to the sound. Pause one second. Say:) Get ready. (Touch the sound.) *The children respond.*

EXERCISE 2

Individual test

(Call on different children to identify more sounds in exercise 1.)

a   n   d   t

o   i   m

a   f   th

Corrections

If any child in the group misidentifies a sound at step *e*, correct as follows:

model ⟶ **1.** (Say:) t.

test ⟶ **2.** (Point to **t**. Pause one second. Say:) Everybody, get ready. (Touch **t** for an instant. Children say: *t*.)

Exercise 2 calls for individual children to identify more sounds. The individual test is very important. You will receive feedback about how well each child has learned the sounds. Make sure that you give turns to the lower-performing children.

The following dialogue illustrates how to handle mistakes on individual turns. The teacher presents an individual turn to Lucy, who makes a mistake at step 4. The teacher corrects the group, then returns to Lucy. This procedure is important. If an individual child makes a mistake, assume that others in the group would make the same mistake. By first correcting the group, you save time, because you won't have to present the same correction to other members of the group.

Read the dialogue out loud. Make sure that you understand why the teacher takes each of the steps that appears in the script.

Note that short vowels are written as aaa and ooo. The ăăă or ŏŏŏ prompting is rarely used after lesson 1.

Script for Exercise 2

1. <u>Teacher:</u> Lucy, your turn to say some of the sounds. (Pause one second.) Get ready. (Touch **d** for an instant.)

2. <u>Lucy:</u> *d.*

3. <u>Teacher:</u> Yes, d. (Point to **a**. Pause one second.) Get ready. (Touch **a**. Hold.)

4. <u>Lucy:</u> *āāā.*

5. <u>Teacher:</u> aaa. (Point to **a**. Pause one second.) Everybody, get ready. (Touch **a**. Hold.)

6. <u>Group:</u> *aaa.*

7. <u>Teacher:</u> Yes, aaa. (Point to **a**. Pause one second.) Lucy, get ready. (Touch **a**. Hold.)

8. <u>Lucy:</u> *aaa.*

9. <u>Teacher:</u> Yes, aaa. (Return to the **d**. Point to **d**.) Starting over. (Pause one second.) Lucy, get ready. (Touch **d** for an instant.)

10. <u>Lucy:</u> *d.*

11. <u>Teacher:</u> Yes, d. (Point to **n**. Pause one second.) Get ready. (Touch **a**. Hold.)

12. <u>Lucy:</u> *aaa.*

13. <u>Teacher:</u> Yes, aaa. (Point to **a**.) (Pause one second.) Get ready. (Touch **a**. Hold.)

14. <u>Lucy:</u> *nnn.*

15. <u>Teacher:</u> Yes, nnn. Good. You said the sounds.

Sound Combinations (Lessons 1–105)

By lesson 103, the children have learned all 40 sounds for the lower-case letter symbols and for the eight joined sound combinations:

th sh ch iñg er oo wh qu.

From lesson 106 through to the end of the program, children learn three sound combinations that are not joined: ar, al, ou.

In the exercise shown from lesson 59, the teacher presents the joined sound combination **ch**. The two letters that make up this sound are connected by a heavy black line. This unique orthography facilitates recognizing sound combinations.

SOUNDS

EXERCISE 1

Teaching ch as in chat

a. (Point to **ch**.) Here's a new sound. It's a quick sound.
b. My turn to say the sound. (Pause. Touch **ch** for an instant, saying:) **ch**. (Do not say **chuh**.)
c. Again. (Touch **ch** and say:) **ch**.
d. (Point to **ch**.) Your turn. When I touch it, you say the sound. (Pause.) Get ready. (Touch **ch**.) *ch*.
e. Again. (Touch **ch**.) *ch*.
f. (Repeat *e* until firm.)

Lesson 59

Sounds (Lessons 106–134)

Remember, the sounds pronunciation guide is on the inside back cover of this guide. Here is an example of the Sounds track format that begins in Reading lesson 106.

- In step *b,* point to the first sound and say Get ready. Then touch the sound. The children are to begin saying the sound as soon as you touch it. They are to continue saying it as long as you touch it.

Rules about Pointing and Touching (Sounds)

1. When pointing, hold your finger about an inch from the page, just below the sound you will touch.

2. Be careful not to cover the sound with your point—all children must be able to see it.

3. Say Get ready after you have pointed to the sound.

4. Pause for one second.

5. Touch just below the sound.

Note: The interval between the end of Get ready and the touch must be timed exactly the same for all tasks so that the children know exactly when you will touch the sound. If you keep the interval between the end of Get ready and the touch constant, there will be far fewer "leading" mistakes (which occur when one child in the group responds before the other and "leads" them with the appropriate response).

SOUNDS
EXERCISE 1

Sounds firm-up

a. (Point to the sounds.) Tell me these sounds.
b. (Point to each sound.) Get ready. (Touch the sound.) *The children say the sound.*
c. (Repeat problem sounds until the children can correctly identify all sounds in order.)

Individual test

(Call on several children to identify one or more sounds.)

er e ā

ē th wh

ch sh y

g h p

Lesson 106

6. Do not cover the sound when you touch it.

7. If the sound is a continuous one—such as *a, m, s, r,* and *o,* which can be pronounced until you run out of breath—touch the sound for 2 seconds (two slow beats).

   If the sound is a stop sound such as *d, t, p,* and *c,* which can be pronounced for only an instant, touch the sound for only an instant.

8. Quickly look up at the children an instant after touching the sound.

9. Move your finger quickly and decisively from the page after touching the sound.

Corrections for Inappropriate Responses to Your Touch

There are two basic types of mistakes that you will probably encounter on this format. The first is an inappropriate response to your touch.

- An inappropriate response to your touch is delaying before saying the sound. (You touch the sound; a moment or two later, some of the children respond.)

- Another inappropriate response is responding before you touch the sound.

- Another is continuing to respond after you have released your touch.

To correct inappropriate responses to your touch:

1. Tell the children what they did. You're early, or You're late, or You didn't say it when I touched it, or I stopped touching it, but you kept saying it. Watch my finger. Get ready. Touch. Children respond as you touch.

2. Repeat the signal until the children are firm.

3. Now you're watching my finger. Let's try it again. Then go on to the next sound.

PRACTICE this correction with another adult, using exercise 1 on page 47 of this guide. The adult who plays the role of the child is to make each of these mistakes: coming in early, coming in late, holding the sound after you have released.

The correction above deals with inappropriate responses to your touch. The other major type of correction deals with misidentification of sounds.

Corrections for Sound-Identification Errors

Use this correction through lesson 20. The correction consists of a model, lead, and test.

> **To correct**
> 1. (Immediately say the correct sound as you continue to touch it. Lift your finger.)
> 2. Say it with me. (Touch the sound and say it with children. Lift your finger.)
> 3. Again. (Repeat until firm.)
> 4. All by yourselves. Get ready. (Touch the sound.) *The children say the sound.*

After lesson 20, the following simplified correction may be used. Notice that the lead step is dropped.

1. *Model:* As soon as you hear a misidentification, say the correct sound loudly, so that all children in the group hear it said the right way.

2. *Test the children:* Your turn. Get ready. Pause one second. Then touch the sound. Listen to the children's responses.

If you are in doubt about the way any child is pronouncing the sound, give the child an individual turn to say the sound.

Note that after correcting a sound-identification error, you return to the first sound on the page and repeat all of the sounds in order. If children make errors, correct errors. Then return to the first sound again. Continue until the children can correctly identify all sounds in order.

PRACTICE correcting sound-identification errors. Work with another adult who plays the role of the child. The adult is to make identification errors when you touch some of the sounds on the format on page 47. Remember to respond as soon as you hear an error. (When working with children, you want all of the children in the group to hear the correct identification, not an incorrect one.)

Track Development

Near the end of Level 1, children work with final-e and long and short vowels (vowel mechanics). By lesson 133, increasing emphasis is placed on vowels in the Sounds track. Make sure the children are quite firm on all vowels, particularly in lessons 133 and 134.

SOUNDS

EXERCISE 1

Sounds firm-up

a. (Point to the sounds.) Tell me these sounds.
b. (Point to each sound.) Get ready. (Touch the sound.) *The children say the sound.*
c. (Repeat problem sounds until the children can correctly identify all sounds in order.)

Individual test

(Call on several children to identify one or more sounds.)

$$a \quad e \quad i$$

$$o \quad u \quad \bar{a}$$

$$\bar{e} \quad \bar{i} \quad \bar{o}$$

Lesson 133

Sound Combinations (Lessons 106–160)

Level 1 introduces three non-joined sound combinations: *ar* (lesson 106), *al* (lesson 125), and *ou* (lesson 140). These combinations are taught in reading-vocabulary exercises.

Sound-Combination Review (Lessons 129–160)

Beginning in lesson 129, the children review the three new sound combinations (*ar, al,* and *ou*) as part of their sound-identification activity. The sound-combination review format appears below.

Critical Behaviors

1. In step *a,* describe the task to the children, telling them to get ready to tell the sound the letter combinations make.

EXERCISE 2

Sound combination review

a. Here are some letters that go together. Get ready to tell me the sound they usually make.

b. (Point to **ar**.) What sound do these letters usually make? (Signal.) *Are.* Yes, **are**.

c. (Repeat *b* with **al**.)

d. (Repeat both sound combinations until firm.)

ar

al

Lesson 129

2. In step *b,* point to *ar* and say, What sound do these letters usually make?

- When pointing, hold your finger about an inch from the page, just below the middle of *ar*. Be careful not to cover parts of either sound.

- Say, What sound do these letters usually make? Do not move your finger as you say this.

- Pause one second after you say the last word in your question *(make).*

- Touch just below the middle of *ar*:

Note: The interval between the end of your question and your touch must be the same interval used between the end of "Get ready" and your touch in the sound-identification format on page 47.

- Touch under the sound combination for only an instant. (Use the same touching procedures you use for stop sounds.) Children are to say the sound combination *ar* quickly. They are not to drag it out.

3. Repeat step *b* of the format for the sound combination *al* (pronounced "all").

- Point to *al*. As you point, say What sound do these letters usually make? Continue to point for one second.

- Then touch just under the middle of *al*. Touch for only an instant. The children respond *all* the moment you touch under the combination.

Corrections: Children make inappropriate responses to your touching. They may also make identification mistakes.

Correct inappropriate responses to the touch using the procedures described on page 48.

If children confuse the combinations (calling *ar* "all,") follow this correction.

1. As quickly as possible, tell the sound combination.

2. Point to the last letter in the combination (*l* in *al* or *r* in *ar*). Say: Tell me this sound.

3. If response is not firm, point to the sound and say: Again, and touch the sound. Repeat until the children are firm on identifying the sound.

4. Point under the combination. What sound do these letters usually make? (Step *b* in format.)

5. Pause one second. Then touch just under the middle of the sound combination . . . Yes, arr. Note that you stress the *rrr* sound to tie in with the correction procedure.

6. Repeat steps 2 through 5 above for the other sound combination, *al.*

If the children fail to respond when you touch the sound combination (step 5), tell them the sound the letters usually make, "Are." Then repeat step *b.* "What sound do these letters usually make?"

Repeat both sound combinations until the children are firm on both.

Note: The first step in all corrections is to tell the children the correct answer. If the children miss a sound, the first step is to tell them the correct sound. If the children miss a word, the first step is to tell them the correct word.

The final sound combination for Level 1, **ou,** is introduced in Lesson 140. Here it is.

EXERCISE 6

Introduce ou as in out

a. (Point to **ou.**) When these letters are together, they usually say (pause) **ou.** What do these letters say? (Signal.) *Ou.* Yes, **ou.**

b. (Repeat *a* until firm.)

Lesson 140

Critical Behaviors

As with **ar** and **al,**

1. Touch just below the middle of **ou.**

2. Children are not to drag out the sound (pronounced ow).

Sound combinations are reviewed until the end of the program.

Reading Vocabulary

Overview

In each lesson, after the children have completed the sounds activities, they work on reading vocabulary activities.

In lesson 1, children review words and word-reading procedures taught in Level K.

1. In lesson 2, two "slightly irregular" words are presented. Children review the word **is.** It is irregular because it is sounded out as **iiiss** (which rhymes with **miss**) but is pronounced **iz.** The teacher directs the children to sound out the word **is,** and then "translates" by saying, Yes, **iz.** We say **iz. Is** it raining today? The word **a** is presented in Story-reading context.

Other slightly irregular words presented in early lessons are **his** and **has.** The purpose of introducing words that are slightly irregular is to make the children aware that not everything they read is perfectly regular. By introducing some words that are not perfectly regular early in the reading program, you alert the children to what will come. Note that children still sound out words—regular or irregular—but they learn to discriminate between how the irregular word is sounded out and how it is pronounced.

2. Highly irregular words are introduced after children have mastered slightly irregular words. The procedure is the same—children always say the sound they have learned for each letter. In sounding out a word such as **was,** they say *wwwaaasss* (rhymes with **gas**). Then you translate, That's how we sound out the word. Here's how we say the word. **Wuz.** After several lessons, the children read the whole word the fast way and <u>then</u> sound it out. The sounding-out decoding skill eliminates guessing. Irregulars are not treated as "sight" words because a particular word, like **was,** is always spelled the same way. The sounding out demonstrates this stable spelling.

3. Children begin to read words the fast way in lesson 6. By lesson 42 children read all words the fast way.

A variety of word-attack skills is taught. The same word may appear in a rhyming format, a sound-out format, a read-the-fast-way format, a build-up format, and a final-e format.

The reading-vocabulary portion of the lesson should take no more than ten minutes early in the program and less later in the program, so that an increasing amount of the lesson time can be spent on the stories. The exercises in this guide will help you teach economically.

Vocabulary Comprehension

Although the emphasis of the reading-vocabulary activities is on decoding, we want to make sure the children understand that they are reading real words. Meaning sentences are not specified for all words. If you feel that a sentence would help the children understand a particular word that may not be well understood in isolation, put it in a sentence. But <u>don't</u> use the meaning sentence as a substitute for decoding. Children do not become facile at decoding words by understanding the words. They become facile at decoding by practicing decoding.

Here is a meaning sentence for the word **meat** (lesson 20): "A hamburger is made of (pause) **meat.**"

Regular Words (Lessons 1–160)

Regular words, such as in the sentence **Pam had a ham,** are easy to read. Each word can be sounded out and said fast without mispronouncing the word. But the number of simple, regular words is very limited. To increase the number of "regular" words (words that children can pronounce the way they are sounded out), *Reading Mastery Plus* uses a modified orthography, or print, which is faded out in Level 2 of the program.

The modified orthography presents three conventions:

1. *Diacritical marks.* Long lines appear over the symbols for the vowels that sound like their letter names (ā, ē, ī, ō, ū). The symbol **a** signals the sound in **at,** while **ā** signals the sound in **ate.**

2. *Small letters.* Small letters appear in some words. Children are taught to sound out only full-size letters, not small ones. The small letters permit many words with silent letters to be spelled correctly. As the children progress through the program, the small letters are increased in size. The examples below illustrate the long lines and small letters:

māil kick ēat have hōme

3. *Joined letters.* If two or more letters function as a single sound, they are joined. The joined letters allow many additional words to become regular words.

shop that her tēacher slīdiñg

Sound It Out—Say It Fast Signal

You will use the Sound It Out—Say It Fast signal to direct the children to sound out words in all sound-out formats through lesson 160. After the children sound out the word, you direct them to "say it fast" or "What word?"

The illustration below demonstrates the correct procedures for presenting the word **sock** from lesson 1. Practice this procedure.

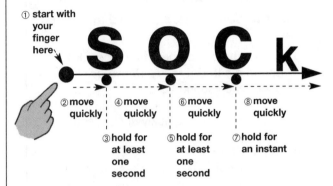

① start with your finger here

② move quickly

③ hold for at least one second

④ move quickly

⑤ hold for at least one second

⑥ move quickly

⑦ hold for an instant

⑧ move quickly

⑨ return to the first ball

⑩ quickly move along arrow for say-it-fast signal

- Hold under the **s** for at least one second; hold under the **o** for at least one second; hold under the **c** for only an instant; move past the **k** (it has no ball under it); and then move quickly to the end of the arrow. The children respond, *sssooc.*

- After you reach the end of the arrow, return to the first ball of the arrow. Say, Say it fast. Pause one second. Then slash from the first ball to the end of the arrow. The children respond, *sock.* Remember, first you talk—then you signal. Practice this timing. Start with your finger on the first ball. Keep your finger on the ball as you say, Say it fast . . . and pause one second. Signal by slashing along the arrow.

Practice exercise 9 from the beginning, with your partner making no mistakes.

EXERCISE 9

Children sound out the word and say it fast

a. (Touch the ball of the arrow for **sock.**) Sound it out. Get ready. (Move quickly under each sound.) *Sssoooc.*
b. (Return to the ball.) Again, sound it out. Get ready. (Move quickly under each sound.) *Sssoooc.*
c. (Repeat *b* until firm.)
d. (Return to the ball.) Say it fast. (Slash.) *Sock.* Yes, what word? (Signal.) *Sock.* Put a (pause) **sock** (pause) on your foot.

SOCk

Lesson 1

Rhyming Words (Lessons 1–104)

The rhyming skill allows the children to read many new words by blending different initial sounds with word endings. A child with good rhyming skills can see that words that rhyme have ending parts that sound alike and look alike.

In rhyming formats, two or more words in a series are presented.

Rhyming—Words that Begin with Continuous Sounds

In lessons 1 through 3, the rhyming part of each word is in red type. The beginning sounds are in black type. Children sound out and then identify the ending part. Then they identify the beginning sound and blend it with the ending part. Here is a format from lesson 2.

READING VOCABULARY—RHYMING

Do not touch any small letters.

EXERCISE 12

Children rhyme with ick

a. (Point to **ick** and **sick.**) These words rhyme.
b. (Touch the ball of the arrow for **ick.** Pause.) Sound it out. Get ready. (Move quickly under each sound.) *iiic.*
c. (Return to the ball.) Again, sound it out. Get ready. (Move quickly under each sound.) *iiic.*
d. (Return to the ball.) Say it fast. (Slash.) *ick.* Yes, **ick.**
e. (Touch the ball of the arrow for **sick.**) The red part of this word is (pause) **ick.** So what does this word rhyme with? (Tap the ball.) *ick.* Yes, **ick.**
   Rhyme with (pause) **ick.** Get ready. (Move quickly under **s.** Hold.) *sss.* (Slash.) *Sick.*
   (Return to the ball.) What word? (Slash.) *Sick.*
   Yes, **sick.** You're not (pause) **sick** (pause) today.
f. (Call on different children to do *e.*)

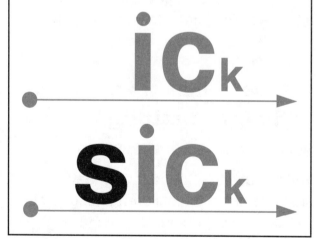

ick

sick

Lesson 2

- *Steps b to d.* Use the same signal as you practiced in the sound it out—say it fast formats on page 53.

Corrections—Step e

1. When you tap the first ball of the arrow, the children may respond by saying *sss* because they are not attending to your question. If they say *sss,* correct by saying: **ick.** It rhymes with **ick.** Listen again. Repeat step *e* from the beginning.

2. When you hold your finger under the **s,** the children are supposed to hold the **sss** until you slash. If a child says *sssick* before you slash, tell the group, I'm still touching under the **sss.** Repeat step *e* from "Rhyme with (pause) **ick.** Get ready," until the children are firm at holding the **sss.**

Rhyming—Words that Begin with Stop Sounds

Words that begin with stop sounds, such as **c, d,** or **t,** are hard for children to sound out because the sound cannot be held for more than an instant. If the sound is held longer, it becomes distorted with an inappropriate vowel sound—**duuuuuu.**

Children Read a Word Beginning with a Stop Sound

This format, which starts at lesson 9, contains fewer prompts than earlier rhyming formats. The children first identify the ending part of the word (which is no longer in red), and then they rhyme.

- *Step a.* Run your finger under **it** to identify the part of the word the children are to sound out. Do not permit them to start sounding out with **h.** If necessary, cover the **h.**

- *Step b.* You say, Say it fast and not What word? because the ending part of a stop-sound word is not always a word by itself (t̲ail, c̲o̲p, h̲e̲).

- *Step d.* Quickly touch **h** for only an instant, and then slash under the rest of the word as the children say *hit.*

- *Step g.* Touch the **h** for only an instant, and then move to **i.** The illustration below shows your behavior for directing the sounding out of this word, which begins (and ends) with a stop sound.

Lesson 9

EXERCISE 17

Children read a word beginning with a stop sound (hit)

a. (Run your finger under **it.**) You're going to sound out this part. Get ready. (Touch **i, t** as the children say *iiit.*)

b. Say it fast. (Signal.) *It.* Yes, this part says (pause) **it.**

c. (Repeat *a* and *b* until firm.)

d. (Touch the ball for **hit.**) This word rhymes with (pause) **it.** Get ready. (Move quickly along the arrow.) *Hit.*

e. What word? (Signal.) *Hit.* Yes, **hit.**

f. (Repeat *d* and *e* until firm.)

g. (Return to the ball.) Now you're going to sound out (pause) **hit.** Get ready. (Quickly touch **h, i, t** as the children say *hiiit.*)

h. What word? (Signal.) *Hit.* Yes, **hit.** Good reading. She **hit** me.

i. (Repeat *g* and *h* until firm.)

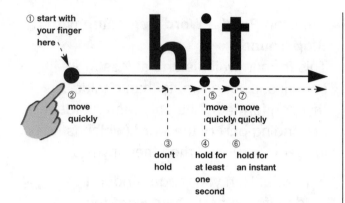

① start with your finger here
② move quickly
③ don't hold
④ hold for at least one second
⑤ move quickly
⑥ hold for an instant
⑦ move quickly

Correction: If children have trouble with step *g,* remind them, You have to say this first sound fast. So I can't stop under it. When I stop under the next sound, say both sounds.

Reading the Fast Way (Lessons 6–42)

The sequence of formats in this track is designed to help the children make the transition from sounding out every word to reading new words without sounding them out. Beginning at lesson 6, the children read a word the fast way after they have sounded out the word and identified it.

- *Step b.* Touch under each sound as the children sound out the word. Slash under the word as the children respond to "What word?"

- *Step e.* Pause at least three seconds. The idea is to build the child's "memory" for handling words. If you proceed too fast from *c* through *e,* very little memory load will be placed on the child. In later formats, the memory load will be further increased until the children are able to remember words consistently from one day to the next.

- *Steps d and e.* Expect to repeat these steps at least one time the first time this format is presented.

Correction

If a child misidentifies the word at step *e,*

Lesson 6

EXERCISE 8

Children sound out the word, then read it the fast way

a. (Touch the ball for **thē.**) Sound it out.
b. Get ready. (Touch **th, ē** as the children say *thththēēē.*)
• (If sounding out is not firm, repeat *b.*)
c. What word? (Signal.) *Thē.* Yes, **thē.**
d. (Return to the ball.) Get ready to read the word the fast way. Don't sound it out. Just tell me the word.
e. (Pause at least three seconds.) Get ready. (Move your finger quickly along the arrow.) *Thē.* Yes, **thē.** Good reading.

> **To correct**
>
> (If the children sound out the word instead of reading it the fast way:)
>
> 1. (Say:) I'll read the word the <u>fast</u> way. **Thē.**
> 2. (Repeat *d* and *e* until firm.)
> 3. (Repeat *a* through *e.*)

f. (Repeat *d* and *e* until firm.)

thē

correct by returning to step *a* and repeating the exercise.

Track Development

In the format for **thē** below, you count to five before directing the children to identify the word. The purpose of the counting is to challenge the children to remember the word in the face of greater "interference."

Lesson 11

EXERCISE 6

Children sound out the word, then read it the fast way

a. (Touch the ball for **thē**.) Sound it out.
b. Get ready. (Touch **th, ē** as the children say *thththēēē*.)
• (If sounding out is not firm, repeat *b*.)
c. What word? (Signal.) *Thē*. Yes, **thē.**
d. (Return to the ball.) Get ready to read the word the fast way. I'm going to count to five. See if you can remember the word.
e. 1, 2, 3, 4, 5. Get ready. (Move your finger quickly along the arrow.) *Thē*. Yes, **thē.** Good reading.
f. Again. (Repeat *e* until firm.)

Some words are in shaded boxes. The children have read these words earlier in the lesson.

Lesson 11

EXERCISE 17

Children read the word in the box the fast way

a. (Touch the ball for **not.**)
b. You're going to read this word the fast way. I'll move down the arrow and stop under the sounds. But don't say the sounds out loud. Just figure out what you're going to say. (Touch under each sound.) *Children do not respond.*
c. (Return to the ball. Pause at least three seconds.) Read it the fast way. Get ready. (Slash.) *Not.* Yes, **not.**

Word identification mistakes are corrected by first directing the children to sound out the word and then repeating the exercise.

A reading vocabulary page from lesson 21
is reproduced below. Exercises 15 and 16
are rhyming tasks.

EXERCISE 15

Children rhyme with sick

Do not touch any small letters.

a. (Touch the ball for **sick**.) Sound it out.
b. Get ready. (Touch **s, i, c** as the children say *sssiiic*.)
• (If sounding out is not firm, repeat *b*.)
c. What word? (Signal.) *Sick.* Yes, **sick**.
d. (Quickly touch the ball for **lick**.) This word rhymes with (pause) **sick**.
   Get ready. (Touch **l**.) *lll.* (Move your finger quickly along the arrow.)
   Lllick.
e. What word? (Signal.) *Lick.* Yes, **lick**.

sick

EXERCISE 16

Children read a word beginning with a stop sound (hāte)

a. (Run your finger under **āte**.) You're going to sound out this part.
   Get ready. (Touch **ā, t** as the children say *āāāt*.)
b. Say it fast. (Signal.) *Ate.* Yes, this part says (pause) **ate**.
c. (Repeat *a* and *b* until firm.)
d. (Touch the ball for **hāte**.) This word rhymes with (pause) **āāt**.
   Get ready. (Move quickly along the arrow.) *Hate.*
e. What word? (Signal.) *Hate.* Yes, **hate**.
f. (Repeat *d* and *e* until firm.)
g. (Return to the ball.) Now you're going to sound out (pause) **hate**.
   Get ready. (Quickly touch **h, ā, t** as the children say *hāāāt*.)
h. What word? (Signal.) *Hate.* Yes, **hate**. Good reading.
   Do you **hate** monsters?
i. (Repeat *g* and *h* until firm.)

lick

EXERCISE 17

Children read a word beginning with a stop sound (cāme)

(Repeat the procedures in exercise 16 for **cāme**.)

hāte

EXERCISE 18

Children read the words the fast way

a. Now you get to read these words the fast way.
b. (Touch the ball for **lick.** Pause three seconds.) Get ready.
   (Move your finger quickly along the arrow.) *Lick.*
c. (Repeat *b* for **sick, hāte,** and **cāme**.)
d. (Have the children sound out the words they had difficulty identifying.)

EXERCISE 19

Individual test

(Call on different children to read one word the fast way.)

cāme

Lesson 21

Children Read the Words the Fast Way

Children reread the words the fast way on some reading-vocabulary pages in lessons 21 to 160. Sometimes the words have been sounded out; sometimes they have been presented in a rhyme series; or sometimes they have been read the fast way. The rereading step is designed to help children with whole-word reading and with remembering words.

Correcting Word-Identification Mistakes in Lists of Words

In lessons 3 to 160, the children read words in columns. If a child misidentifies one of the words in a column, use the correction procedure below. Use the same procedure whether the word was presented in a sound-out format, a rhyming format, or in a read-the-fast-way format. As in all corrections, correct the group.

Here are the steps in the correction procedure:

1. Identify the word. That word is. . . .

2. Direct the group to sound out and identify the word. Everybody, sound it out . . . Get ready . . . What word?

3. Direct the group to return to the first word in the column. Starting over . . . or Back to the first word in the column . . .

4. Return to the ball for the first word on the page; pause several seconds; then ask What word? for each word on the page.

If the mistake occurs on an individual test in which a child is reading only one word, correct with steps 1 to 4 above. Present additional individual turns, then return to the child who missed the word and have that child sound out and identify the word.

Children Read the Fast Way

Beginning at lesson 42, the children read all the words on the page the fast way and then read the words in a new, random order as specified in the format. Beginning at lesson 42, most words will be taught in this format.

Lesson 42

EXERCISE 13

Children read the fast way

a. Get ready to read these words the fast way.
b. (Touch the ball for **this.** Pause three seconds.) Get ready. (Signal.) *This.*
c. (Touch the ball for **that.** Pause three seconds.) Get ready. (Signal.) *That.*
d. (Repeat c for **thē.**)

EXERCISE 14

Children read the fast way again

a. Get ready to do these words again. Watch where I point.
b. (Point to a word. Pause one second. Say:) Get ready. (Signal.) *The children respond.* (Point to the words in this order: **thē, that, this.**)
c. (Repeat b until firm.)

EXERCISE 15

Individual test

(Call on different children to read one word in exercise 14 the fast way.)

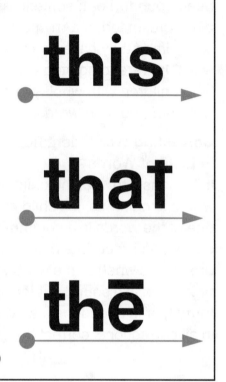

Here is a page from lesson 42.

- Treat the page as a unit. The children must be able to read all the words on the page correctly before moving to the next page.

- Follow the specified variation in order when the children reread the words. Varying the original order will show you just how firm the children really are on all the words.

- In the rereading, pause one second after pointing to a word before signaling for the children to say the word. If you signal without pausing, they will probably have difficulty responding correctly.

Irregular Words (Lessons 35–160)

Before lesson 35 you introduced slightly irregular words, such as **has, is, a.** Now you will introduce somewhat more irregular words, such as **was, saw, said.** In *Reading Mastery Plus,* a word is irregular if it is sounded out one way and pronounced (said fast) another.

An irregular word is introduced in stages through several lessons. In the first stage, the word is sounded out and then pronounced as it is usually said. In the next stage, the word is identified by reading it the fast way, and then sounding it out. The word then appears on reading-vocabulary pages to be read the fast way.

Lesson 35

EXERCISE 8

Children sound out an irregular word (said)

a. (Touch the ball for **said**.) Sound it out.
b. Get ready. (Quickly touch each sound as the children say *sssaaaiiid*.)

> **To correct**
>
> (If the children sound out the word as **ssseeed:**)
> 1. (Say:) You've got to say the sounds I touch.
> 2. (Repeat *a* and *b* until firm.)

c. Again. (Repeat *b* until firm.)
d. That's how we <u>sound out</u> the word. Here's how we <u>say</u> the word. **Said.** How do we <u>say</u> the word? (Signal.) *Said.*
e. Now you're going to <u>sound out</u> the word. Get ready. (Touch each sound as the children say *sssaaaiiid*.)
f. Now you're going to say the word. Get ready. (Signal.) *Said.*
g. (Repeat *e* and *f* until firm.)
h. Yes, this word is **said**. She **said,** "Hello."

Children Sound Out an Irregular Word (First Format)

- *Step d.* Emphasize the words "sound out" and "say." Pause slightly to set off the words. "That's how we (pause) <u>sound out</u> the word. Here's how we (pause) <u>say</u> the word. **Said.** How do we (pause) <u>say</u> the word?" Signal by slashing along the arrow.

- *Steps e and f.* Repeat these steps in sequence at least two times. With very low-performing children, you may have to present the sequence four or five times before the children are firm. Expect these children to have difficulty with the first two or three irregular words that are introduced.

Corrections

1. In step *e,* if the children sound out the word the way it is pronounced, use the correction in the format.

2. In step *f,* if the children begin to sound out the word when told to say the word or if they say the wrong word, correct as follows:

step f ⟶ Now you're going to say the word. Get ready. (Signal.)

mistake → Children say *sssaaaiiid.* Correct by saying, That word is **said.** Say the word. Get ready. (Signal.) *Said (sed).* Now sound out the word. Get ready. (Signal.) *Sssaaaiiid.* Let's try it again. **Return to step a.**

Children Sound Out an Irregular Word (Second Format)

After three lessons the irregular word is taught with this format (from lesson 38).

Lesson 38

EXERCISE 7

Children identify, then sound out an irregular word (said)

a. (Touch the ball for **said.**) Everybody, you're going to read this word the fast way. (Pause three seconds.) Get ready. (Move your finger quickly along the arrow.) *Said.* Yes, **said.**
b. Now you're going to sound out the word. Get ready. (Quickly touch **s, a, i, d** as the children say *sssaaaiiid.*)
c. Again. (Repeat *b.*)
d. How do we say the word? (Signal.) *Said.* Yes, **said.**
e. (Repeat *b* and *d* until firm.)

Listen, Sound-Out Format (Third Format)

This format (from lesson 112) is used to introduce some words that are quite difficult to say fast after they have been sounded out.

• *Step a.* Be sure to pause three seconds to give the children thinking time.

Corrections: Use the same corrections as for the first irregular-word format.

Critical Behaviors

• In step *a,* tell the children the word and test them on the pronunciation of the word.

• In step *b,* the children sound out the word.

EXERCISE 9

Listen, sound out

a. (Point to **circle.**) I'll tell you this word. (Pause.) **Circle.** What word? (Signal.) *Circle.* Yes, **circle.**
b. (Touch the ball for **circle.**) Sound it out. Get ready. (Quickly touch **c, i, r, c, l** as the children say *kiiirrrclll.*)

> **To correct**
>
> (If the children do not say the sounds you point to:)
> 1. (Say:) You've got to say the sounds I point to.
> 2. (Repeat *b* until firm.)

c. What word? (Signal.) *Circle.* Yes, **circle.**
d. (Repeat *b* and *c* until firm.)

circle

Lesson 112

Corrections: The most frequent mistake comes in step *b* when the children say "sssurrclll" instead of "kiiirclll." (Note that the word is irregular only in the pronunciation of the first two letters.)

To correct sounding out of irregular words:

1. Stop the children as soon as you hear a sound pronunciation error. Say the word as quickly as possible.

2. Touch under the mispronounced sound. Say: What sound?

3. Then say: You've got to say the sounds I point to.

4. Repeat the sounding out (step *b*) until the children are firm.

Special Word-Analysis Formats

Beginning with lesson 42, children read the vocabulary words the fast way, except in the following special word-analysis formats.

Ending Build-Ups (Lessons 70–160)

kiss

kissed

The children read the first word, *kiss.* You touch the ball for **kiss** and say, Yes, this word is **kiss.** You quickly touch the ball for **kissed** and say, So this must be kiiiiissssssss . . . and point to the **d** before touching it. When you touch the **d,** the children say *kissed.* Then they sound out the word. You signal for the sounding-out as you would if the word were on an arrow like the one below.

kissed

Move quickly from the **k** to the **i,** then to between the two **s**'s, and then to the **d.**

In teaching this particular build-up, avoid referring to the ending as "the e-d ending." Such a reference might lead the children to mispronounce the ending. In some of the words the children read, the ending is pronounced **d** as in **rained;** in others it's pronounced **t** as in **kissed.** If children pronounce **kissed** with a **d** sound, say Yes, **kisst.** What word?

Last-Part First-Part Words Beginning with Two Consonants (Lessons 71–160)

Here's an example from lesson 106.

swam

In lesson 106, the last-part, first-part format is introduced. This format is used for words that involve initial consonant blends that are difficult.

To correct

(Have the children sound out and tell what word.)

swam

EXERCISE 8

Last part, first part

a. (Cover **s**. Point to **wam**.) Read this part of the word the fast way. (Pause two seconds.) Get ready. (Signal.) *Wam.* Yes, **wam.**

b. (Uncover **s**. Point to **s**.) First you say sss. (Move your finger quickly under **wam**.) Then you say (pause) **wam.**

c. (Touch the ball for **swam**.) Get ready. (Move to **s**, then quickly along the arrow.) *Ssswam.*

d. Say it fast. (Signal.) *Swam.* Yes, what word? (Signal.) *Swam.* Yes, **swam.** Good reading.

e. (Repeat *c* and *d* until firm.)

Lesson 106

Critical Behaviors

1. In step *a,* cover *s* and point to *wam.*

- Practice covering *s* so that you do not conceal other parts of the word.

- When you point to *wam,* run your finger under the letters *w-a-m.*

- Say, Read this part of the word the fast way.

- Pause two seconds. Point under the letter *w.* Say, Get ready. Then slash under *wam.* After the children respond *wam,* say, Yes, wam.

2. In step *b,* uncover *s.* Point to *s* and say, First you say *sss.* Move your finger quickly under *wam* as you say, Then you say *wam.*

3. In step *c,* touch the ball for *swam* and say, Get ready. Then move quickly under *s* and hold as the children say "sss." Then quickly slash under *wam* as the children continue to say "swam." The children's response to the word is "ssswam."

4. In step *d,* return to the ball and say, Say it fast. Signal by slashing under the word. The children say "swam."

Corrections

1. If children are weak in saying *ssswam* in step *c,* repeat steps *b* and *c* until the children are firm.

2. If children are weak in saying the word fast in step *d,* repeat steps *c* and *d* until firm.

PRACTICE this format with another adult. First practice the steps when the person working with you makes no mistakes. Then practice it when the person pauses between the parts, saying "sss—wam" instead of "ssswam."

Two-Part-Word Format

In lesson 131, the first two-part-word format is introduced. This type of format is used throughout the program to teach the children how to analyze parts of words, including endings. The format requires the teacher to cover the last part of the word as the children read the first part. Then the teacher uncovers the remainder of the word, and the children read the entire word.

inside

EXERCISE 6

Two-part word

a. (Cover **sīde.** Point to **in.**) Everybody, tell me what this part of the word says. Get ready. (Signal.) *In.*

b. (Uncover **sīde.** Touch the ball for **insīde.**) Now tell me what the whole word says. Get ready. (Signal.) *Inside.* Yes, **inside.**

c. (Repeat exercise until firm.)

Lesson 131

Critical Behaviors

1. In step *a,* cover the last part of the word so that you don't obscure any letter in the first part. (You can cover the ending with a piece of paper if you find it more convenient.)

• With your free hand, point to *in.* (Point slightly below the letter *i.*) Say Everybody, tell me what this part of the word says. Get ready. Signal by touching between *i* and *n.*

2. In step *b,* uncover the ending of the word. Touch the ball for the word and say Now tell me what the whole word says. Pause to allow the children to look at the word. Get ready. Signal by slashing right along the arrow. Yes, inside.

Corrections for step a

In step *a,* the children may make the mistake of telling you the first sound in the word rather than the first part of the word, *in.*

To correct:

1. Underscore in with your finger. This is the part I want to know about. Everybody, tell me what this part of the word says. Get ready . . . .

2. Continue with step *b* of the format. Repeat the task until the children are firm.

Corrections—step b

In step *b,* the children may make the mistake of failing to identify the whole word appropriately.

To correct:

1. First consider that you may not have given them enough time before saying "Get ready" and signaling. Try step *b* again, this time with a longer pause.

2. If the children still misidentify the word, have them sound out the word and answer the question "What word?"

3. Then return to step *a* of the format and repeat all steps.

Here is an example from lesson 139.

himself

EXERCISE 6

Two-part word

a. (Cover **self.** Point to **him.**) Everybody, tell me what this part of the word says. Get ready. (Signal.) *Him.* Yes, **him.**

b. (Uncover **self.** Touch the ball for **himself.**) Now tell me what the whole word says. Get ready. (Signal.) *Himself.* Yes, **himself.**

c. (Repeat exercise until firm.)

Lesson 139

Sound-Combination ar (lesson 106)

In lesson 106, the basic sound-combination format is introduced. The heading of the exercise indicates the sound combination involved: *ar*.

- In exercise 4, the teacher identifies what the letters say, and tests the children: What do these letters say?

- In exercise 5, the teacher points to the bar that is under *ar* and asks, What do these letters say? The teacher then tells the children to read the first word the fast way.

- In step c, the teacher points to *ar* in the word *barking* and asks, What do these letters say?

- The teacher then tells the children to read the word the fast way.

Critical Behaviors for exercise 4

1. Point between *a* and *r* before you say, When these letters are together, they usually say (pause) *are*.

2. Remember to pause before saying *are* in the above statement.

3. After you ask What do these letters say? signal by touching just under the middle of *ar*. (See pages 50 and 51.)

4. Repeat step 3 until firm. Make sure that children are pronouncing *are* appropriately.

EXERCISE 4

Introduce ar as in shark

a. (Point to **ar**.) When these letters are together, they usually say (pause) **are.** What do these letters say? (Signal.) *Are.* Yes, **are.**

b. (Repeat *a* until firm.)

EXERCISE 5

ar words

a. (Point to **ar** in **arf**.) What do these letters say? (Signal.) *Are.* Yes, **are.**

b. (Touch the ball for **arf**.) Read this word the fast way. Get ready. (Signal.) *Arf.* Yes, **arf.**

c. (Repeat *a* and *b* for **barking**.)

Lesson 106

Critical Behaviors for exercise 5

As soon as children are firm on exercise 4, move quickly to step *a* in exercise 5.

1. Point to the bar under *ar* in *arf.* Move your finger back and forth along the bar. As you point to the bar, ask, What do these letters say?

2. Pause one second. Signal by touching the bar between *a* and *r.* When you touch the bar, the children are to respond, "Are."

3. Next, touch the ball of the arrow. Say Read this word the fast way. Pause two seconds. Get ready. Signal by slashing quickly along the arrow to the right. As you slash, children are to say "arf" at a normal speaking rate.

Critical Behavior for Step c

Step c involves the same steps as Exercise 4, steps a and b.

PRACTICE presenting Exercises 4 and 5 in order. Remember to move quickly from exercise to exercise.

Corrections: The children may fail to identify the words in exercise 5.

To correct:
1. Tell the children the word.

2. Touch the ball of the arrow. Sound it out. Get ready.

3. Move under *b ar k ing* as the children say *barkiiing.* Note that the children are to identify the *ar* combination as *are,* not as *aaarrr* or *air.* They identify the *ing* combination as *iiing.*

- When moving under *ar,* go to the middle of the bar, between *a* and *r.*

- Do not hold under *ar* for more time than the children need to say *are.* (An instant.)

- If children misidentify *ar* in sounding out, repeat exercise 4 of the format. Then repeat the sounding out.

4. After children have sounded out the word appropriately, return to the ball of the arrow. Say: What word? Slash quickly to the right as children say *barking.*

5. Return to exercise 4 on the format page and repeat both exercises in order until the children are firm on every step.

Sound Combinations al, ou (lessons 125 and 140)

In lessons 125 and 140 the sound combinations *al* and *ou* is introduced. The combination is introduced in the formats shown below.

Critical Behaviors

Follow the procedures specified on page 50. Remember to pronounce *al* as "all" and *ou* as "ow."

---

al

ball

EXERCISE 11

Introduce al as in ball

a. (Point to **al**.) When these letters are together, they usually say (pause) **all.** What do these letters say? (Signal.) *All.* Yes, **all.**

b. (Repeat *a* until firm.)

EXERCISE 12

al word

a. (Point to **al** in **ball**.) What do these letters say? (Signal.) *All.* Yes, **all.**

b. (Touch the ball for **ball.**) Read this word the fast way. Get ready. (Signal.) *Ball.* Yes, **ball.**

Lesson 125

EXERCISE 6

Introduce ou as in out

a. (Point to **ou**.) When these letters are together, they usually say (pause) **ou.** What do these letters say? (Signal.) *Ou.* Yes, **ou.**

b. (Repeat *a* until firm.)

ou

EXERCISE 7

ou word

a. (Point to **ou** in **out**.) What do these letters say? (Signal.) *Ou.* Yes, **ou.**

b. (Touch the ball for **out**.) Read this word the fast way. Get ready. (Signal.) *Out.* Yes, **out.**

out

EXERCISE 8

ou word

a. (Point to **ou** in **shout**.) What do these letters say? (Signal.) *Ou.* Yes, **ou.**

b. (Touch the ball for **shout**.) Read this word the fast way. Get ready. (Signal.) *Shout.* Yes, **shout.**

shout

Lesson 140

Correcting Words with Taught Sound Combinations

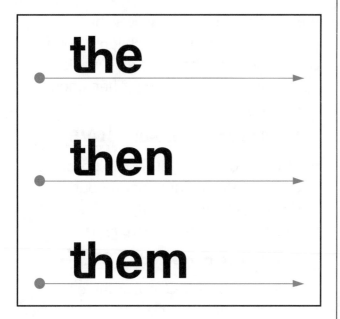

Corrections—Words

- If children misidentify any word in the list, correct in this way:

1. The word is ____. What word?

2. Point to *th*. What do these letters say?

3. Touch ball for word. Sound it out. Get ready. Move under *th*. Then touch remaining full-sized letters or joined sounds. Children are to identify the *th* as "ththth" when they sound out the word.

4. When sounding out is firm, ask: What word?

5. Return to the word *the* and repeat for each word.

Samples:

Word	*Children sound out*	*What word?*
the	thththēēē	the
then	thththeeennn	then
them	thththeeemmm	them

Practice the sound-out correction with the words above and with the words *when* and *what.* (Remember that *what* is irregular. It is sounded out "whwhwhaaat," but pronounced "whut" or "whot.")

Correcting Words with Taught Sound Combination and -ed Ending:

If the word contains a sound combination that has been taught, use a similar correction.

- **Word to be corrected:** **called**

1. The word is **called.** What word? (Signal.) *Called.*

2. Cover the *ed* ending. Point to *al* in *called.* What do these letters say? Children respond *all.* Yes, **all.**

3. Touch ball of arrow. Sound it out. Get ready.

4. Move under *c, al.* Children say *call.*

5. Return to ball. What does the first part say? Slash right. Children respond *call.* Yes, **call.**

6. Uncover *ed* ending. Touch ball of arrow. What does it say now? Slash right. Children pronounce word as it is normally pronounced, *calld.* Yes, **called.**

PRACTICE the correction with the words below. The underscored parts show you what to point to first. (The words you are working with in the teacher presentation materials may not be underscored.)

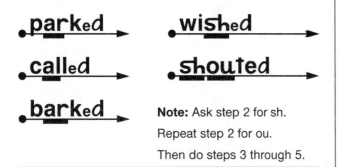

Note: Ask step 2 for sh.
Repeat step 2 for ou.
Then do steps 3 through 5.

Correcting Irregular Words with -*ed* Ending:

If the word is irregular, follow the procedure of having the children sound out and identify the word as it would appear without an ending. Then uncover the ending.

- **Word to be corrected:** **loved**

For the word *loved,* you would cover only the *d,* have the children sound out "Illlooovvveee" and identify the first part (*love*). You would then uncover *d.*

- **Word to be corrected:** **touched**

For the word *touched,* cover the *ed* and have the children sound out and identify *touch.* Then uncover the *ed.*

Follow this procedure (covering *ed*) for the words *wanted* and *looked.*

Hard-Words in Textbook Format (lessons 108, 113, 127, 142)

Beginning in lesson 108, the children are presented with lists of "hard words." These are mostly words that have been presented in the program but often give the poor reader some trouble. "Hard word" exercises appear in lessons 108, 113, 127, and 142.

Critical Behaviors

The children read words from their textbooks. This exercise involves individual reading from the textbook. Each child in the group reads every word in one of the columns. You proceed from one column to the next in order, calling on a different child to read each column.

Keep track of the children who miss more than one word when reading a column.

READING HARD WORDS
EXERCISE 4
Hard words in reader

a. You're going to read hard words today. Look at page 5. ✓
b. If you can read all of the words in a column without making a mistake, you'll get_____. (Reward the children with stars, points, and so on.)
c. (Call on a child.) Read the words in the first column. Start at the top and go down the column. Everybody, touch the words that are being read. Raise your hand if you hear a mistake.
d. (Call on a different child to read the second column.)
e. (Give each child a turn at reading one column of words. Praise the children who read each word in the column without making a mistake. Children who make a mistake must repeat the word until firm.)

> **To correct**
> 1. (Immediately say the correct word.)
> 2. (Tell the child who made the mistake:) Touch that word. (Pause.) What word?
> 3. (Then tell the child:) Now go back to the top of the column and read the words again.

Lesson 108 Presentation Book C

līkₑd	barkiñg	when
swim	that	thereₑ
fōr	hēreₑ	other
get	shē	funny
got	they	hōrsₑ
end	whereₑ	cāmₑ
and	how	giveₑ
at	whȳ	trȳiñg
ātₑ	dōn't	rīdiñg
ēat	didn't	hard

Lesson 108 Textbook

Procedures for Firm-up on Hard-Words Days

- Keep all children in the group until each child has had a first turn. Then dismiss children who made no mistakes in reading their column of hard words. Instruct them to do their seatwork for the lesson.

- Keep the other children and work with them.

Present the following firm-up procedure for children who make more than one mistake on a column of words.

1. Instruct the children who miss more than one word to study all the words on the page until they can read every word without making a mistake. Allow the children about two minutes to study the words.

2. Direct each child to read all the hard words individually to you. Tell the child not to hurry, to point to each word, and to read the word the fast way (without sounding out). *It is very important for the children to point to each word as they read it.*

- If a child misidentifies a word, tell the child to sound out the word and then answer the question, What word? Then tell the child to return to the first word on the page and read all of the words in order.

- If a child misidentifies a sound or sound combination when sounding out a word, tell the child the sound or sound combination. Then have the child sound out the word again. After the sounding out is firm, ask, What word?

- If a child reads all words without making mistakes, praise the child for good reading. Do not scold the child for having missed words before.

- If a child makes more than one mistake in reading all words on the page, write each word on a card, mix up the cards, and present the cards to the child. A child who is considered firm on the words can go through the stack two times without making mistakes. *Remember to write all the words with the same letters and lines that appear in the* Reading Mastery Plus *program.* For example, write *here* this way

hēre

and *where* this way—

wher_e

Track Development

Use the firm-up procedures above for every lesson that contains hard words. On hard word days, there is no other reading vocabulary and there are no stories. Use these hard-word days to diagnose specific problems and correct those problems. The minimum firm-up is specified above. If it is apparent that some children are weak on sounds, on sounding out, or on reading the fast way, a more elaborate firming procedure would be implied. Children should not proceed in the program if they are not firm on all hard words and on the operations they have been taught for reading words. Hard words exercises are actually in-program mastery tests. (See In-program Mastery Tests, pages 216–222.)

Vowel Mechanics

Toward the end of Level 1 the major thrust of the Reading Vocabulary tracks is to teach children how to read words such as *rode* and *made* that have a final *e* and a long-vowel sound and how to discriminate between these words and regularly spelled short-vowel words (such as *mad* and *rod*).

Initially the children are presented with Reading Vocabulary words that follow the long-vowel rule but that are written in *Reading Mastery* orthography:

This procedure strengthens identification of the words.

In lesson 143, the children are introduced to the rule about the final *e*: If there is an *e* on the end of the word, you say the name of this letter (pointing to the first vowel in the word).

Note that the rule makes reference to the <u>name of this letter</u>.

The children apply the rule about the final *e* to words that are presented with no lines over the vowel and a full-sized *e*.

Teach the long-vowel-rule formats very carefully and present enough individual turns to give you feedback about how firm the children are. If the long-vowel exercises have not been taught well, the lower-performing children may have difficulties in Level 2.

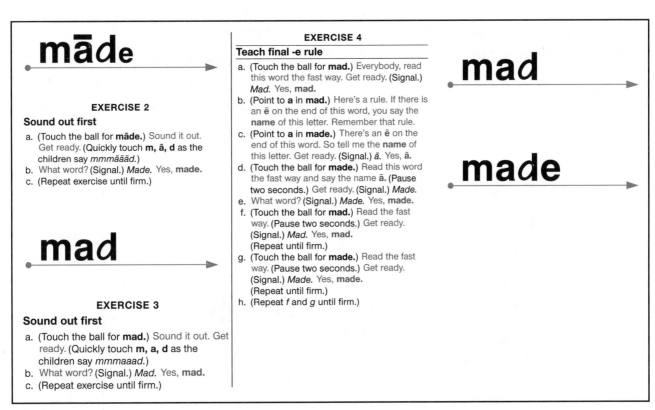

Lesson 143

Long-Vowel-Rule Format (lesson 143)

The first reading-vocabulary formats that deal with the long-vowel rule appear on page 73.

Note that the first two words are repeated. In the first appearance of *made* (exercise 2), a long line and a small *e* are present. In the second appearance (exercise 4), there is no long line and the *e* is full-sized.

- In step *b* of exercise 4 (titled *Teach final-e rule*), the teacher points to the *a* in *mad* and presents the rule about the final *e*: If there is an *ē* on the end of this word, you say the name of this letter.

- In step *c*, the teacher applies the rule to the word *made*. The teacher points to the *a* in *made* and tells the children, There's an *ē* on the end of this word. So tell me the name of this letter. Get ready. (Signal.)

- In step *d*, the children read the word the fast way, saying the name *ā*.

- In steps *f* and *g*, the children reread *mad* and *made* the fast way.

Critical Behaviors for Exercise 4

1. Fast pacing of the steps in this exercise is critical. In step *b*, remember to stress the word *name* in the rule. The discrimination between the "sound" and the "name" will be easier if you stress, ... You say the name of this letter.

PRACTICE saying the rule so that you can present it in step *b* without looking at the book. Say the rule as if it is very important. (It is.)

2. In step *c*, present the rule in parts. Pause after you say, There's an *ē* on the end of this word. If you wish, you can ask the children, Do you see it? Or even ask one of the children to touch it.

Then say, So tell me the name of this letter. Get ready. Signal by touching just under the *a*.

Corrections for Exercise 4

- In step *a*, if the children make mistakes on reading *mad*, use the standard

---

EXERCISE 4

Teach final -e rule

a. (Touch the ball for **mad**.) Everybody, read this word the fast way. Get ready. (Signal.) *Mad.* Yes, **mad**.

b. (Point to **a** in **mad**.) Here's a rule. If there is an *ē* on the end of this word, you say the **name** of this letter. Remember that rule.

c. (Point to **a** in **made**.) There's an *ē* on the end of this word. So tell me the **name** of this letter. Get ready. (Signal.) *ā.* Yes, *ā*.

d. (Touch the ball for **made**.) Read this word the fast way and say the name *ā*. (Pause two seconds.) Get ready. (Signal.) *Made*.

e. What word? (Signal.) *Made.* Yes, **made**.

f. (Touch the ball for **mad**.) Read the fast way. (Pause two seconds.) Get ready. (Signal.) *Mad.* Yes, **mad**. (Repeat until firm.)

g. (Touch the ball for **made**.) Read the fast way. (Pause two seconds.) Get ready. (Signal.) *Made.* Yes, **made**. (Repeat until firm.)

h. (Repeat *f* and *g* until firm.)

mad ⟶

made ⟶

Lesson 143

sound-out correction. Then repeat step *a* of the format.

- In step *c,* the children may say the sound *aaa,* not the name.

  To correct:
  1. Tell the children: You said the sound. I want the <u>name</u>. What's the name?

  2. Repeat steps *b* and *c* of the format.

- In step *d,* some children will make mistakes when trying to say the word (particularly the first time the format is presented).

  To correct:
  1. Immediately tell the children the word. **Made.**

  2. Relate the pronunciation to the rule. I said **ā** when I read the word. Listen: **māāāāāde.** Hear the **ā**?

  3. Repeat steps *c* and *d* of the format until firm.

- In step *f,* children may make mistakes. They read *mad* as *made.*

  To correct:
  1. The correction is the standard sound-it-out, what-word correction.

  2. Then repeat steps *f* and *g* until the children are quite firm on both words.

PRACTICE presenting the format and the corrections in steps *c, d,* and *f.*
Work with another adult who makes the mistakes. Work on the corrections until you can execute them without referring to the format or to this guide.

Track Development

Practice Final-e Rule (lesson 146)
Vowel-rule exercises similar to the one above are presented in lessons 143–145. In lesson 146, the children are introduced to a format that requires less teacher prompting. The format from lesson 147 is shown below.

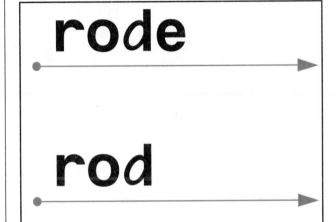

EXERCISE 4

Practice final -e rule
a. (Touch the ball for **rode.**) Everybody, is there an **ē** on the end of this word? (Signal.) *Yes.*
b. (Point to **o** in **rode.**) So tell me what you say for this letter. (Signal.) *ō.*
c. (Touch the ball for **rode.**) Everybody, read this word the fast way and remember to say ō. Get ready. (Signal.) *Rode.* Yes, **rode.**
d. (Touch the ball for **rod.**) Everybody, is there an **ē** on the end of this word? (Signal.) *No.*
e. (Point to **o** in **rod.**) So tell me what you say for this letter. (Signal.) *ooo.*
f. (Touch the ball for **rod.**) Everybody, read this word the fast way and remember to say **ooo.** Get ready. (Signal.) *Rod.* Yes, **rod.**
g. (Repeat *a* through *f* until firm.)

Lesson 147

rode → rod →

EXERCISE 4
Practice final -e rule

a. (Touch the ball for **rode**.) Everybody, is there an ē on the end of this word? (Signal.) *Yes.*

b. (Point to **o** in **rode**.) So tell me what you say for this letter. (Signal.) *ō.*

c. (Touch the ball for **rode**.) Everybody, read this word the fast way and remember to say ō. Get ready. (Signal.) *Rode.* Yes, **rode.**

d. (Touch the ball for **rod**.) Everybody, is there an ē on the end of this word? (Signal.) *No.*

e. (Point to **o** in **rod**.) So tell me what you say for this letter. (Signal.) *ooo.*

f. (Touch the ball for **rod**.) Everybody, read this word the fast way and remember to say **ooo**. Get ready. (Signal.) *Rod.* Yes, **rod.**

g. (Repeat *a* through *f* until firm.)

Critical Behaviors

1. In step *c*, do not hurry the children. Pause before saying "Get ready."

- Touch the ball for *rode*. Say "Everybody, read this word the fast way and remember to say ō." Pause for two seconds while the children figure out what they will say. If you fail to pause, some children will have trouble.

- "Get ready." Signal by slashing right.

2. Step *g* is critical, particularly if children made any mistakes in reading the two words. Repeat all steps—*a* through *f*—until the children can perform without making a mistake. If you follow this procedure the first time the format appears, you will discover that the children require very few corrections on subsequent vowel-rule exercises.

Corrections

- In step *a*, the children may respond weakly or incorrectly when asked, "Everybody, is there an ē on the end of the word?"
  To correct step a:
  1. Touch the e. Ask: What is the name of this letter? The children respond ē.

  2. Ask: Where is this ē? . . . . Yes, on the end of this word.

  3. Repeat step *a*.

- In step *b*, the children may say the sound *ooo* in response to "So tell me what you say for this letter."
  To correct step b:
  1. Point to *o* and say: If there is an ē on the end of this word, you say the **name** of this letter? What's the name of this letter? The children respond ō. Yes, ō.

  2. Repeat steps *a* and *b*.

- In step *c*, the children may say *rod*.
  To correct step c:
  1. Immediately tell the children the word. **Rode.**

  2. Repeat steps *b* and *c* until firm.

- In step *e*, the children may say the name ō instead of the sound *ooo* when asked about what they say for the letter.
  To correct step e:
  1. Say the correct sound immediately. ooo.

  2. Repeat step *e*.

  3. Repeat steps *a* and *b*, *d* and *e* until the children are firm on all steps.

PRACTICE the above corrections for steps *a*, *b*, *c*, and *e*. They are very important.

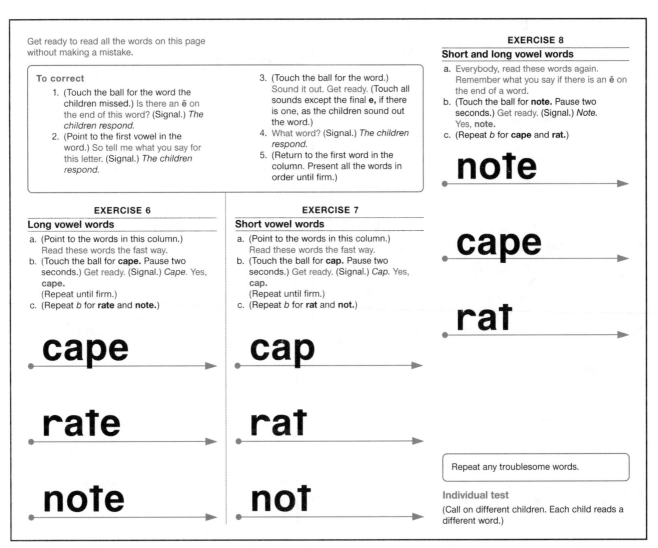

Get ready to read all the words on this page without making a mistake.

To correct

1. (Touch the ball for the word the children missed.) Is there an ē on the end of this word? (Signal.) *The children respond.*
2. (Point to the first vowel in the word.) So tell me what you say for this letter. (Signal.) *The children respond.*
3. (Touch the ball for the word.) Sound it out. Get ready. (Touch all sounds except the final **e,** if there is one, as the children sound out the word.)
4. What word? (Signal.) *The children respond.*
5. (Return to the first word in the column. Present all the words in order until firm.)

EXERCISE 6
Long vowel words

a. (Point to the words in this column.) Read these words the fast way.
b. (Touch the ball for **cape.** Pause two seconds.) Get ready. (Signal.) *Cape.* Yes, **cape.**
(Repeat until firm.)
c. (Repeat *b* for **rate** and **note.**)

cape

rate

note

EXERCISE 7
Short vowel words

a. (Point to the words in this column.) Read these words the fast way.
b. (Touch the ball for **cap.** Pause two seconds.) Get ready. (Signal.) *Cap.* Yes, **cap.**
(Repeat until firm.)
c. (Repeat *b* for **rat** and **not.**)

cap

rat

not

EXERCISE 8
Short and long vowel words

a. Everybody, read these words again. Remember what you say if there is an ē on the end of a word.
b. (Touch the ball for **note.** Pause two seconds.) Get ready. (Signal.) *Note.* Yes, **note.**
c. (Repeat *b* for **cape** and **rat.**)

note

cape

rat

Repeat any troublesome words.

Individual test
(Call on different children. Each child reads a different word.)

Lesson 149

Long-Vowel Words, Short-Vowel Words (lesson 149)

In lesson 149, a new vowel-rule format is introduced. This format involves a column of long-vowel words, a column of short-vowel words, and a column of short- and long-vowel words.

Corrections: The correction procedure for all words is specified in the box on the format page.

PRACTICE the correction in the box in the format above. Note that step 3 of the correction involves sounding out the misidentified word. When sounding out words that have a final *e,* <u>you do not touch the final e.</u> If the children are to sound out the word *cape,* you touch *c, a,* and *p.* In the word *note,* you touch *n, o,* and *t.* Practice the correction with these words:

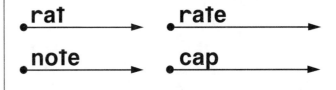

rat → rate

note → cap

- Expect the children to have trouble with exercise 8, in which they read a mix of short- and long-vowel words. You can reduce errors by pausing at least two seconds before saying "Get ready" and signaling.

- If the children make errors on any word, correct, and then return to exercise 6 and present exercises 6, 7, and 8 until the children are perfectly firm.

Track Development
Practice Final-e Rule (lesson 152)
In lesson 152, two new *Practice final-e rule* formats are introduced. In the first format, the children are asked to distinguish when they will say the long vowel sound and when they will not. Then the children read the words the fast way.

Critical Behaviors
To signal for a response in steps *b* and *c*:

1. Point to the ball of the arrow.

2. Ask "Are you going to say the name $\bar{a}$ when you read this word?"

3. Signal by touching the ball. Do not slash right.

Correction: Follow the correction specified in the format.

---

ate

at

EXERCISE 3

Practice final -e rule

a. (Point to **ate** and **at**.) You're going to say the name $\bar{a}$ when you read one of these words.

b. (Point to **ate**.) Are you going to say the name $\bar{a}$ when you read this word? (Signal.) *Yes.*

c. (Point to **at**.) Are you going to say the name $\bar{a}$ when you read this word? (Signal.) *No.*

> **To correct**
>
> 1. You say the name $\bar{a}$ in the word with the $\bar{e}$ on the end.
> 2. (Point to the word.) Is there an $\bar{e}$ on the end of this word? (Signal.) *The children respond.*
> 3. So are you going to say the name $\bar{a}$ when you read this word? (Signal.) *The children respond.*
> 4. (Repeat *b* and *c*.)

d. (Repeat *b* and *c* until firm.)

e. Read these words the fast way.

f. (Touch the ball for **ate**. Pause two seconds.) Get ready. (Signal.) *Ate.* Yes, **ate**.

g. (Touch the ball for **at**. Pause two seconds.) Get ready. (Signal.) *At.* Yes, **at**.

h. (Repeat *f* and *g* until firm.)

Lesson 152

The second *Practice final-e rule* format introduced in lesson 152 involves both reading the fast way and sounding out. This format is shown in exercise 9 below.

Note that in step *c*, you touch *h, e,* and *r*. You do not touch the final *e*.

here

EXERCISE 9

Practice final -e rule

a. (Point to the first **e** in **here.**) Look at this letter and remember the rule about the ē at the end of a word.
b. (Touch the ball for **here.**) Read this word the fast way. (Pause two seconds.) Get ready. (Signal.) *Here.* Yes, **here.**
c. (Touch the ball for **here.**) Sound it out. Get ready. (Quickly touch **h, e, r** as the children say *hēēērr.*)
d. What word? (Signal.) *Here.* Yes, **here.**
e. (Repeat *b, c,* and *d* until firm.)

Lesson 152

Track Development
The third *Practice final-e rule* format that appears in Level 1 is similar to the format for exercise 9, but the children do not sound out the word after reading it the fast way.

Read the Fast Way (lesson 155)
Beginning in lesson 155, words that have a long vowel and a final *e* appear in a *Read the fast way* format.

EXERCISE 11
Read the fast way

a. Read these words the fast way.
b. (Touch the ball for **smiled.** Pause two seconds.) Get ready. (Signal.) *Smiled.* Yes, **smiled.**
c. (Repeat *b* for **more, like, liked, those,** and **here.**)

smiled

more

like

Lesson 155

Corrections: If the children make mistakes in reading words without *d* endings (*more, like*), follow this procedure:

1. **Ask:** Is there an *e* on the end of this word?

2. **Point to the first vowel in the word.** So what are you going to say for this letter?

3. **Touch ball.** Sound it out. Get ready.
   Touch sounds of all letters except the
   final *e.* Children are to sound the first
   vowel by sounding the name, not the
   sound.

   (When touching the letters, hold each
   letter for one second unless it is a stop
   sound.)

4. **Then ask:** What word?

**PRACTICE the sound-out correction
with these words:**

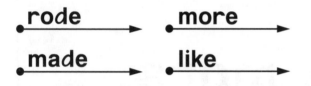

___

Procedures for Rereading Vocabulary Words

In most lessons, children read fifteen to
twenty-five words, arranged in columns on
two or three pages. Later in the program,
instructions for directing the children to
reread the words appear at the end of
each page. For all but the last page in the
reading-vocabulary exercises, the teacher
repeats any troublesome words, and then
presents individual tests by calling on
different children to read a word from the
page.

The last page of later reading-vocabulary
lessons directs the teacher to call on
individual children to read a <u>column</u> of
words.

All words should be read the fast way on
the individual test. If the column contains
only one or two words, the child should

read additional words from an adjacent
column.

Praise children who read all words with
no errors. Encourage children whose
performance is improving. Column
reading samples each child's reading
progress. If a child is tested at least
several times a week, the teacher
receives good information on the child's
progress.

Story Reading (Lessons 1–160)

The content of the stories is based on two
main criteria: First, the words used in the
stories are coordinated carefully with the
words introduced in the reading-
vocabulary presentations. Words are
generally presented in the reading-
vocabulary presentation for a few days
before they are introduced in the stories.
Second, the stories and art are designed
to be interesting, amusing, and appealing
to the children.

All story-reading exercises are part of the
structured lesson. They follow the sounds
and reading-vocabulary exercises. The
allotted lesson time permits the group to
read each story more than one time.
Initially, the stories are not the major part
of the reading lesson. By lesson 21,
however, most of the lesson time is spent
on story reading.

The stories increase in length from three
words in lesson 1 to more than two
hundred words by lesson 160. At the end
of Level 1 reading instruction, children in
Reading Mastery Plus are able to read

stories that are more sophisticated than those presented in other reading programs.

Overview

The major topics in the story track are outlined in the scope and sequence chart on pages 32–33. In this story section of the guide, each topic is described and teaching techniques and corrections are provided.

Sounding Out Words (Lessons 1–20)
During this lesson range, children sound out each story word and then say it fast. The children sound out three words on their worksheets in lessons 1 to 6. Four-word stories start in lesson 7.

In lessons 1 to 20, the children learn the skills they need to make the transition from sounding out to reading the fast way.

Reading Words the Fast Way (Lessons 21–160)
The children identify whole words when they read the fast way. Whole-word reading begins in reading vocabulary at lesson 6. In story 21, the children read sentences the fast way. By lesson 42 in reading vocabulary, the children read most words the fast way. In stories 53 through 160, the children no longer sound out words. Sounding out continues to be used in the correction procedure through lesson 105.

Individual checkouts begin at lesson 54. For a checkout, each child reads part of the story the fast way. You time the reading. A rate and accuracy criterion is specified.

Comprehension (Lessons 1–160)
Comprehension of reading-vocabulary words begins in Level 1 with the introduction of "meaning" sentences. Comprehension skills are taught within the Level 1 story track through the oral questions you present, through discussion of the pictures for the stories, and through written questions on the worksheets.

Pictures. In lessons 1 to 45, the story and the picture related to the story are not on the same page. Children use the words they read to predict something about the content of the picture. Then they look at the picture as you ask questions. At this point in the program, the emphasis is on making sure the children comprehend what they read. They first read the words; then they look at the picture. They do not use "picture cues" to help them figure out words because pictures do not imply specific words.

Oral Questions. From lessons 21 to 160, you ask comprehension questions during the reading of the story. The questions and the points at which they are to be asked are specified. Many questions deal with *who, what, where, when, why,* and *how.* For another type of question, you summarize story events and ask the children to predict what will happen next. For questions that can be answered directly from the words in the story, you signal for a group response. For questions that call for divergent responses—such as, "What do you think?"—you call on individual children.

Written Questions. From lessons 77 to 160, children answer written questions about the story. These questions are on the worksheets.

Read the Items. From lessons 96 to 142, the children play a game called Read the Items. The items are not intuitively obvious, and therefore call for careful teaching and understanding. For example, children read, "If the teacher says 'go,' stand up." To play the game, the children must remember the instructions because you will say different things, such as "stand up" and "go." (Children are to respond only to "go" for this item.)

Additional Skills (Lessons 1–160)

Through a series of exercises in lessons 1 through 160, children learn a set of skills that facilitate their whole-word reading and sentence reading. These exercises include practice in word finding, sentence saying, period finding, quotation finding, question mark finding, reading the title, word practice, and review of troublesome words including final-e words and words with **ar, al, ou.**

Student Materials for Story Reading

The children's stories for lessons 1 through 36 are in Workbook A. The children's stories for lessons 37 through 105 are in the Storybook and stories for lessons 106 through 160 are in the Textbook.

Every fifth lesson, beginning at lesson 41–105, has an extra take-home worksheet page on which one of the children's stories is duplicated. You tell the children, "I'll give you a bonus take-home for doing a good job." The children color the picture and take the story home.

Multiple-part stories begin at lesson 86. The second part of a story begins with a summary of what happened during the first part.

How to Conduct Group Story Activities

After the children have completed the sounds and reading vocabulary activities of each lesson, they read a story. The teacher directs the reading and presents comprehension questions that are specified in the teacher-presentation script for the lesson.

For the story reading:

1. Seat children so that all are close to you. In lessons 1–36, children need to be close enough to see your Workbook. Sit so that you can observe whether each child's finger is pointing to the words and can see whether each child's mouth is forming the words.

2. Seat the higher-performing children on the ends of the group. Place the lower-performing children in the middle of the group.

3. Give all children lap boards or large books on which to place their worksheets, storybook or textbook.

4. Do not allow the children to turn the page to look at the picture until you tell them to turn the page.

5. Each time you give an instruction to point, quickly check to see that each child is pointing appropriately.

6. During reading, make sure that the children look at the words, not at you.

7. Use an audible signal to elicit their responses.

8. Make sure you listen most frequently to the lowest-performing children in the group.

Sounding Out Words (Lessons 1–20)

Children Sound Out Each Word and Say It Fast

During lessons 1 to 6, the children read three-word stories on their worksheets. The illustration below presents the words **the fat rat.** The children sound out each word and then say the words fast. Then individual children read one of the words. You model reading the first two words the fast way. The children use the words as a basis for predicting what they will see in a picture on the other side of the worksheet. The children look at the picture and answer some questions that relate to it.

Worksheet 1

Worksheet 1

STORY

EXERCISE 18

First reading—children sound out each word and say it fast

Do not let the children look at the picture until exercise 22.

a. Everybody, touch the ball for the first word. ✓
Sound it out. Get ready. (Tap for each sound.) *Thththēēē.*

b. Again, finger on the ball. ✓
Sound it out. Get ready. (Tap for each sound.) *Thththēēē.*
Say it fast. (Signal.) *Thē.*
Yes, what word? (Signal.) *Thē.*

c. Touch the box for the next word. ✓
Sound it out. Get ready. (Tap for each sound.) *Fffaaat.*

d. Again, back to the box. ✓
Sound it out. Get ready. (Tap for each sound.) *Fffaaat.*
Say it fast. (Signal.) *Fat.*
Yes, what word? (Signal.) *Fat.*

e. Touch the box for the next word. ✓
Sound it out. Get ready. (Tap for each sound.) *Rrraaat.*

f. Again, back to the box. ✓
Sound it out. Get ready. (Tap for each sound.) *Rrraaat.*
Say it fast. (Signal.) *Rat.*
Yes, what word? (Signal.) *Rat.*

EXERCISE 19

Second reading—children sound out each word and say it fast

a. Get ready to read the story again.
Everybody, finger on the first ball. ✓
Sound it out. Get ready. (Tap for each sound.) *Thththēēē.*

b. Again, finger on the first ball. ✓
Sound it out. Get ready. (Tap for each sound.) *Thththēēē.*
Say it fast. (Signal.) *Thē.*
Yes, what word? (Signal.) *Thē.*

c. Touch the box for the next word. ✓
Sound it out. Get ready. (Tap for each sound.) *Fffaaat.*

d. Again, back to the box. ✓
Sound it out. Get ready. (Tap for each sound.) *Fffaaat.*
Say it fast. (Signal.) *Fat.*
Yes, what word? (Signal.) *Fat.*

e. Touch the box for the next word. ✓
Sound it out. Get ready. (Tap for each sound.) *Rrraaat.*

f. Everybody, touch the ball for the first word. ✓
(Tap for each sound.)
Say it fast. (Signal.) *Thē.* Yes, **thē.**

c. Everybody, touch the box for the next word. ✓
(Tap for each sound.)
Say it fast. (Signal.) *Fat.* Yes, **fat.**

d. Everybody, touch the box for the next word. ✓
(Tap for each sound.)
Say it fast. (Signal.) *Rat.* Yes, **rat.**

e. (Call on different children. Each child reads one word from *b, c,* or *d.*)

EXERCISE 21

Teacher and children read the fast way

a. (Hold up side 1 of your worksheet. Point to the words on the arrow. Touch under **rat.**)
Everybody, this word is (pause) **rat.** What word? (Signal.) *Rat.*
Yes, **rat.** Remember that.

b. We're going to read this story the fast way.

c. (Point to **thē fat.**) I'll read these words the fast way.

d. (Point to **rat.**) When I touch this word, you're going to say . . . . (Signal.) *Rat.*
Yes, **rat.**

e. (Repeat *d* until firm.)

f. (Touch the first ball of the arrow.) Reading the fast way. (Pause three seconds. Touch under **thē** and say:) **thē.** (Touch under **fat** and say:) **fat.**

g. (Then touch under **rat.**) *Rat.*

h. (Repeat *f* and *g* until firm.)

i. Yes, **thē fat rat.**

EXERCISE 20

Individual test

a. Everybody, follow along with your finger as I call on different children to read one of the words.

EXERCISE 22

Picture comprehension

a. What do you think you'll see in the story picture? (Signal.) *Thē fat rat.*

b. (Repeat *a* until firm.)

c. Yes, the picture will show (pause) **thē fat rat.**

d. Turn your worksheet over and look at the picture.

e. (Ask these questions:)
1. What's that rat got around its neck? (Call on a child. Idea: *A bib.*)
2. Where's the cheese that's supposed to be in the rat trap? (Call on a child. Idea: *The rat ate it.*)
3. Do you think that rat likes to eat cheese? (Call on a child. Accept appropriate responses.)
4. What kind of food do you like to eat best? (Call on a child. Accept appropriate responses.)

Worksheet 1, Side 2

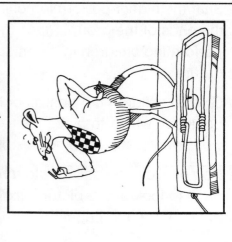

Worksheet 1, Side 1

thē fat rat

Exercise 18   Teaching Techniques

- Do not let the children look at the picture until exercise 22. You want them to read the story words before they relate the words to the picture. Enforce this rule.

- *Step a.* Be sure that the children are touching the first ball. Pause about two seconds between taps. Check to see that the children are touching under each sound as you tap. The children are not to stop between the sounds when they say them.

- *Step b.* Give an audible signal—a clap, snap or tap—for the children to say the word fast. They must be looking at their papers, not at you.

- *Step c.* Be sure that the children are touching the box for the next word.

Exercises 20–22   Teaching Techniques

- *Exercise 20.* Check to see that all the children are following along with their fingers as different children read one of the words. You may have to move some children's fingers.

- *Exercise 21.* Be sure the children are looking at your worksheet as you model how to read the word the fast way.

- *Exercise 22, step a.* Be sure the children are looking at you.

- *Exercise 22, step e.* The children should be looking at the picture. Do not signal. Let different children respond. But do not let the discussion continue for more than about ten seconds.

Corrections: Correct sound misidentification by telling (modeling) the correct sound and repeating the step in which the mistake occurred.

Correct touching errors by physically moving the children's fingers and repeating the step. If children stop between the sounds, present a model by calling on an individual to sound out the word.

If children cannot say a word fast, correct by changing the task into an oral task. Then direct the children to sound out and identify the word on their worksheet.

Remember to follow each correction with a repetition of the step that was missed.

Below are a series of correction procedures for word-identification errors on group reading or on individual tests. If you compare the procedures, you'll see that they are similar to each other, with only slight variations. For group reading, the last step in the correction in all lessons involves repeating the **sentence** that was missed.

For an individual test, however, in lessons 1 to 39, the last step in the correction involves repeating the **word** that was missed, while in lessons 40 to 160, the last step involves repeating the **sentence** that was missed.

Learn these correction procedures and refer back to them as you work through the story formats in this guide.

Individual Test, Lessons 1–39
Correction for Word-Identification Errors
The correction involves the following steps:

1. Identifying the word

2. Directing the group to sound out and identify the word

3. After giving other children individual tests, requiring the child who made the mistake to sound out the word and identify it

Worksheet 1

the fat rat

Individual test on the word **rat** (lesson 1, exercise 20, step d). Lola makes a mistake at step 4.

1. <u>Teacher:</u> Everybody, touch the box for the last word. Check children's responses. Lola, sound it out. Get ready. Tap for each sound, pausing about two seconds between taps.

2. <u>Lola:</u> *Rrraaat.*

3. <u>Teacher:</u> Say it fast. (Signal.)

4. <u>Lola:</u> *Fat.*

5. <u>Teacher:</u> That word is **rat.** Everybody, finger on the last box. ✔ Sound it out. Get ready. Tap for each sound, pausing about two seconds between taps.

6. <u>Group:</u> *Rrraaat.*

7. <u>Teacher:</u> Everybody, say it fast. (Signal.)

8. <u>Group:</u> *Rat.*

9. <u>Teacher:</u> Yes, **rat.** Continue with exercise 20. After completing exercise 20, return to Lola.

10. <u>Teacher:</u> Point to the box for **rat.** Lola, touch the box for this word. ✔ Sound it out. Get ready. Tap for each sound, pausing about two seconds between claps.

11. <u>Lola:</u> *Rrraaat.*

12. <u>Teacher:</u> Say it fast. (Signal.)

13. <u>Lola:</u> *Rat.*

14. <u>Teacher:</u> Yes, **rat.** Good. You said it fast.

Group Reading, Lessons 1–160
Correction for Word Identification Errors

Worksheet 6

the rat āte.

The correction involves returning to the beginning of the sentence and rereading the sentence. Here are the steps:

1. Identify the word. That word is. . . .

2. Direct the group to sound out and identify the word. Everybody, sound it out. Get ready . . . What word?

3. Direct the group to return to the first word of the sentence (to the ball) and read the entire sentence. Starting over, or Back to the first word (of the sentence).

Until the words **period** and **sentence** have been taught, you will have to show the children where to start reading.

Individual Test, Lessons 40–160
Correction for Word-Identification Errors

Storybook 40

> a little fish sat on a fat fish.

The correction involves returning to the beginning of the sentence and rereading the sentence. Here are the steps:

1. Identify the word. That word is. . . .

2. Direct the group to sound out and identify the word. Everybody, sound it out. Get ready . . . What word?

3. Require the child who made the mistake to sound out the word and identify it. Sound it out. Get ready . . . What word?

4. Direct the child to return to the first word of the sentence and read the entire sentence. Back to the first word of the sentence.

The words **sentence** and **period** have been taught by lesson 40.

Sounding Out Words Track Development

Boxes Between the Words (Lessons 1–32)

Boxes between the words on the line keep the children from running the words together. You establish the terminology of "first word" and "next word" by having the children touch the beginning ball for the first word and sound the word out. Then they touch the box for the next word and sound it out.

Only lesson 1 has balls under the sounds in the words, but you continue to tap for each sound and the children continue to touch under the sounds. The stories get longer in lessons 7 to 32. The boxes move above the line in lesson 3 and gradually get smaller until they are phased out in lesson 33.

Teacher and Children Read the Fast Way (Lessons 1–20)

In lessons 1 to 20, you and the children read part of the story the fast way. You provide a strong model of inflection and whole-word reading. The lower-performing children, especially, need this strong model; so be sure to teach these exercises to criterion.

Lesson 3

EXERCISE 17

Teacher and children read the fast way

a. (Point to the words on the arrow. Touch under **on.**) Everybody, this word is (pause) **on.** What word? (Signal.) *On.* Yes, **on.** Remember that.
b. We're going to read this story the fast way.
c. (Point to **it is.**) I'll read these words the fast way.
d. (Point to **on.**) When I touch this word, you're going to say . . . . (Signal.) *On.* Yes, **on.**
e. (Repeat *d* until firm.)
f. (Touch the ball of the arrow.) Reading the fast way. (Pause three seconds. Touch under **it is** and say:) It is . . . .
g. (Then touch under **on.**) *On.*
h. (Repeat *f* and *g* until firm.)
i. Yes, **it is on.**

Worksheet 3

- *Step a.* After you ask, What word? move to the end of the arrow. The children should respond *on.*

- *Step d.* Signal the children to complete the sentence. Watch your voice cue and your timing. Say, When I touch this word, you're going to saaaaaay. . . . and move to the end of the arrow.

- *Step f.* After you say, Reading the fast way, be sure to pause for three seconds. Move quickly to **it** and say **it.** (If you move slowly, the children may try to respond with you.) Then move quickly to **is** and say **is.**

- *Step g.* Move more slowly to **on.** Children are to respond the instant you stop under the word, not before.

- Repeat steps *f* and *g* until the children are firm. Then say, Yes, it is on.

Correction

Use this correction procedure for step *g* if the children begin to sound out the word instead of saying it fast.

model ⟶ **1.** Immediately say the word **on.**

lead ⟶ **2.** Repeat steps *f* and *g,* responding with the children at step *g.* Repeat the lead.

test ⟶ **3.** Repeat step *f.* Then present step *g.* Do not respond with the children.

delayed test ⟶ **4.** Say, Let's do it again. Return to step *a* and present the format. Do not lead the children at step *g.*

Dotted Arrows Between the Lines (Lessons 7–20)

Beginning with lesson 7, the stories are printed on two lines.

Worksheet 7

The dotted arrow from the first line to the second line is a prompt for the children. Some children have a tendency to go from the end of the first line to the end of the second line. The dotted arrow prompts children to begin the next line at the left. The dotted arrow is dropped at lesson 21, after the children have mastered the convention of proceeding from line to line.

Lesson 7

> **STORY**
> **EXERCISE 18**
>
> **Children follow the arrow to the bottom line**
>
> a. (Do not let the children look at the picture until exercise 22.)
> b. (Hold up Worksheet 7. Point to the story.) These words are on two lines. Watch me touch all the words.
> c. (Touch **this** and **is**.) Now I follow the arrow to the ball on the next line. (Follow the arrow.)
> d. Now I touch the rest of the words. (Touch **not** and **me**.)
> e. (Repeat *b* through *d* two times.)
> f. Your turn. Finger on the ball of the top line. ✓
> g. Touch the words when I tap. Get ready. (Tap for **this** and **is**.) *The children touch* **this** *and* **is**.
> h. Now follow the arrow to the next ball. ✓
> i. (Repeat *f* through *h* until firm.)
> j. Touch the words on the bottom line when I tap. Get ready. (Tap for **not** and **me**.) *The children touch* **not** *and* **me**.
> k. This time you're going to touch all the words in the story. Finger on the ball of the top line. ✓
> Get ready. (Tap for **this** and **is**.) ✓
> l. (Do not tap for **not** until the children have followed the arrow to the ball on the bottom line. Then tap for **not** and **me**.) ✓
> m. (Repeat *k* and *l* until firm.)

- *Step f.* Be sure to refer to the first line as the top line and stress the word **top**. You are using the word first in connection with **first word** and **first sound**.

- *Step g.* The children may start to sound out the word rather than pointing and touching. Stress the word **touch**. Repeat step *g* until students touch without sounding out the word.

- *Step l.* If the children do not move their finger to the ball of the second line, you may have to tell them, "Go to the next ball," or "Follow the arrow to the next ball." Remember to present the delayed test after any corrections. Repeat steps *k* and *l* until firm.

Reading The Fast Way
(Lessons 21–160)

Throughout the word-reading activities in the reading-vocabulary and story tracks, the emphasis is on increasing the children's ability to decode without sounding out words. The steps that lead to whole-word reading are sequenced so that the children are able to relate the attack skill of sounding out words to the skill of remembering words. Children do

Lesson 21

STORY

Do not tap for any small letters.

EXERCISE 20

First reading—children sound out each word and tell what word

a. (Do not let the children look at the picture until exercise 22.)
b. Get ready to read the story. First word. ✓
c. Get ready. (Tap for each sound.) *Hēēē.* What word? (Signal.) *He.* Yes, **he.**
d. Next word. ✓
e. Get ready. (Tap for each sound.) *Aāāt.* What word? (Signal.) *Ate.* Yes, **ate.**
f. (Repeat *d* and *e* for the remaining words in the story.)

EXERCISE 21

Second reading—children reread the story and answer questions

a. This time you'll read the story and I'll ask questions. Back to the first word. ✓
b. (Repeat *c* through *f* in exercise 20. Ask the comprehension questions below as the children read.)

After the children read:	You say:
He ate a fig.	What did he eat? (Signal.) *A fig.*
And he is sick.	How does he feel? (Signal.) *Sick.* Why? (Signal.) *Because he ate a fig.*

> **To correct**
>
> (If the children do not give acceptable answers, have them reread the sentence that answers the question. Then ask the question again.)

EXERCISE 22

Picture comprehension

a. What do you think you are going to see in the picture? (Call on a child. Ideas: *a sick boy; boy eating a fig.*)
b. Turn your worksheet over and look at the picture.
c. (Ask these questions:)
 1. Is he eating a fig? (Signal.) *No.*
 2. Why is he sick? (Signal.) *He ate a fig.*
 3. What is that thing in his mouth? (Call on a child.) *A thermometer.* Yes, a thermometer.
 4. What's the doctor going to do to make him feel better? (Call on a child. Accept appropriate responses.)

EXERCISE 23

Word finding

a. Turn your worksheet back to side 1. Everybody, look at the words in the top line. One of the words is **he.**
b. Get ready to touch **he** when I tap. (Pause three seconds.)
c. (Repeat *b* for these words: **fig, hē, āte, fig, āte, fig, hē, āte, hē, fig, āte.**)

EXERCISE 24

Children read the first sentence the fast way

a. Everybody, now you're going to read part of the story the fast way. Finger on the ball of the top line. ✓
b. Move your finger under the sounds of the first word and figure out the sounds you're going to say. Don't say the sounds out loud. Just figure out what you're going to say. ✓
 (Prompt children who don't touch under the sounds. Pause five seconds.) Read the word the fast way. Get ready. (Tap. Say *he* with the children.) *He.*
c. Next word. Move your finger under the sounds and figure out the sounds. ✓
 (Pause five seconds.) Read the word the fast way. Get ready. (Tap. Say *ate* with the children. *Ate.*)
d. (Repeat *c* for the words **a, fig.**)
e. Let's read the words the fast way again. Everybody, finger on the ball of the top line. ✓
 Figure out the first word and get ready to read it the fast way. Say the sounds to yourself. (Pause five seconds.) What word? (Tap.) *He.* Yes, **he.**
f. Figure out the next word. Say the sounds to yourself. (Pause five seconds.) What word? (Tap.) *Ate.* Yes, **ate.**
g. (Repeat *f* for the words **a, fig.**)

EXERCISE 25

Individual test

a. Everybody, finger on the ball of the top line. ✓
b. We're going to have different children read. Everybody's going to touch the words.
c. Everybody, touch the first word. ✓
d. (Call on a child.) Reading the fast way. Get ready. (Tap.) *He.*
e. Next word. ✓
f. Everybody reading. Get ready. (Tap.) *Ate.*
g. Next word. ✓
h. (Call on a child.) Get ready. (Tap.) *A.*
i. (Repeat *e* and *f* for **fig.**)

Worksheet 21, Side 1

> hē ▪ āt. ▪ a ▪ fig.
> and ▪ hē
> is ▪ sic.

Worksheet 21, Side 2

not lose the sounding-out ability. They simply add the ability to remember words. This combination gives them the tools they need to figure out new words and the strategy they need to note the details of words and remember them.

Reading the Fast Way, Lesson 21

Starting with lesson 21, a number of changes appear in the procedures for reading the worksheet story. On the first reading of the story, the children use familiar procedures to sound out each word one time and tell what word.

On the second reading of the story, you ask questions at specified points in the reading.

After the second reading, the children look at the picture, and you ask questions about it.

Next, the children play word finding with three words that appear in the top line of the story.

Then, the children read the first sentence the fast way—a new activity.

Finally, you present a new format for individual turns. You intersperse group reading and individual reading.

Exercise 20. Sounding Out Words That Begin with Stop Sounds

The children sound out each word only one time before they identify the word. Before lesson 13 you tapped for each sound, pausing two seconds between taps as the children hold each sound. But the word **hē** begins with a stop sound, and there is no way the children can hold a stop sound until they say the sound that follows. If you pause two seconds between taps, the children must either

pause between the stop sound and the next sound or mispronounce the stop sound. To guide the sounding out, you must tap for **h** and then quickly for **ēēē**. Children should not stop between the sounds as they say . . .

Children: hēēē

Note that the children say both sounds in response to your second tap.

For the word **him,** you would tap for **h;** tap quickly for **iii** as the children say **hiii;** and tap quickly for **mmm.**

Exercise 23. Word Finding

Word-finding activities started at lesson 3 as a transition activity between sounding out words and reading words the fast way.

In lesson 21, exercise 23, an abbreviated form of the activity is presented.

- *Step a.* Make sure that children are looking at the words and not at you or at their neighbor's story.

- *Step b.* Make sure they are pointing to the appropriate word before you signal.

- *Step c.* Present the series until the children are firm.

Correction

If the child touches a wrong word, have the child sound out and identify that word.

Sound out the word you're touching.

Get ready . . . What word?

Is that the word **fig?**

Look for the word fig, **fffiiig.**

Exercise 24. Children Read the First Sentence the Fast Way

This is a new kind of reading exercise. Children reread the first sentence the fast way. <u>You tap one time for each word.</u>

- *Step b.* If children don't move their fingers under the sounds, guide their fingers.

  Pause five seconds before saying, "Read the word the fast way." Count to yourself or softly tap your foot five times. You must pause long enough before saying, "Get ready," to allow the children to figure out the word. Some children will audibly sound out the word as they point to the sounds. This behavior is quite acceptable. If the children sound out too loudly, tell them to whisper. But allow them to go through the familiar steps of sounding the word out.

  Say, "Get ready," tap, and say **he** with the children.

- *Steps c and d.* Repeat the procedures for the remaining words in the first sentence.

- *Step e.* Note that you ask, "What word?" and tap, but you do <u>not</u> lead by saying the word with the children. You reinforce by saying, "Yes, **he.**"

- *Steps f and g.* Repeat the procedures for the remaining words in the first sentence.

Correction: Use the same correction procedure you used for word-identification errors on page 59.

Reading the Fast Way Track Development

In lessons 21 to 32, the children read the first sentence the fast way.

In lesson 33, the children are taught to find the periods and to say a sentence.

In lessons 33 to 36, the children read the first two sentences the fast way.

In lesson 37, the children reread the entire story the fast way.

In lessons 53 to 160, the children read the story the fast way on the first reading.

Lesson 33

EXERCISE 20

Period finding

a. Turn you worksheet back to side 1. Everybody, we're going to read all the words in the first sentence the fast way.
b. (Point to the first word.) The first <u>sentence</u> begins here and goes all the way to a little dot called a period. So I just go along the arrow until I find a period.
c. (Touch **shē.**) Have I come to a period yet? (Signal.) *No.*
   (Touch **is.**) Have I come to a period yet? (Signal.) *No.*
   (Touch **in.**) Have I come to a period yet? (Signal.) *No.*
   (Touch **thē.**) Have I come to a period yet? (Signal.) *No.*
   (Touch **rāin.**) Have I come to a period yet? (Signal.) *Yes.*
d. Again. (Repeat *b* and *c* until firm.)
e. Everybody, put your finger on the ball of the top line. ✓
f. Get ready to find the period for the first sentence. Go along the arrow until you find that period. ✓

EXERCISE 21

Children read the first sentence the fast way

a. Everybody, get ready to read all the words in the first sentence the fast way.
b. Touch the first word. ✓
   (Pause three seconds.) Get ready. (Tap.) *She.*
c. Next word. ✓
   (Pause three seconds.) Get ready. (Tap.) *Is.*
d. (Repeat *c* for the words **in, thē, rāin.**)
e. (After the children read **rain** say:) Stop. That's the end of the sentence.
f. Let's read that sentence again, the fast way.
g. First word. ✓
   Get ready. (Tap.) *She.*
h. Next word. ✓
   Get ready. (Tap.) *Is.*
i. (Repeat *h* for the words **in, thē, rāin.**)
j. (After the children read **rain** say:) Stop. You've read the first sentence.

EXERCISE 22

Children read the second sentence the fast way

a. Everybody, put your finger on the period after rain. ✓
b. Now move along the arrows until you find the next period. ✓
c. (Repeat *a* and *b* until firm.)
d. Put your finger on the period after rāin.
e. Get ready to read all the words until we come to the next period.
f. Starting with the first word after rāin. ✓
   (Pause three seconds.) Get ready. (Tap.) *She.*
g. Next word. ✓
   (Pause three seconds.) Get ready. (Tap.) *Has.*
h. (Repeat *g* for the remaining words in the second sentence.)
i. (After the children read **sack** say:) Stop. You've read the sentence.
j. Let's read it again. Go back to the period after **rāin.** ✓
   Get ready to read all the words in the sentence.
k. First word. ✓
   Get ready. (Tap.) *She.*
l. Next word. ✓
   Get ready. (Tap.) *Has.*
m. (Repeat *l* for the remaining words in the second sentence.)

Worksheet 33

. shē is in thē rāin. ⟶
. shē has a sacₖ. ⟶

Exercise 20. Period Reading

In exercise 20, you introduce the words **period** and **first sentence.** In exercise 21, steps *e* and *j*, you tell the children that they have come to the end of the sentence. After you have presented these two exercises for several lessons, the children will understand the relationship between a period and a sentence.

Exercise 21. Children Read the First Sentence the Fast Way

- *Step b.* Practice the timing. Say, "Touch the first word." Scan the children's pointing fingers. Watch their mouths forming the words. Pause three seconds. Say, "Get ready." Tap.

- *Steps c and d.* As soon as the children respond, say, "Next word" . . . Scan . . . Pause three seconds . . . Say, "Get ready" . . . Tap.

- *Steps g and h.* Continue to use the three-second pause, although it is not specified.

Exercise 22. Children Read the Second Sentence the Fast Way

Maintain your three-second pause in steps *f* through *h* before you tap for each word. Reduce the length of the pause in steps *j* through *m.*

- *Step j.* A signal is not specified for finding a period. The reason is that all children cannot be expected to find the period at the same time. Some children will move along the line faster than others. In the first few presentations, you may have to tell the children, "Go ahead. Do it."

Lesson 33

EXERCISE 23

Individual test

a. Everybody, finger on the ball of the top line. ✓
b. We're going to have different children read the fast way. Everybody's going to touch the words.
c. First word. ✓ (Call on a child. Tap.) *The child responds.*
d. Next word. ✓ (Call on a child. Tap.) *The child responds.*
e. (Repeat *d* for the remaining words in the first sentence.)

EXERCISE 24

Sentence saying

a. Good reading. Listen to the whole sentence. (Repeat the sentence at a normal speaking rate.)
b. Your turn. Say all the words in that sentence without looking. (Signal.) *The children repeat the sentence at a normal speaking rate.*
c. (Repeat *b* until firm.)

Exercise 24. Sentence Saying

This exercise requires children to remember the words in a sentence. They should say the sentence at a normal, brisk pace with an inflection that conveys the meaning of the sentence. The group should repeat the sentence until all words are properly sequenced and the inflection is appropriate.

If a child omits a word, says the words out of sequence, or inflects inappropriately, repeat the sentence. Then have the children repeat the sentence.

Additional Sentence-Reading Activities

At lesson 40 you introduce quotations; the children answer questions on the first and second reading of the story; and individual children read whole sentences the fast way.

Quotation Finding

Lesson 40

Quotation finding

a. (Pass out Storybook.)
b. Open your book to page 7. ✓
c. (Point to the quotation marks around the word **wow** in the second sentence.) These marks show that somebody is saying something. He's saying the word between these marks.
d. (Point to the quotation marks around **that fat fish is mom** in the last sentence.) These marks show that somebody is saying something. He's saying all the words between these marks.
e. (Point to the quotation marks around **wow**.) Everybody, touch these marks in your story. ✓
   Somebody is saying the word between those marks.
f. (Point to the quotation marks around **that fat fish is mom**.) Everybody, touch these marks in your story. ✓
   Somebody is saying all the words between those marks.
g. (Repeat *e* and *f* until firm.)

Storybook 40

Quotations are in red type in the first several stories. The sentence-saying practice has prepared the children for repeating what is said within quotation marks.

- *Steps c and d.* Be sure that you show the children the quotation marks and the word or words between the marks. You can point with two fingers to the set of quotation marks, or you may want to prop the book so you can point to the marks with both hands.

  When you refer to the words "between the marks," run a finger under the word or words to which you refer.

- *Steps e and f.* Do not signal. Watch to make sure that the children touch the marks. You may have to help them by placing their index fingers on the quotation marks.

Answering Questions (Comprehension)

Lesson 40

EXERCISE 24

Quotation finding

a. (Pass out Storybook.)
b. Open your book to page 7. ✓
c. (Point to the quotation marks around the word **wow** in the second sentence.) These marks show that somebody is saying something. He's saying the word between these marks.
d. (Point to the quotation marks around **that fat fish is mom** in the last sentence.) These marks show that somebody is saying something. He's saying all the words between these marks.
e. (Point to the quotation marks around **wow.**) Everybody, touch these marks in your story. ✓
Somebody is saying the word between those marks.
f. (Point to the quotation marks around **that fat fish is mom.**) Everybody, touch these marks in your story. ✓
Somebody is saying all the words between those marks.
g. (Repeat e and f until firm.)

EXERCISE 25

First reading—children read the story and answer questions

a. You're going to read the story and I'll ask questions.
b. (Tap for the sounds in each word as the children sound out each word one time and tell what word. Present the items below as the children read.)

After the children read:	You say:
The little fish said,	Now we're going to read what he said.
"Wow."	What did the little fish say? (Signal.) *Wow.*
The little fish said,	Now we're going to read what he said.
"That fat fish is Mom."	What did he say? (Signal.) *That fat fish is Mom.*

If the children do not respond on signal at a normal speaking rate, correct by presenting a model, and then a test, as you did for sentence saying on page 94. Then present a delayed test by asking the question again.

Individual Children Read a Sentence the Fast Way

Lesson 40

EXERCISE 28

Individual test

a. I'm going to call on different children to read a whole sentence the fast way. Everybody's going to touch the words.
b. First word of the story. ✓ (Call on a child to read the first sentence. Do not tap for each word.)
c. (Call on a child to read the second sentence. Do not tap for each word.)

• Individual children read at their own rate; you do not tap. Other children follow along.

• Praise children who read rapidly and accurately. Praise children who read with inflection. Praise children who are trying hard and doing well.

• Provide several individual tests. Be sure to call on some lower-performing children.

Question Mark Finding

Lesson 44

EXERCISE 18

First reading—question mark finding

(Have the children reread any sentences containing words that give them trouble. Keep a list of these words.)

a. (Pass out Storybook.)

b. Open your book to page 15 and get ready to read. ✓

c. (Tap for the sounds in each word of the first sentence the children sound out each word one time and tell what word.)

d. (After the children read **shē was not mad at him,** say:) Everybody, move along the lines until you come to the next period. Oh, oh. There's no period in this sentence. There's a funny mark called a question mark.

e. Everybody, touch the question mark. ✓

f. There's a question mark in this sentence because this sentence asks a question. Everybody, get ready to read the question.

g. Finger on the first word. ✓
   (Tap for the sounds in each word of the sentence as the children sound out each word one time and tell what word.)

h. (After the children read **did shē hit him?** say:) Everybody, say that question. *The children repeat the question at a normal speaking rate.*

i. Yes, **did she hit him?** Let's read the next sentence and find out.

j. Finger on the first word. ✓
   (Tap for the sounds in each word of the sentence as the children sound out each word one time and tell what word.)

k. Did she hit him? (Signal.) *No.*

l. Everybody, get ready to read the next sentence. (Repeat *g* through *k* for the sentences: **did shē hug him? nŏ, nŏ, nŏ.**)

m. Everybody, get ready to read the next sentence. (Repeat *g* and *h* for the last sentence: **did shē kiss him?**)

n. Did she kiss him? We'll find out later.

o. (After the first reading of the story, print on the board the words that the children missed more than one time. Have the children sound out each word one time and tell what word.)

p. (After the group's responses are firm, call on individual children to read the words.)

Storybook 44

shē was not mad at him. did
shē hit him? nō, nō, nō. did shē
hug him? nō, nō, nō. did shē
kiss him?

This format teaches the difference between the question mark and the period. The children read each question in the story, say the question at a normal speaking rate, and read the answer.

Children Read the Fast Way Without Sounding Out   (Lessons 53–160)

Major changes take place during these lessons. The children no longer sound out during story reading except as a correction. During group story reading, the group reads the fast way. Individual children read sentences. You present individual checkouts and time each child reading the whole story or part of the story without sounding out.

Procedures for Lessons 53–64

Lesson 54

> **STORY 54**
> **EXERCISE 20**
> **First reading—children read the story the fast way**
> (Have the children reread any sentences containing words that give them trouble. Keep a list of these words.)
> a. (Pass out Storybook.)
> b. Open your book to page 37 and get ready to read. ✓
> c. We're going to read this story the fast way.
> d. Touch the first word. ✓
> e. Reading the fast way. First word. (Pause three seconds.) Get ready. (Tap.) *Thē.* ✓
> f. Next word. ✓
> (Pause three seconds.) Get ready. (Tap.) *Old.*
> g. (Repeat *f* for the remaining words in the first sentence. Pause at least three seconds between taps. The children are to identify each word without sounding it out.)
> h. (Repeat *d* through *g* for the next two sentences. Have the children reread the first three sentences until firm.)
> i. (The children are to read the remainder of the story the fast way, stopping at the end of each sentence.)
> j. (After the first reading of the story, print on the board the words that the children missed more than one time. Have the children sound out each word one time and tell what word.)
> k. (After the group's responses are firm, call on individual children to read the words.)

Storybook 54

> thē ōld gōₐt had an ōld cōₐt.
>
> thē ōld gōₐt said, "I will ēₐt this ōld cōₐt." sō shē did.
>
> "that was fun," shē said. "I ātₑ thē ōld cōₐt. and now I am cōld."
>
> now thē ōld gōₐt is sad.

- Keep a list of troublesome words for word practices at steps *j* and *k.*

- *Steps b through g.* These procedures are similar to those you used for reading the fast way in lessons 33 to 52.

- *Step h.* You direct the reading and rereading of the first three sentences until the children are firm. Pause at least three seconds before signaling for each word. If the children are firm at reading one word every three seconds, they will be likely to maintain their rate through the rest of the story.

Note that the children reread any sentences that are not firm. Some children will have difficulty reading the fast way at this specified rate. You can pause longer than three seconds before words that you know might take longer to figure out, such as new words, words beginning with a stop sound, or words children had trouble with during the reading-vocabulary exercises.

The simplest way to determine an appropriate rate for group reading is to direct individual children to read the passage. Note the amount of time each child requires for different words. Based on their performance, adjust the timing of your signal so that it is slow enough for about eighty percent of the children's individual performances. If some children are consistently very slow (requiring more than five seconds per word), provide additional firming before proceeding in the program.

- *Step i.* Children are to stop at the end of each sentence. On the second reading you will ask questions at the end of some sentences.

Procedures for Lessons 65–160

Beginning with story 61, the stories have titles. In the first story exercise for lessons 61 through 64, you hold up your storybook, point to the title, and say, These words are called the title of the story. These words tell what the story is about.

Lesson 65

STORY

EXERCISE 19

First reading—children read the story the fast way

(Have the children reread any sentences containing words that give them trouble. Keep a list of these words.)

a. (Pass out Storybook).
b. Open your book to page 68. ✓
c. Everybody, touch the title of the story and get ready to read the words in the title the fast way.
d. First word. ✓
   (Pause two seconds.) Get ready. (Tap.) *Al.*
e. (Tap for each remaining word in the title.)
f. (After the children have read the title, ask:) What's this story about? (Signal.) *Al and Sal.* Yes, **Al and Sal.**
g. Everybody, get ready to read this story the fast way.
h. First word. ✓
   (Pause two seconds.) Get ready. (Tap.) *Al.*
i. (Tap for the remaining words in the first sentence. Pause at least two seconds between taps.)
j. (Repeat *h* and *i* for the next two sentences. Have the children reread the first three sentences until firm.)
k. (The children are to read the remainder of the story the fast way, stopping at the end of each sentence.)
l. (After the first reading of the story, print on the board the words that the children missed more than one time. Have the children sound out each word one time and tell what word.)
m. (After the group's responses are firm, call on individual children to read the words.)

Storybook 65

- *Step h.* Some children may touch the first word of the title instead of the first word of the story. Firm the discrimination by telling the children, You're not touching the first word of the story. Hold up your storybook and touch the first word of the story. Here's the first word of the story. Everybody, touch it . . . Listen: Everybody, touch the first word of the title. Get ready . . . Listen: Everybody touch the first word of the story. Get ready . . .

- *Step i.* Here are some guidelines for tapping.

(1) Slow the pace for the first word in every line after the first line. Do this by saying, Next word as soon as the children read the last word of a line. Then say, Get ready . . . Tap. Make sure that the children are touching under the first word of the line before you tap (clap) for the words.
(2) Slow the pace before troublesome words.
(3) Use the individual tests and individual rate and accuracy checkouts to determine whether the children are reading the words in the group reading or are being led. If their rates on individual tests or checkouts are typically slower than the rate you establish for the group reading, your rate is too fast. If they make a number of errors on individual tests, they are probably being led during the group reading. (See In-program tests.)
(4) Make sure that children point under the words that are being read—both on group and individual turns. Watch the children's mouths as they form the

words and observe whether they are pointing appropriately.

(5) Except for words that are preceded by "Get ready . . ." all words must be presented at a constant rate. The children benefit by knowing how much time they have to prepare the next word and the rate at which you expect them to read.

Individual Children or the Group Read Sentences on the First Reading (Lessons 86–117)

Lesson 86

EXERCISE 21

Individual children or the group read sentences to complete the first reading

a. I'm going to call on different children to read a sentence. Everybody, follow along and point to the words. If you hear a mistake, raise your hand.

b. (Call on a child.) Read the next sentence. (Do not tap for the words. Let the child read at his own pace, but be sure he reads the sentence correctly.)

> **To correct**
> Have the child sound out the word. Then return to the beginning of the sentence.

c. (Repeat *b* for most of the remaining sentences in the story.) (Occasionally have the group read a sentence. When the group is to read, say:) Everybody, read the next sentence. (Pause two seconds.) Get ready. (Tap for each word in the sentence. Pause at least two seconds between taps.)

After the group is firm on the title and the first three sentences, you call on individual children to read a sentence. Intersperse some group turns. Children raise their hand if they hear a mistake. Use the corrections on page 86 to correct the group or the individual.

Story-Reading Format from Lesson 106 (Questions on Second Reading)

From lesson 106 through the end of the program children read stories from the textbook. These stories appear in Reading Presentation Book C and are coded to the questions you ask.

Although the page is set up differently, you use the same steps for story reading as used earlier:

1. The children read the title, a word at a time. Children read the fast way (without sounding out each word before identifying it).

2. Next, the children read the story the fast way, a word at a time. The title and first three sentences are read in unison, with the teacher tapping as a signal for each word.

3. After the children have read the first three sentences, the teacher calls on individual children, each to read one of the following sentences. From time to time, the teacher directs the group to read.

When the individual children read, the teacher does not tap.

When the group reads, the teacher taps for each word.

4. The children reread the story after they are firm on the first reading.

5. On the second reading, the teacher presents comprehension questions.

6. The last task dealing with the story is picture comprehension. The children refer to the story picture and answer questions.

Lesson 106

Textbook

STORY
EXERCISE 14

First reading—title and three sentences

a. (Pass out Textbook.)
b. Everybody, open your reader to page 1.
c. Everybody, touch the title.
d. I'll tap and you read each word in the title the fast way.
e. First word. ✓
   (Pause two seconds.)
   Get ready. (Tap.) *Arf.*
f. Next word. ✓
   (Pause two seconds.)
   Get ready. (Tap.) *The.*
g. (Repeat f for the remaining word in the title.)
h. Everybody, say the title. (Signal.) *Arf the shark.* Yes, **Arf the shark.**

i. Everybody, get ready to read this story the fast way.
j. First word. ✓
   (Pause two seconds.) Get ready. (Tap.) *Arf.*
k. Next word. ✓
   (Pause two seconds.) Get ready. (Tap.) *Was.*
l. (Repeat k for the remaining words in the first three sentences. Have the children reread the first three sentences until firm.)

EXERCISE 15
Remaining sentences

a. I'm going to call on different children to read a sentence. Everybody, follow along and point to the words. If you hear a mistake, raise your hand.
b. (Call on a child.) Read the next sentence.

> **To correct** word-identification errors (**from,** for example)
>
>   1. That word is **from.** What word? *From.*
>   2. Go back to the beginning of the sentence and read the sentence again.

c. (Call on a different child.) Read the next sentence.
d. (Repeat c for most of the remaining sentences in the story.)
e. (Occasionally have the group read a sentence. When the group is to read, say:) Everybody, read the next sentence. (Pause two seconds. Tap for each word in the sentence. Pause at least two seconds between taps.)

---

arf the shark[1]

arf was a barking shark. arf was a little shark, but she had a big bark that made the other fish swim away.[2]

a shark swam up to arf and said, "you are a shark. let's play."

arf was happy. "arf, arf," she said.[3] and the other shark swam far, far away. arf was not happy now.[4]

another shark swam up to arf. "you are a shark," he said. "let's play."

arf was happy. "arf, arf," she said. and the other shark swam far, far away. arf was not happy now.

then a big, big fish that liked to eat sharks swam up to the other sharks.[5]

"help, help," they yelled.[6]

but the big fish was swimming after them very fast.

stop[7]

Second reading—sentences and questions

a. You're going to read the story again. This time I'm going to ask questions.
b. Starting with the first word of the title. ✓ Get ready. (Tap as the children read the title.)
c. (Call on a child.) Read the first sentence.

> **To correct** word-identification errors (**from,** for example)
> 1. That word is **from.** What word? *From.*
> 2. Go back to the beginning of the sentence and read the sentence again.

d. (Call on a different child.) Read the next sentence.
e. (Repeat d for most of the remaining sentences in the story.)
f. (Occasionally have the group read a sentence.)
g. (After each underlined sentence has been read, present each comprehension question specified below to the entire group.)

[1] What's this story about? (Signal.) *Arf the shark.*
[2] Who was Arf? (Signal.) *A little shark.*
[3] What did Arf say? Let's hear you say it like Arf said it. (Signal.) *Arf, arf.*
[4] Why wasn't she happy? (Call on a child. Accept appropriate responses.)
[5] What did the big fish like to eat? (Signal.) *Sharks.* Let's see if the big fish eats any.
[6] Why did the sharks yell? (Call on a child. Idea: *They were scared; a big fish that liked to eat sharks was swimming toward them.*)
[7] Is this the end of the story? (Signal.) *No.* Right. We stop now. What do you think will happen? (Call on a child. Accept reasonable responses.) We'll find out next time.

Picture comprehension

a. Look at the picture. ✓
b. (Ask these questions:)
  1. Show me the shark you think is Arf. ✓
  2. What does it look like Arf is doing? (Call on a child. Accept reasonable responses.)
  3. What is that big fish doing? (Call on a child. Accept appropriate responses.)
  4. What would you do if you were Arf? (Let the children comment for ten seconds. Then comment briefly.)

From lesson 106 the comprehension questions are specified in the teacher presentation material. A reduced copy of the children's story appears boxed in Reading Presentation Book C. The sentences about which questions are to be asked are *underlined* and numbered in blue. The questions that the teacher asks are numbered in blue.

- The number 1 for question 1 appears in blue at the bottom of the page. That question is, What's this story about? Children say: *Arf the Shark.*

  Confirm the correct response. Yes, it's about a shark named Arf.

- After the children have read "Arf was a little shark, but she had a big bark that made the other fish swim away" (which is underlined and numbered[2]), you ask question 2. Who was Arf? Children say: *A little shark.*

Note that there are three basic types of questions presented during the second reading.

Type one. A response that involves a few words. The response for this type of question is always indicated in the text. Often variations of the response that is specified for the question are perfectly acceptable.

Type two. The children repeat a sentence or what somebody said in a quote. (Question 3, for example. After the children read "'Arf, arf' she said," the teacher asks, "What did Arf say?") The answer: "Arf, arf." *The children must produce these responses verbatim.* Questions of this type are very important. They help children learn to remember facts and sequences that are presented in stories.

Type three. The children express an opinion or summarize events that were discussed in more than one sentence of the story. For example, question 6: "Why wasn't she happy?" Note that the response to the question, "Why wasn't she happy?" is not specified. When you see the words *the children respond* or *accept reasonable responses,* you may expect more than one correct answer.

If children give an acceptable response to *type one* or *type three* questions, accept the response even if it is not the response specified in the text. For the *type two* questions, however, hold the children to a very firm criterion. Make sure that every child is saying the sentence appropriately and is including every word.

Corrections for Exercise 16 (Comprehension Errors)

In the step *g* of exercise 16, the children answer comprehension questions. They can make many different types of mistakes. Here are the most common mistakes and how to correct them.

Drony Responses

Children may answer questions as if they are reading the answer. For example, after the children read the title, the teacher asks, "What's this story about?" The children respond by saying 'Arf——the——Shark."

Correction for Drony Responses

1. Tell the children what they did: You're not reading now. You're talking to me. I'll answer the question. Listen: What's this story about? **Arf the shark.**

2. Test the children. Your turn. What's this story about? **Children say,** *Arf the shark.*

3. Praise the children. Now you're talking the right way.

4. Provide children with a *model* of an appropriate response. Take note when children use a drony response and model a faster paced voice in directions and signals.

Grammatical Mistakes

Another typical mistake is that the children use inappropriate grammatical structures. For example, the children read: "He went to the store." Teacher asks, "Where did he go?" Children: "He go to the store."

Correction for Grammatical Mistakes

1. Acknowledge that the children got the right information. Yes, that's right.

2. *Model* the appropriate way to answer the question: He <u>went</u> to the store.

3. *Test.* Everybody, say that.

Critical Behaviors for Exercise 16 (Individual and Group Reading and Comprehension)

The focus of exercise 16 is on comprehension. You direct the group in the second reading of the story.

1. The group reads the title in unison.

2. Then you call on different children each to read a sentence.

3. As the children read the story you ask specified comprehension questions. These are indicated in the teacher directions for the second reading. The boxed story that appears in the format indicates when different questions are to be presented.

• The title of the story in the format is underlined and followed by a 1 (<u>arf the shark</u>[1]), which means that you ask question one *after the children have read the title.*

Information Mistakes

The children may not be able to say all the words in a long sentence that has been read haltingly.

Correction for Information Mistakes

1. Read the sentence to the children at a more normal speaking rate. Listen to the sentence: . . . .

2. Repeat the question.

3. If children still have trouble, follow the *model-lead-test* procedure.

   Model: First say the sentence.
   Lead: Then say it with the children.
   Test: Then have the children say it without your lead.

4. Repeat the lead and test steps until the children are firm.

Questions with More Than One Answer

When presenting questions that admit to various answers (such as question 6), not all the children will be producing the same response. Permit the children to respond together. However, to make sure that individual children within the group are giving appropriate answers, call on different children after the group responds:

After reading the part of the story, present the question again.

Call on at least three children to answer these questions.

Story Reading Format from Lesson 118 (Questions on First and Second Readings)

In lesson 114, a story-reading format is introduced in which questions are presented to the children on both the first and second reading of the story. The sample format is for story 118.

Two types of items are introduced on the <u>first</u> reading:

1. Questions that ask about what a character in the story said.

2. Items that relate to directions that are given to the reader. For example, the story tells the reader, "Tell Spot what the man said." (Question 7.) This is a direction which calls for a reader response.

The items that are to be presented on the first reading are listed under exercise 14, step f. Notice the use of two colors, one for first-reading items, another for items that appear on second readings.

Lesson 118

STORY

EXERCISE 13

First reading—title and three sentences

a. Look at the story on page 33. ✓
b. Everybody, touch the title of the story and get ready to read it the fast way.
c. Get ready. (Tap.) *Spot.*
d. Everybody, say the title. (Signal.) *Spot.*
e. Everybody, get ready to read this story the fast way.
f. First word. ✓ (Pause two seconds.) Get ready. (Tap.) *This.*
g. Next word. ✓ (Pause two seconds.) Get ready. (Tap.) *Is.*
h. (Repeat *g* for the remaining words in the first three sentences. Have the children reread the first three sentences until firm.)

---

spot [1]

this is a stōry of a dog

nāmₑd spot. [2] spot did not hēₐr

well. [3] the other dāy shē went to

a stōrₑ to get some bōnₑs. [4] the

man in the stōrₑ said, "it is a

fīnₑ dāy." [5]

 "whaт did you sāy?" spot

askₑd. [6]

 tell spot whaт the man said. [7]

 the man got some bōnₑs fōr

spot. hē said, "pāy mē a dīmₑ

fōr thēsₑ bōnₑs." [8]

 spot askₑd, "whaт did you

sāy?"

 tell spot whaт the man said. [9]

 spot did not hēₐr the man

and the man was gettіภg mad at

spot. [10] the man said, "givₑ mē a

dīmₑ fōr thēsₑ bōnₑs." [11]

 spot askₑd, "whaт did you

sāy?"

 tell spot whaт the man said. [12]

 spot said, "it is тīmₑ fōr mē

to lēₐvₑ. sō I will pāy you a

dīmₑ fōr the bōnₑs and I will

gō hōmₑ."

 sō spot gāvₑ the man a dīmₑ. [13]

then shē took the bōnₑs hōmₑ

and had a fīnₑ mēₐl of bōnₑs.

 the end

See first reading questions below step *f.*

EXERCISE 14

Remaining sentences and questions

a. I'm going to call on different children to read a sentence. Everybody, follow along and point to the words. If you hear a mistake, raise your hand.
b. (Call on a child to read the title and the first sentence.)
c. (Call on a different child.) Read the next sentence.

> **To correct** word-identification errors (**from,** for example)
>
> 1. That word is **from.** What word? *From.*
> 2. Go back to the beginning of the sentence and read the sentence again.

d. (Repeat *c* for most of the remaining sentences in the story.)
e. (Occasionally have the group read a sentence. When the group is to read, say:) Everybody, read the next sentence. (Tap for each word in the sentence.)
f. (After each underlined sentence has been read, present each comprehension question specified below to the entire group.)

[1] What's this story going to be about? (Signal.) *Spot.*
[2] What is Spot? (Signal.) *A dog.*
[3] Did Spot hear well? (Signal.) *No.* She does not hear well. So we'll have to repeat things for Spot.
[5] What did the man say? (Signal.) *It is a fine day.* (Repeat the question until the children give a firm response.)
[7] Everybody, tell Spot what the man said. (Signal.) *It is a fine day.*
[8] Everybody, what did the man say now? (Signal.) *Pay me a dime for these bones.* (Repeat the question until the children give a firm response.)

[9] Everybody, tell Spot what the man said. (Signal.) *Pay me a dime for these bones.*
[11] Everybody, what did the man say? (Signal.) *Give me a dime for these bones.* (Repeat the question until the children give a firm response.)
[12] Everybody, tell Spot what the man said. (Signal.) *Give me a dime for these bones.*

EXERCISE 15

Second reading—sentences and questions

a. You're going to read the story again. And I'm going to ask more questions.
b. Starting with the first word of the title. ✓ Get ready. (Tap as the children read the title.)
c. (Call on a child.) Read the first sentence.

> **To correct** word-identification errors (**from,** for example)
>
> 1. That word is **from.** What word? *From.*
> 2. Go back to the beginning of the sentence and read the sentence again.

d. (Call on a different child.) Read the next sentence.
e. (Repeat *d* for most of the remaining sentences in the story.)
f. (Occasionally have the group read a sentence.)
g. (After each underlined sentence has been read, present each comprehension question specified below to the entire group.)

[4] Why did she go to the store? (Signal.) *To get some bones.*
[6] What did Spot ask? (Signal.) *What did you say?* Why did Spot ask that? (Call on a child. Idea: *Because she didn't hear well.*)
[10] Why do you think the man was getting mad at Spot? (Call on a child. Accept reasonable responses.)
[13] How much did Spot pay for the bones? (Signal.) *A dime.*

EXERCISE 16

Picture comprehension

a. Look at the picture. ✓
b. (Ask these questions:)
   1. Why do you think Spot has her paw on her ear like that? (Let the children comment for ten seconds. Then comment briefly.)
   2. What is Spot carrying? (Signal.) *Bones.*
   3. What do you think that man is saying? (Call on a child. Idea: *Give me a dime for those bones.*)
   4. What do you think Spot wants to do with those bones? (Let the children comment for ten seconds. Then comment briefly.)

The last exercise dealing with the story on each lesson is picture comprehension. For this task, the children refer to the story picture and answer questions that are based on the content of the story and the details that are present in the picture.

Workbook story pictures (lessons 1–37) are always on the second page. The illustrations to some Storybook and Textbook stories appear on the same page as the text. For other stories, the picture is on the next page. When the picture is on the next page the comprehension activities involve prediction questions that require the children to tell what they think they will see in the picture. For stories in which the picture is on the same page as the text, prediction questions do not appear.

Lesson 40

EXERCISE 27

Picture comprehension

a. What do you think you'll see in the picture? (Call on a child. Idea: *a little fish sitting on a fat fish or sitting on his mom.*)
b. Turn the page and look at the picture.
c. (Ask these questions:)
  1. What's the little fish doing? (Call on a child. Idea: *He's sitting on a fat fish.*)
  2. Which fish is Mom? (Call on a child: Idea: *the fat fish.*)
  3. What would you do if a little fish sat on you? (Call on a child. Accept appropriate responses.)

Storybook 40, Story picture

Lesson 109

EXERCISE 15

Picture comprehension

a. What do you think you'll see in the picture? (Call on child. Accept reasonable responses.)
b. Turn the page and look at the picture. ✓
c. (Ask these questions:)
   1. Look at the cow boy on the cow. Does he look happy? (Signal.) *No.*
   2. Why are those other cow boys pointing at him? (Call on a child. Accept reasonable responses.)
   3. What would you say if you saw a cow boy riding a cow? (Let the children comment for ten seconds. Then comment briefly.)

Textbook 109, Story picture

Critical Behaviors

The questions in the picture comprehension activities are designed to allow the children to express themselves. But you must draw a line between letting the children elaborate about things that are important to them and keeping the lesson moving.

1. A good procedure is to present the questions to the group, allowing more than one child to talk at the same time. Then call on individual children to respond.

2. If you find it difficult to allow all the children to respond when they are giving different answers, simply call on different children.

3. Do not allow wrong answers. If the children have trouble identifying some of the things that are illustrated, tell them what you think they are. Also accept responses that are different from the ones you would give but that seem acceptable.

Read the Items (Lessons 96–142)

Read the items is a vehicle for teaching and testing comprehension skills. The items the children read are designed so that the children must read every word and remember the instructions given in the item. The exercises are presented so that you can test the children to make certain that they are reading carefully and comprehending. The first formats have only one item.

- *Exercise 23, step h.* Pause after the word **now.** This helps the children divide the statement into parts that relate to the two comprehension questions you wil ask in exercise 24.

- *Exercise 23, steps i and j.* Be sure the children repeat what they have read at a normal speaking rate.

- *Exercise 24, step b.* Do not insist that the children read silently. They may whisper or read in a low voice.

- *Exercise 24, steps c and d.* Give the children some thinking time in steps *c* and *d.* Hold the last word that you say in step *c*—**nowwww.**

Correction: The corrections for exercises 24 and 25 are specified in the formats. You correct the children by referring them to the item for the answer to the question.

Lesson 97

Storybook

READ THE ITEM
EXERCISE 23

Children read item 1

a. (Pass out Storybook.)
b. Open your book to page 163. ✓
c. (Point to the title **rēad the ītem.**) Everybody, touch this title. ✓
d. I'll read the title. You point to the words I read. (Pause.) Get ready. **Read** (pause) **the** (pause) **item.**
e. Your turn to read the title. First word. ✓
   Get ready. (Tap for each word as the children read: *read the item.*)
f. Everybody, say the title. (Pause and signal. Without looking at the words, the children say *read the item.*) (Repeat until firm.)
g. You're going to read the item. Touch item 1 and get ready to read. ✓
h. First word. (Tap for each word as the children read: *If the teacher says "Now," hold up your hand.*) (Repeat three times or until firm.)
i. Everybody, get ready to say item 1 with me. (Pause and signal. Without looking at the words, you and the children say:) *If the teacher says "Now," (pause one second) hold up your hand.* (Repeat four times or until firm.)
j. All by yourselves. Say item 1. (Signal.) *If the teacher says "Now," hold up your hand.* (Repeat four times or until firm.)

Storybook 23

---
rēad the Ītem

1. if the tēacher says "now," hōld up your hand. →

EXERCISE 24
Children reread item 1 and answer questions

a. Everybody, touch item 1 again. ✓
b. Read item 1 to yourself. Raise your hand when you know what you're going to do and when you're going to do it.
c. (After the children raise their hands, say:) Everybody, what are you going to do if I say "**Now**"? (Signal.) *Hold up my hand.*

To correct	1. Everybody, read item 1 out loud. (Tap as the children read each word.) 2. What are you going to do if I say "**Now**"? (Signal.) *Hold up my hand.*

d. Everybody, when are you going to **hold up your hand**? (Signal.) *If the teacher says "Now."*

To correct	1. Everybody, read item 1 out loud. (Tap as the children read each word.) 2. When are you going to **hold up your hand**? (Signal.) *If the teacher says "Now."*

e. (Repeat *c* and *d* until firm.)

EXERCISE 25
Children play the game

a. Everybody, touch item 1. ✓
b. Read the item to yourself. Raise your hand when you know what you're going to do and when you're going to do it.
c. (After the children raise their hands, say:) Let's play the game. Think about what you're going to do (pause) and when you're going to do it.
d. (Hold out your hand. Pause.) Get ready. **Now.** (Pause. Drop your hand.) *The children hold up their hands immediately.*

To correct	1. What did I say? (Signal.) *Now.* 2. What are you supposed to do if I say "**Now**"? (Signal.) *Hold up my hand.* 3. (If the children's responses are not firm, have them read item 1 aloud.) 4. (Repeat exercise 25.)

Read-the-Items "Fooler" Format (Lessons 121 to 134, 142)

Beginning in lesson 121, a variation of read the items is introduced in which "foolers" occur. A "fooler" is a game situation in which the teacher performs the wrong action. The children are not to respond. The fooler is presented after the children have read the items, said the items, and answered the comprehension questions. The purpose of the foolers is to teach the children how to apply a "rule" appropriately. The "fooler" format from lesson 121 is shown on the next page.

Critical Behaviors for Exercise 10 (Preparation for the game)

1. In step *e,* the children say the item *(When the teacher stands up, say "Stand up").*

2. In step *f,* the teacher asks, "What are you going to say when I stand up?" The children respond, "Stand up."

3. In step *g,* the teacher asks, "What are you going to say when I touch my ear?" The children respond, "Nothing."

4. In steps *h* and *i,* the teacher asks two more similar questions that help firm the children on what they are going to do.

Perhaps the most critical behavior in presenting fooler tasks is <u>pacing</u>. You move very quickly after the children say the rule (step *e* in exercise 10).

Textbook

READ THE ITEM
EXERCISE 10

Read the item

a. (Pass out Textbook.)
b. Open your reader to page 41. ✓ Get ready to read the item.
c. Finger under the first word of the item. ✓
d. Get ready. (Tap. Tap for each word in item 1. Repeat until firm.)
e. Everybody, get ready to say the item. (Pause. Signal.) *When the teacher stands up, say "Stand up."* (Repeat until firm.)
f. What are you going to say when I stand up? (Signal.) *"Stand up."* Right.
g. What are you going to say when I touch my ear? (Signal.) *Nothing.* Right.

> **To correct**
> 1. (Give the answer.)
> 2. (Then have the children read the item aloud.)
> 3. (Repeat the question.)

h. What are you going to say when I say "**Stand up**"? (Signal.) *Nothing.* Right.
i. What are you going to say when I stand up? (Signal.) *"Stand up."*

Lesson 121

Textbook

READ THE ITEM
EXERCISE 10

Read the item

a. (Pass out Textbook.)

b. Open your reader to page 41. ✓
Get ready to read the item.

c. Finger under the first word of the item. ✓

d. Get ready. (Tap. Tap for each word in item 1. Repeat until firm.)

e. Everybody, get ready to say the item. (Pause. Signal.) *When the teacher stands up, say "Stand up."* (Repeat until firm.)

f. What are you going to say when I stand up? (Signal.) *"Stand up."* Right.

g. What are you going to say when I touch my ear? (Signal.) *Nothing.* Right.

> **To correct**
> 1. (Give the answer.)
> 2. (Then have the children read the item aloud.)
> 3. (Repeat the question.)

h. What are you going to say when I say "**Stand up**"? (Signal.) *Nothing.* Right.

i. What are you going to say when I stand up? (Signal.) *"Stand up."*

Lesson 121

EXERCISE 11

Fooler game

> **To correct mistakes on foolers**
> 1. What did I (say, do)? (Signal.)
> 2. Everybody, read the item out loud. First word. Get ready. (Tap for each word.)
> 3. Does the item tell you what to do when I (say, do _____)? (Signal.) *No.*
> 4. So you don't do anything. I fooled you.
> 5. (Repeat the fooler game.)

a. Let's play the game and see if I can fool you.

b. My turn. (Hold your hand out. Pause. Touch your ear. Pause. Drop your hand. Praise the children who do nothing.)

c. My turn. (Hold your hand out. Pause. Say:) Stand up. (Pause. Drop your hand. Praise the children who do nothing.)

d. My turn. (Hold your hand out. Pause. Stand up. Pause. Drop your hand.) *The children are to say "Stand up" immediately.* (Praise the children who say "Stand up.")

> rēad the Ītem
>
> when the tēₐcher stands up, sāy "stand up."

Critical Behaviors for Exercise 11 (Fooler game with the children)

1. In exercise 11, pause before presenting each action. Aside from that pause, move quickly.

- In step *a*, say the instructions quickly.

- In step *b*, do not be elaborate in your praise. "Good job. I couldn't fool you. Let's keep going."

- Move to step *c*. If you go slowly, the children will forget the item and make mistakes.

2. If the children require some firming on the questions at the end of exercise 10, repeat the item before presenting exercise 11. "Let's play the game and see if I can fool you. Remember the item: When the teacher stands up, say 'Stand up.'"

3. At this point, you may want low performers to repeat the rule several times before playing the game.

4. Also, for these low-performing children you may want to present the steps in the exercise with more structure.

- For example, you would present step *b* this way: "My turn": Hold your hand out. (Pause.) Touch your ear. "Everybody, tell me what I did." (Signal.) The children respond, "You touched your ear."

  "Yes, I touched my ear. Now show me what you do when I touch my ear." (Pause.) "Get ready." (Drop-hand signal.)

- You would present step *c* this way: "My turn." Hold your hand out. (Pause.) Say "Stand up." Say "Everybody, tell me what I said." (Signal.) The children respond, "Stand up."

- "Yes, I said 'Stand up.' Now show me what you do when I say 'Stand up.'"

If the children are low performers, practice presenting the fooler exercises in this way. When the children catch on to the format, return to the format that appears in the Teacher Presentation Book.

Corrections: The corrections for exercise 10 and exercise 11 are specified in the format. Follow these corrections if children make mistakes.

PRACTICE the corrrection in exercise 11 before working with the children. The words that go in the blank of step 3 describe a wrong action that you did. If you just said "Stand up" (a wrong action), the wording of step 3 would be: "Does the item tell you what to do when I say 'Stand up?'"

If you just touched your ear (a wrong action), the wording of step 3 would be: "Does the item tell you what to do when I touch my ear?"

Use this correction when the children respond to any wrong action that you perform in the fooler game.

Worksheet Activities

Overview

The worksheets support many skills that are taught in the Reading lessons and shape the children's ability to work independently. Each worksheet presents four or more different activities and will usually occupy the children in independent work for ten to twenty minutes. The worksheets for lessons 1 to 36 also contain the words and stories that the children read.

Worksheets should be taken home and shown to parents. This serves an important function when the children begin to read. It allows children to relate what goes on in school to what goes on at home. It provides parents with a potential basis for praising their child's performance in school. Equally important, it shows parents on a day-to-day basis what is happening in school and what their child is being taught. The worksheet activities extend and reinforce the teacher-directed activities.

When new comprehension worksheet activities are introduced, they are teacher-directed. After one or two days of such direction, the children work on the activities independently. When the children work independently, they should work with as little help from you as possible. Early in the program, some children may need help with writing. Work with these children and praise them for progress in working independently.

The Work Check

Check the children's worksheets each day. Mark errors in pencil or in some way that your marks can be erased so the parent will see a corrected paper. Set up a simple rule that children must have everything corrected on their worksheets before they take them home. Pay close attention to the worksheets. The children's performance on their worksheets reflects how well they have learned a particular skill. If you see a pattern of errors, reteach that skill.

Rewarding the Children

Set up a point system for rewarding children who complete their independent work with few errors during the allotted time.

For no errors on the worksheet 10 points
For 1 to 3 errors 2 points
For more than 3 errors 0 points

Make a chart that shows the number of points that each child earns each day. At the end of the week, have an awards ceremony at which the children can exchange their points for tangible rewards. These can be inexpensive puzzles or games, class parties or special certificates of award that the children can take home, stating that "John earned 26 points this week for hard work on his worksheets."

A reasonable number of points to qualify a child for the awards ceremony is 26.

Summary of Independent Activity

After the children have learned how to do a particular kind of exercise, it becomes part of their independent activity. At the end of each lesson you indicate to the children which exercises they will complete independently. These activities are specified for you in the last exercises for each lesson.

Worksheet Track Development

The worksheet comprehension activities shown on the scope and sequence chart on pages 32 and 33 are developed in a sequence of increasing complexity. The exact steps for teaching all worksheet activities are detailed in exercises that appear at the end of each lesson in the presentation books.

The worksheet formats in the presentation books are self-explanatory, and easy to follow. You should become familiar with them before teaching the worksheet activities. The first time a new format appears in the presentation book, its title has lines above and below it. Follow the directions carefully during the days you present the task to the children. Your careful, exact presentation will pay off in fewer errors when the children begin doing the tasks independently.

The following worksheet activities will be discussed in this guide: writing, pair relations, reading comprehension, picture comprehension, and following directions.

Sound Writing (Lessons 1–120)

The Sound Writing track begins in lesson 1 and continues through lesson 120. The sound writing section of the worksheet displays a model sound on the left of each line. The children are to copy that sound on each empty block on the line. The children practice the sounds they have already learned.

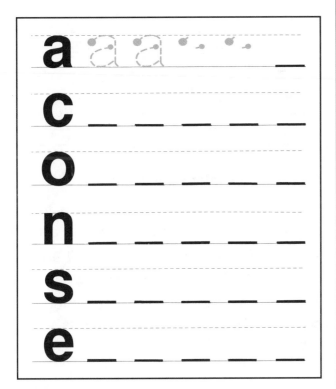

Worksheet 7

A light dotted line helps the children make the small and tall letters the appropriate height. The dotted mid-line is discontinued after lesson 105.

h _ _ _	i _ _ _
n _ _ _	a _ _ _
m _ _ _	o _ _ _

Worksheet 107

Here is the basic teacher presentation for sound-writing exercises.

Sound writing

a. (Point to the sound-writing exercise.) Here are the sounds you're going to write today. I'll touch the sounds. You say them.
b. (Touch each sound.) *The children respond.*
c. (Repeat the series until firm.)

Note that the children respond by saying **sounds,** not letter names. (Letter names is a *Reading Mastery Plus*, Level K track.)

In step *b,* when you touch **a** on your worksheet, children respond with *aaa.* If children respond with the letter name or the word **a,** immediately correct them: **Aaa.** That's the sound. What sound? (Touch **a.**) *Aaa.*

I'll touch the sounds. You say them. (Repeat the series until firm.)

Story Copying and Sentence Copying (Lessons 1–143)

These worksheet exercises teach the children to copy an entire story, later part of a story, and finally a sentence that is similar to a sentence in the story. In the first exercise, at lesson 1, the children copy directly beneath the story. They trace the letters by following dots on the first line. In early lessons, blocks appear between the words, and there are lines (macrons) over the long vowels. All the letters in the words the children write are full-size. Blocks are printed to show the children where they are to write each word.

Worksheet 6

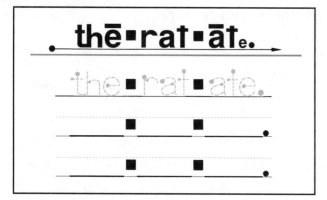

It is not critical for children to copy the long lines when they write the sentence on the lines below the sentence to be traced. It is important, however, that all letters are full-sized.

Watch the children carefully to be sure they are writing the letters small enough to fit into the available space. Be sure that they complete one word at a time. The children may try copying a whole row of the first letter, then a row of the next letter, and so on. This defeats the purpose of the exercise—to practice writing whole words.

Starting at lesson 37, children write a sentence related to the story and illustrate it. Illustrating story art becomes a plain paper activity from lesson 66 through 105.

The writing exercises reinforce the sounds and words being taught. They are not intended to be a handwriting program.

Pair Relations and Matching

Pair Relations (Lessons 1–89)

Children who complete the pair-relations exercises are in a good position to understand the kind of workbook activities they will encounter in a variety of school subjects and on standardized tests. For all pair relations, sound symbols must be paired with the appropriate symbol or an illustration paired with the appropriate word or sentence. The examples below show some of the various types of pair-relations exercises in the program.

Worksheet 1

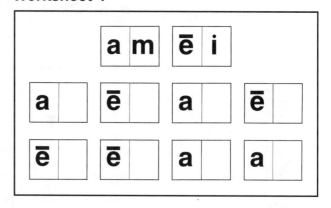

Children complete the pairs.

The purpose of the above exercise is to show the children that pairs such as a/m can be repeated. Each time the pair appears, it must say a/m: aaa, mmm.

The exercise below is introduced after sixteen days of practice with sounds cross-out and circle games.

Worksheet 17

Children cross out the incorrect pairs.

Worksheet 68

Children draw lines through sentences that do not apply, leaving the correct pair.

Worksheet 72

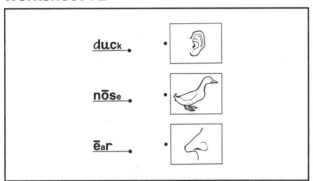

Children connect the correct pairs.

Matching Sounds and Words (Lessons 1–65)

Before children connect words with corresponding pictures (lesson 72, above), they work on matching games that involve sounds and words. In lessons 1 to 10, children match letters with each other. In lessons 11 to 36, children match words. The final variation, in lessons 37 to 65, shows a word in one column and a line to a blank write-on line in the other column. Children write the missing word in the blank.

Worksheet 11

fat. | .sad

is. | .the

the. | .fat

sad. | .is

Reading Comprehension and Story Items

Reading Comprehension (lessons 66–141)

The Reading Comprehension track begins in lesson 66 and continues through lesson 160. The reading comprehension exercises consist of several sentences below which are items about the content of the sentences. The children complete the items by circling the appropriate word for each item. The vocabulary is "safe" in the sense that all words were taught earlier in the program.

The first written reading-comprehension items presented require the children to complete each sentence by circling the appropriate word.

Worksheet 66

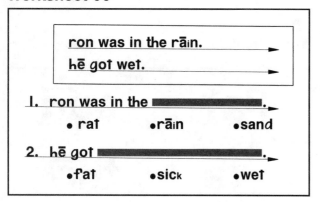

Worksheet 106

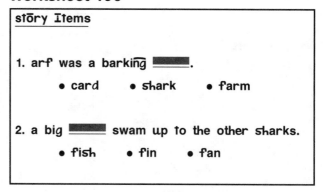

Initially, the blank in each item occurs only at the end of the sentence and involves only a single word. Later, the blank occurs in the middle of the sentence (a harder task) and may involve a response that contains more than one word. The children read several sentences in the first reading-comprehension exercises. By lesson 141, the children read two stories, about twenty-five words each.

This format extends the skills mastered in the matching exercises, the sentence-saying exercisees, and the comprehension exercises presented in connection with reading the story. In picture-comprehension items, starting at lesson 90, the children use their spelling and comprehension skills to complete two sentences for a given picture.

Story Items (lessons 77–142)

Comprehension items that deal with the story the children have just read begin on lesson 77. The story-items exercises from lesson 77 through 143 involve circling the appropriate word to complete the item.

Note that the blanks for story items 1 and 2 on the worksheet are designed so that children will not write in them.

Beginning in lesson 109, the story-item work is no longer teacher-directed.

Reading Comprehension (lesson 142–160)

In lesson 142, the children begin writing responses to reading-comprehension items. (On preceding tasks in reading-comprehension items, the children had merely circled the answers.) The teacher presentation and the children's material for the reading-comprehension story from lesson 142 are shown below.

Note that in the children's material, the blanks are open to provide space for the children to write the answers.

- In steps *b* through *d* of the teacher presentation format, the children read the story about the girl who went out for the running team.

- In step *e*, the teacher tells them that they will write answers in the blanks.

- In step *f*, the children read item 1. (*The girl went out for the running blank.*)

- In step *g*, the children answer the question.

- In step *h*, they write the answer in the blank.

- In steps *i* through *k*, they do item 2 with the teacher.

- In step *l*, they do items 3 and 4 on their own.

Note: There are two reading-comprehension stories in lesson 142, both of which are teacher-directed. This is the only lesson in which the children receive the structured instructions. In following lessons, the children are to work on their own. It is therefore important to make sure that the children are firmed in lesson 142. If they are not, monitor their reading-comprehension work in lessons 143 and 144.

EXERCISE 7

Read story, answer items

a. (Point to the second story.) Everybody, touch this story on your worksheet. ✓

b. Read the fast way. First word. ✓ Get ready. (Tap.) *A.*

c. Next word. ✓ Get ready. (Tap.) *Girl.*

d. (Repeat *c* for the remaining words in the story.)

e. Let's do the items for that story. From now on, you're going to write your answers in the blanks. Don't circle the answers. Just write them in the blanks.

f. Everybody, read item 1. First word. ✓ Get ready. (Tap for each word as the children read: *The girl went out for the running blank.*)

g. Everybody, what goes in the blank? (Signal.) *Team.*

h. Write that answer in the blank. ✓

i. Everybody, read item 2. First word. ✓ Get ready. (Tap for each word as the children read: *Did the boys think she could run fast?*)

j. What's the answer? (Signal.) *No.*

k. Write that answer in the blank. ✓

l. Everybody, do items 3 and 4 on your own. Remember—write the answers in the blanks. ✓

Lesson 142

Worksheet 142

> a girl went out for the runnin̄g t̄eam.
> the boys on the t̄eam said, "that girl thinks she can run fast."
> the girl ran faster than the boys. then she said, "h̄o, h̄o."
>
> 1. the girl went out for the runnin̄g _____.
>   ● n̄ose ● fast ● t̄eam
> 2. did the boys think she could run fast? _____
>   ● yes ● no
> 3. who ran faster? _____
>   ● the boys ● the girl ● the t̄eam
> 4. what did the girl s̄ay after she ran? _____
>   ● "he, he" ● "ha, ha" ● "h̄o, h̄o"

Story Items (lesson 143)

In lesson 143, the story items are changed so that the children respond by writing answers in the blanks, not by circling answers. (At this point, the reading comprehension and the story items follow the same form. There are blanks in every item. The children write the appropriate answer in the blank.)

The teacher presentation and the story items for lesson 143 are shown below.

Story items

(Point to the story-items exercise.) Today you're going to write the answers in the blanks. Remember, don't circle them. Write them.

Lesson 143

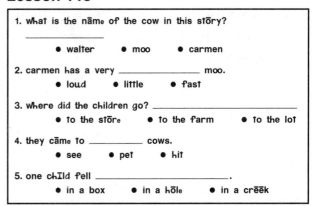

> 1. what is the n̄ame of the cow in this st̄ory?
>   _____
>   ● walter ● moo ● carmen
> 2. carmen has a very _____ moo.
>   ● loud ● little ● fast
> 3. where did the children go? _____
>   ● to the st̄ore ● to the farm ● to the lot
> 4. they c̄ame to _____ cows.
>   ● see ● pet ● hit
> 5. one child fell _____.
>   ● in a box ● in a h̄ole ● in a cr̄eek

Worksheet 143

If possible, monitor the children when they work the story items in lesson 143. If they circle items, show them the blanks and say, "These blanks are open so that you can write in them. That's what you're supposed to do. Find the right answer and write it in the blank."

Spelling Conventions for Reading Comprehension and Story Items

In some of the reading-comprehension activities, the children must compose the answer (not copy it). Follow these rules with regard to their spelling of words:

1. If the word has occurred in the spelling program, the children should be held accountable for spelling it accurately.

2. If the word appears in the choices that are presented with the item, the children should spell the word accurately.

3. The words *yes* and *no* are to be spelled accurately.

4. If the words are in the reading-comprehension story, the children should find the words and spell them accurately.

5. If the item involves writing words that are not on the Worksheet and that have not been presented in the spelling program, do not expect the children to spell all words accurately. Accept phonetic spelling.

Corrections of Spelling Mistakes

If the misspelled word occurs in the reading-comprehension activity, follow this correction:

1. Ask the child to identify the misspelled word.

2. Say: Find that word in the story.

3. After the child finds the word, say: Now write the word the way it is written in the story.

If the misspelled word is one that occurred earlier in the spelling program, have the child spell the word, following the spelling-program format shown below. Then have the child write the word.

If the children make mistakes in writing the word, use this correction procedure:

1. (Model) Here are the sounds in the word **stop.** Listen. **sss** (pause) **t** (pause) **ooo** (pause) **p.**

2. (Test) Write the word.

When spelling by letter names begins, use the same correction procedure (model, test), but refer to letter names instead of sounds.

Spelling correction

Award points or some other form of reinforcement for children who make 0 to 2 spelling mistakes on their Worksheet (limited only to words that the children have been taught or should copy).

Picture Comprehension

Writing Words for Pictures (lessons 90–120)

The worksheet Picture Comprehension track begins on lesson 90 and continues through lesson 120, then doesn't resume again until story-picture items start at lesson 156.

This track involves writing and should not be confused with the story-reading picture comprehension track. Here is the student Worksheet from lesson 91.

Worksheet 91

Following Instructions (lessons 113–160)

The Following Instructions track begins in lesson 113 and continues through lesson 160. There are two types of following-instructions exercises:

- Following Instructions Type 1 (lessons 113–155)
- Following Instructions Type 2 (lessons 142–160)

The Following Instructions track is very important. The exercises are similar to those in Read the Items in that they require the children to read each instruction very carefully and then do what the instructions say. A major difference between Following Instructions and the textbook Read the Items is that the children do the workbook Following Instructions by themselves (after three teacher-directed introductions in lessons 113, 114, and 115).

The Following Instructions Type 1 presentation and the student material from lesson 113 are shown below.

Worksheet 113

- In steps *e* through *h,* the children read both items and answer the questions presented by the teacher.

- In step *i,* the children are instructed to read the instructions to themselves, then do what the instructions tell them to do.

Critical Behaviors

1. Watch the children to make sure that they actually reread the items before responding.

2. Make sure that they do item 1 first and item 2 next.

Corrections

The most frequent problem among low performers is that they don't know prepositions, such as *in.* They may make the letters *on* the circle and box, not *in* the circle and box.

To correct:

1. Hold up worksheet. Everybody, I'm going to touch. Tell me if I touch in the circle.

2. Touch over the circle. Is this in the circle?

3. Touch next to the circle. Is this in the circle?

4. Touch in the middle of the circle. Is this in the circle?

If children don't respond appropriately, tell them the answer and repeat the examples (in a different order) until the children are firm.

Worksheet

FOLLOWING INSTRUCTIONS

The children will need pencils.

EXERCISE 5

Box and circle items

Children call letters by sounds, not letter names.

a. (Hold up Worksheet 113.)
b. (Point to the circle.) Everybody, touch this circle. ✓
c. (Point to the box.) Everybody, touch this box. ✓
d. Everybody, touch instruction 1 next to the circle and the box. ✓
e. Reading the fast way. First word. ✓
Get ready. (Tap for each word as the children read:) *Make rrr in the circle.*
f. What does the instruction tell you to do? (Signal.) *Make rrr in the circle.*

> **To correct**
>
> (Tell the children the answer.)
> (Then repeat *e* and *f.*)

g. Everybody, get ready to read instruction 2 next to the circle and the box.
First word. ✓
Get ready. (Tap for each word as the children read: *Make sss in the box.*)
h. What does this instruction tell you to do? (Signal.) *Make sss in the box.*
i. (Point to the instructions.) Everybody, read these instructions to yourselves. Then do what the instructions tell you to do. ✓

Lesson 113

Then:

1. Everybody, touch in the circle on your worksheet. **Check.**

2. Everybody, touch in the box on your worksheet. **Check.**

3. Repeat steps 2 and 3 until firm.

4. Repeat the following instructions format beginning with step *d.*

Following Instructions Type 1 (lesson 121)

Beginning in lesson 118, the children are presented with a single object (either a box or a circle). They must discriminate between different prepositions to handle these exercises. The following Worksheet is from lesson 121.

```
1. māke  m  in the circle.

2. māke  a  ōver the circle.

3. māke  r  under the circle.
```

Worksheet 121

Corrections

Note: If children have preposition problems, use a variation of the procedure outlined above.

First firm the children on two prepositions, *in* and *over.*

1. Hold up your worksheet. Everybody, I'm going to touch. Tell me if I touch in the circle or over the circle.

2. Touch over the circle. Where did I touch?

3. Touch above original touch. Where did I touch?

4. Touch in the circle. Where did I touch?

5. Repeat the examples (in mixed order until the children are firm).

6. Then have them touch in the circle and over the circle on their worksheet. Check children's responses.

7. After children are firm on *in* and *over,* introduce *under.* ("Tell me if I touch in the circle or over the circle or under the circle.")

• If children continue to make mistakes, require them to circle the word in the instruction that tells where they will make the symbol. "Item 1 tells where. Does it say *in,* or *over,* or *under?* Circle the word that tells." Check work.

Beginning with lesson 123, items are introduced that involve a vocabulary that is less predictable than that in earlier items.

```
1. māke a circle ōver the box.

2. māke  s  in the box.

3. māke  r  ōver the circle.
```

Worksheet 131

Note that the first item involves both the words *circle* and *box.*

Critical Behaviors for Later Following Instructions

The most frequent type of errors that children make results from carelessness. They do the items quickly and often make errors. To prevent these errors, challenge the children:

• "Remember, these items are hard. They're so hard that you probably can't do all of them without making a mistake no matter how hard you try. You really have to read these instructions carefully."

• When children don't make mistakes, act somewhat surprised. "I didn't think you could do those hard, hard instructions. I don't know how you do it."

If you set up the following-instructions exercises in this way (and follow a similar procedure for other exercises in which children tend to make mistakes), the carelessness mistakes will quickly diminish. Note that you may still have to teach the children things they don't know, particularly the meaning of prepositions to low-performing children.

Following Instructions (lesson 135)

The first activity that deals with word-writing is following instructions in lesson 135. The format is similar to earlier following-instructions tasks, except the children write words, not letters or numbers.

1. māke the word sun in the circle.

2. māke the word cat under the circle.

Worksheet 135

If the children are firm on preceding following-instructions tasks, they should have no trouble with this exercise. The teacher instructions appear in only one lesson (135). It is a good idea to watch the children as they work the following instructions in lessons 136 and 137. If the children ask how to work the exercises, <u>do not tell them</u>. Instead, instruct them to read the instructions aloud. Then say, "Do what those instructions tell you to do."

Teacher instructions and the children's activity for the following-instructions exercise in lesson 135 are shown here.

Worksheet 135

FOLLOWING INSTRUCTIONS

The children will need pencils.

EXERCISE 20

Box and circle items

Children call letters by sounds, not letter names.

a. (Pass out Worksheet 135 to each child.)
b. (Point to the first circle on side 1.) Everybody, touch this circle. ✓
c. Everybody, touch instruction 1 next to the circle.
d. Reading the fast way. First word. ✓ Get ready. (Tap for each word as the children read: *Make the word **sun** in the circle.*)
e. What does this instruction tell you to do? (Signal.) *Make the word **sun** in the circle.*

> **To correct**
>
> (Tell the children the answer.)
> (Then repeat *d* and *e*.)

f. Everybody, get ready to read instruction 2 next to the circle. First word. ✓ Get ready. (Tap for each word as the children read:) *Make the word **cat** under the circle.*
g. What does this instruction tell you to do? (Signal.) *Make the word **cat** under the circle.*
h. (Point to the instructions.) Everybody, read the instructions to yourselves. Then do what the instructions tell you to do. ✓
i. You'll follow the instructions for the other circle later.

Lesson 135

FOLLOWING INSTRUCTIONS
EXERCISE 8

Read sentence, follow instructions

a. (Point to the sentence in the first box on side 2.)

b. Everybody, touch this sentence on your worksheet. ✓

c. I'll read the instructions above the sentence in the box. Listen: **Read this sentence.** That's what you're going to do.

d. Everybody, read the sentence in the box. First word. Get ready. (Tap for each word as the children read: *The dog was fat.*)

e. Everybody, say that sentence without looking. (Signal.) *The dog was fat.* (Repeat until firm.)

f. Touch instruction 1 below the sentence in the box. ✓

g. Read that instruction. First word. Get ready. (Tap for each word as the children read: *Circle the word* **was.**)

h. What are you going to do? (Signal.) *Circle the word* **was.**

i. You're going to circle the word **was.** Everybody, the word **was** is in the box. Touch the word **was.** ✓

j. What are you going to do to the word was? (Signal.) *Circle it.*

> **To correct**
> 1. (Have the children read instruction 1 below the box.)
> 2. (Then ask:) What are you going to do to the word **was**?

k. Everybody, touch instruction 2 below the sentence in the box. ✓

l. Read that instruction. First word. Get ready. (Tap for each word as the children read: *Make a line over the word* **the.**)

m. What are you going to do? (Signal.) *Make a line over the word* **the.**

n. You're going to make a line over the word **the.** Everybody, touch the word **the** in the box. ✓

o. What are you going to do to the word **the**? (Signal.) *Make a line over it.*

> **To correct**
> 1. (Have the children read instruction 2 below the box.)
> 2. (Then ask:) What are you going to do to the word **the**?

p. Everybody, read instruction 1 to yourself and do what it tells you to do. ✓

q. Everybody, read instruction 2 to yourself and do what it tells you to do. ✓

r. Everybody, you'll follow the instructions for the other sentences later.

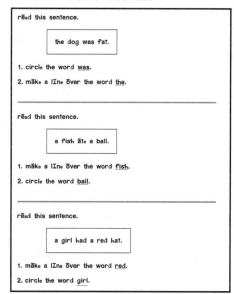

Worksheet 142

Lesson 142

In lesson 142, variations of instructions are introduced for two worksheet activities: Following Instructions and Reading Comprehension.

Following Instructions (lesson 142)

The teacher presentation and the children's material for the new following-instructions activity are shown here.

PRACTICE presenting the format and the corrections that are specified. If the children have mechanical troubles (finding the items under the box, finding the words in the box), repeat the exercise after correcting the mistakes.

If the children make mistakes on the items for the first following-instructionns sentence, structure the presentation on the second sentence. Remember the structured teacher presentation runs for only one lesson. During this lesson, make the children as firm as posssible.

Picture Comprehension

Story-Picture Items (lessons 156–160)

The Story-Picture Items track begins in lesson 156 and continues through lesson 160.

The Story-Picture Items track involves questions similar to those presented in the picture-comprehension activities that are introduced every day after the story has been read.

The teacher-presentation format and the story-picture item from lesson 156 are shown in the next column.

Critical Behaviors

1. In step *c,* the teacher reads the instructions. *(Look at the picture on page 142 of your reader.)* When reading the instructions, read slowly so the children can follow along.

2. In step *d,* the children read as the teacher taps.

3. In step *e,* the children tell what they are to do, and they look at the picture.

4. In steps *f* and *g,* the children read item 1. *(Does the girl look happy or sad?)*

5. In step *h,* the children look at the picture and and answer the question, "Does the girl look happy or sad?"

6. In step *i,* the children write the answer in the blank.

EXERCISE 21

Story picture

a. (Point to the story-picture items exercise on side 2.)

b. Here's something new on your worksheet today. Everybody, touch the instructions. ✓

c. My turn to read the fast way. (Read:) Look at the picture on page 142 of your reader. ✓

d. Your turn to read the instructions the fast way. First word. ✓ Get ready. (Tap for each word as the children read: *Look at the picture on page 142 of your reader.*)

e. Everybody, what do the instructions tell you to do? (Signal.) *Look at the picture on page 142 of my reader.* Do it. ✓

f. Everybody, touch item 1 below the instructions. ✓

g. Read the fast way. First word. ✓ Get ready. (Tap for each word as the children read:) *Does the girl look happy or sad?*

h. Look at the picture on page 142. ✓ Does the girl look happy or sad? (Signal.) *Happy.* Yes, she looks **happy.**

i. Write the answer in the blank. ✓ (Accept phonetic spelling.)

Lesson 156

---

look at the picture on page 142 of your reader.

1. does the girl look happy or sad? _____

Worksheet 156

Corrections

Expect low-language children to have trouble understanding the word <u>or</u> in step *h.* If children have trouble with *or,* follow this correction:

1. Verbally present a series of <u>or</u> questions about the picture. Is the girl sitting or standing? . . . Is the girl sleeping or awake? . . . Is the girl big or little? . . . Is the girl happy or sad?

2. When the children are firm on all questions, have them reread item 1 again. Then ask: Does the girl look happy or sad?

3. After they are firm on answering the question, tell them: Write the answer in the blank.

LANGUAGE

		5	10	15	20	25	30	35	40	45	50
Actions											
Classification											
Word Skills	Opposites										
	Definitions										
	Synonyms										
	Contractions										
Sentence Skills	How–Who–What–Where–When–Why										
	Questioning Skills										
	Verb Tense										
	Statements										
Reasoning Skills	Same–Different										
	True–False										
	Can Do										
	Only										
	Description										
	Analogies										
	If–Then										
Directional Skills	From–To										
	Map Reading										
Information	Days, Months, Seasons										
	Materials										
Applications	Absurdities										
	Temporal Sequencing										
Story-Related Activities	Storytelling Details										
	Sequencing Events										
	Data Collection										
	Extrapolation										
	Putting On a Play										
	Skills (Days, Months, Bleep Talk)										
	Story Completion										
Worksheet Tracks	Coloring										
	Part-Whole										
	Locations										
	Writing Opposites										
Literature Lessons											

Language Scope and Sequence

55 60 65 70 75 80 85 90 95 100 105 110 115 120 125 130 135 140 145 150 155 160

Language Tracks

Much of what children learn in the Language portion of *Reading Mastery Plus,* Level 1 is an extension of skills and information presented in *Reading Mastery Plus,* Level K. The difference between the Level 1 and Level K language programs is that the Level 1 program, in addition to dealing with more sophisticated concepts, stresses visualization and mental operations more than *Reading Mastery Plus,* Level K. The scope and sequence on pages 126 and 127 shows the major skills that are taught in the Language lessons.

In *Reading Mastery Plus,* Level 1 there are no illustrations for the main part of the teacher-directed activities. Children work from verbal information. Another difference is the amount of time devoted to the work on language. In *Reading Mastery Plus,* Level K, language was the primary emphasis, and reading was secondary. In *Reading Mastery Plus,* Level 1, Reading is the primary program and Language is secondary, which means that the Language lessons are not as extensive as those for Reading.

In *Reading Mastery Plus,* Level 1, there are two different types of Language lessons. Special story lessons occur in every lesson that ends in the digits 1 and 6—1, 6, 11, 16, 21, 26, etc. Regular lessons occur in all other lessons.

The regular lessons present 5 or 6 teacher-directed exercises followed by two worksheet exercises. These lessons address a variety of building-block skills that provide children with instructional literacy. In lesson 5, for instance, children do **actions, classification,** responses to directions involving **where** and **when, calendar facts,** and **opposites.** Then they do worksheet activities involving **part-whole** and **classification.**

The special lessons tend to be longer than the regular lessons because they provide a continuation of the sequence that appears in the regular lessons. In addition, they provide exercises involving story grammar, sequencing, and activities associated with retelling and acting out stories.

Actions

The actions track starts in lesson 5 and continues throughout *Reading Mastery Plus,* Level 1. The first exercise in most lessons is an action routine. Routines consist of directions for children to perform specific actions, and questions and instructions that require them to describe what they did, are doing, or will do.

The primary purpose of the action routines is to reinforce and review concepts in an enjoyable routine. The concepts presented include many that were taught in *Reading Mastery Plus,* Level K, such as **prepositions; tense; some, all, none; same, different; and, or**; and **pronouns.**

New concepts are introduced through special action exercises. The first exercises in the following tracks are action tasks: **can do, synonyms,** and **from–to.** These tracks are discussed elsewhere in this guide.

The objectives of the action routines are:

1. To provide the children with practice that does not smack of drill. Action exercises are fun.

2. To promote facility in the use of specific concept words.

3. To induce facility in saying a variety of statements, applied to both new and familiar settings.

4. To provide you with immediate feedback about the children's performance. If they don't understand the instructions for performing an action, you are able to identify the problem immediately.

This is the first Actions routine, from lesson 1.

EXERCISE 1

ACTIONS

a. Let's play some action games.
- Everybody, you're going to hold up your foot **and** touch your ears at the same time. Get ready. (Signal.) ✓
- What are you doing? (Signal.) *Holding up my foot and touching my ears.*

b. Say the whole thing. Get ready. (Signal.) *I am holding up my foot and touching my ears.*
- (Repeat step b until firm.)

c. Everybody, you're going to touch your chin and hold up your **feet**. Get ready. (Signal.) ✓
- What are you doing? (Signal.) *Touching my chin and holding up my feet.*

d. Say the whole thing. Get ready. (Signal.) *I am touching my chin and holding up my feet.*
- (Repeat step c until firm.)

e. Here's another game. I'm going to do something. See if you can figure out what I'm going to do.

f. Listen: I'm going to shake my head or shake my foot or wave.
- What am I going to do? (Signal.) *Shake your head or shake your foot or wave.*

g. (Repeat step f until firm.)

h. Yes, I'm going to shake my head or shake my foot or wave.
- Am I going to wave? (Signal.) *Maybe.*
- Am I going to shake my foot? (Signal.) *Maybe.*
- Am I going to shake my arm? (Signal.) *No.*
- Am I going to shake my head? (Signal.) *Maybe.*

i. Here I go. (Shake your head.)
- Did I shake my head? (Signal.) *Yes.*
- Did I wave? (Signal.) *No.*
- Did I shake my foot? (Signal.) *No.*

j. (Repeat steps h and i until firm.)

Teaching notes: Keep your pacing brisk—say your lines quickly. A brisk pace is critical with all the action tasks.

Do not allow the children to lead you. If you do not require them to respond on signal, you will find yourself slowing the pace of the task, waiting for each child to perform an action before presenting the next instruction.

In step a, after giving the instruction, pause only long enough for the children to perform the action. Then immediately ask the question, What are you doing?

Always make sure that the children are performing the action while they are answering the question What are you doing? They must still be performing it when they say the whole thing. Otherwise, the children will have serious problems with past tense actions.

Make sure the children do **not** respond with a complete statement in step a. They should say *Holding up my foot and touching my ears* not *I am holding up my foot and touching my ears.* If necessary, lead them through this response several times.

In step b, lead the children through the statement as many times as necessary so that they can make the statement without your help. You may have to repeat the statement several times.

Do not proceed to steps e–i, until the children have mastered steps a–d. Make sure the children are responding together and on signal to all steps of this task on the first day it is presented.

To correct: If a child does not follow your instruction correctly, point to a child who has and say, Look, John is holding up his foot and touching his ears. If the child still does not perform the action, help him. For example, take his hands and move them to his ears.

Model the question and correct answer in steps a and b, and steps c and d. If the children respond with a complete statement in steps a and c, repeat the pairs of steps until the children respond without error.

Correct errors in a perfunctory manner and then return to the beginning of the section in which the error occurred.

If the children are hesitant to respond or are being led by some of the group, return to the beginning of the series. Give the instruction, pause two seconds, then give a very precise signal. Repeat until all the children are initiating the responses and are responding on signal.

In this format from lesson 8, the children play a game. They are to respond only if the teacher does exactly the action specified in the first part of the rule. If the teacher does anything else, they are to do nothing.

<hr>

EXERCISE 1

ACTIONS

a. We're going to learn a rule and play some games.

b. Listen to this rule: If the teacher touches the floor, say **yes.**
- Listen again. If the teacher touches the floor, say yes.
- Everybody, say the rule. Get ready. (Signal.) *If the teacher touches the floor, say yes.*

c. (Repeat step b until firm.)

d. Tell me, what are you going to say if I touch the floor? (Signal.) *Yes.*
- Are you going to say **yes** if I touch the floor? (Signal.) *Yes.*
- Are you going to say **yes** if I touch my head? (Signal.) *No.*
- Are you going to say **yes** if I say "Touch the floor"? (Signal.) *No.*

e. Now we're going to play the game.

f. Let's see if I can fool you. Get ready. (Pause.) (Touch your head.) (Signal.) (The children should not say anything.)
- Get ready. (Pause.) (Touch the floor.) (Signal.) *Yes.*
- See if I can fool you this time. Get ready. (Pause.) **Yes.** (Signal.) (The children should not say anything.)
- Get ready. (Pause.) (Touch the floor.) (Signal.) (Children say *yes.*)

g. (Repeat step f until firm.)
- That's the end of the game.

Teaching notes: In step b, present the rule as follows: If the teacher touches the floor, say **yes.**

Make sure that all the children can say the rule before leaving step b.

Present the questions in step d quickly.

Present the last part of the exercise, steps d–g, as a game. Challenge the children. Let them know you would like to fool them.

To correct: If the children have trouble saying the rule, repeat the model, lead, and test procedure specified in step b.

If the children make errors in step d, correct them and return to the beginning of the step. Then do the entire task again.

Classification

The classification track starts in lesson 1 and continues throughout *Reading Mastery Plus,* Level 1. The classification track has a number of objectives, each of which is important for later in the program. These include:

1. Teaching the names of common classes, such as **furniture** and **vehicles.**

2. Setting the stage for the definitions exercises. A definition is constructed by first naming a class for the object to be defined, then by indicating how it is different from the other members of that class.

3. Teaching the relationship between larger and smaller classes, as follows:

   • An object belongs to a number of classes. For example, a yellow pencil is in the classes of yellow pencils, pencils, writing tools, and tools. A larger class has more kinds of things in it. A small class, such as yellow pencils, has only one kind of thing in it; a large class, such as tools, has many different kinds of things in it—pencils, rulers, pliers, and so on.

   • There is a logical test for determining which of two classes is the larger: The larger class has more kinds of things in it. For example, if all trucks are removed from the class of trucks, nothing is left; if all trucks are removed from the class of vehicles, however many vehicles are left. Therefore, the class of vehicles has more kinds of things in it than the class of trucks.

4. Showing children a new way that objects are the same. For example, a pair of pliers and a pencil are the same because both are tools.

The first classification exercises in *Reading Mastery Plus,* Level 1 review the rules for common classes—**containers, vehicles, food, tools, clothing.**

Here's the classification exercise from lesson 1.

EXERCISE 1

CLASSIFICATION

Containers

a. This is the first language lesson. When we do language lessons, you're going to talk. You're going to name things and learn about things like opposites and rules. You'll learn facts about places and things. You'll learn about the calendar, difficult words, and a lot of other things. Remember to follow my directions and work hard.

• Let's start with a rule for containers.

b. Listen: If it's made to hold things, it's a container.

• Say the rule. Get ready. (Signal.) *If it's made to hold things, it's a container.*

• Again. Say the rule. Get ready. (Signal.) *If it's made to hold things, it's a container.*

• (Repeat step b until firm.)

c. Listen: If something is made to hold things, it is a container. If something is not made to hold things, it is not a container.
d. A box is made to hold things, so what do you know about a box? (Signal.) *It's a container.*
- A cup is made to hold things, so what do you know about a cup? (Signal.) *It's a container.*
- A basket is made to hold things, so what do you know about a basket? (Signal.) *It's a container.*
- A suitcase is made to hold things, so what do you know about a suitcase? (Signal.) *It's a container.*
- Is a knife made to hold things? (Signal.) *No.*
- So what do you know about a knife? (Signal.) *It's not a container.*
e. I'll name some things. You tell me if they are containers.
- Listen: a log. Tell me: container or not container. (Signal.) *Not container.*
- Listen: a bike. Tell me. (Signal.) *Not container.*
- Listen: a cabinet. Tell me. (Signal.) *Container.*
- Listen: a jar. Tell me. (Signal.) *Container.*
- Listen: a pencil. Tell me. (Signal.) *Not container.*

Teaching notes: In step b, you present a rule for containers—**if it's made to hold things, it's a container.** Children learned this rule in *Reading Mastery Plus,* Level K.

In step d, you provide children with information they need to classify objects as containers.

Require solid responses from the children. In step b, they should say the rule correctly. If you're not sure of how firm they are in saying the rule, call on individual children after you direct the group to repeat the rule. In step d, they are applying the rule about containers. If they make mistakes, correct by referring to the rule for containers. For instance, A

suitcase is made to hold things, so what do you know about a suitcase? If children say, *It's a suitcase,* remind them of the rule: Listen, if it's made to hold things, it's a container. A suitcase it made to hold things. So a suitcase is a container. Then repeat the wording for the question the children missed: Listen, a suitcase is made to hold things, so what do you know about a suitcase?

It's important for the children to hear how they should go about figuring out the answer to the questions you ask. Practice starting with a rule and giving information and drawing conclusions about whether the thing is a container. If it's made to hold things, it's a container. A box is made to hold things. So a box is a container.

Here are the rules for the classes children learned in *Reading Mastery Plus,* Level K:

> If it is made to take you places, it is a **vehicle.**
>
> If you can eat it, then it's **food.**
>
> If you put things in it, it's a **container.**
>
> If you can wear it, it's **clothing.**
>
> If it has walls and a roof, it's a **building.**
>
> If it grows in the ground, it is a **plant.**
>
> If it helps you do work, it's a **tool.**

Children review these rules through lesson 14. Here's the review exercise from lesson 14.

CLASSIFICATION

a. I'm going to name some objects. Tell me a class these objects are in. (Accept all reasonable responses, but then suggest the response given.)

b. Listen: glass, suitcase, purse, box, bottle. Everybody, what class? (Signal.) *Containers.* Yes, containers.

• Listen: plane, train, bus, car, boat. Everybody, what class? (Signal.) *Vehicles.* Yes, vehicles.

• Listen: saw, rake, screwdriver, pliers, ax. Everybody, what class? (Signal.) *Tools.* Yes, tools.

• Listen: bread, burgers, butter, beans. Everybody, what class? (Signal.) *Food.* Yes, food.

c. (Repeat step b until firm.)

d. I'm going to name a class. See how many objects you can name in that class. Listen: containers. (Call on different children. Accept all reasonable responses.)

• I'm going to name another class. See how many objects you can name in that class. Listen: vehicles. (Call on different children. Accept all reasonable responses.)

• I'm going to name another class. See how many objects you can name in that class. Listen: tools. (Call on different children. Accept all reasonable responses.)

Teaching notes: For this exercise, you name different objects. Children name the class for all the objects. Make sure that children's responses are firm on the classes. If they have a good idea of the objects that are in a class like vehicles, they will be in a good position to learn the new classification operations scheduled for *Reading Mastery Plus,* Level 1.

Starting in lesson 23, they start learning about bigger classes and smaller classes. The test for the size of a class is the different kinds of things that are in the class. A class with more kinds of things in it is bigger than a class with fewer kinds of things in it.

Here's the exercise that introduces bigger–smaller class in lesson 23.

CLASSIFICATION

a. You're going to learn about bigger classes and smaller classes.

• Here's the rule: The bigger class has more kinds of things in it.

• Everybody, say that rule. Get ready. (Signal.) *The bigger class has more kinds of things in it.*

b. Listen to these classes: children, girls, baby girls.

• Everybody, say those three classes. Get ready. (Signal.) *Children, girls, baby girls.*

c. The biggest class is children. It has boys in it. It has girls in it, and it has baby girls in it. What's the biggest class? (Signal.) *Children.*

• Are there girls in that class? (Signal.) *Yes.*

• Are there baby girls in that class? (Signal.) *Yes.*

• Are there boys in that class? (Signal.) *Yes.*

• Say the three classes again. Get ready. (Signal.) *Children, girls, baby girls.*

• Which class is the biggest? (Signal.) *Children.* Yes, the biggest class is children.

d. The next biggest class is girls. It has girls and baby girls in it, but it doesn't have boys in it.

• Say the three classes again. Get ready. (Signal.) *Children, girls, baby girls.*

• Which class is the biggest? (Signal.) *Children.*

• Which class is the next biggest? (Signal.) *Girls.*

• Are there girls in that class? (Signal.) *Yes.*

• Are there baby girls in that class? (Signal.) *Yes.*

• Are there boys in that class? (Signal.) *No.*

e. The smallest class is baby girls. It has only baby girls in it, not older girls or any boys.

f. I'll tell you what is in a class. You tell me which class it is.
- Listen: This class has boys and girls and baby girls. Which class is that? (Signal.) *Children.*
- Listen: This class has only baby girls in it. What class is that? (Signal.) *Baby girls.*
- Listen: This class has girls and baby girls in it. But it doesn't have any boys in it. Which class is that? (Signal.) *Girls.*

g. (Repeat step f until firm.)

Teaching notes: These are nested classes, which means that everything inside the smallest class is in the middle-sized class and inside the biggest class. Some children have trouble learning the structure, but if you bring them to a solid criterion of mastery on the first few appearances of the bigger-class exercises, they'll catch on. The program provides for children lots of practice in applying what they learn about these classes.

The strategy for presenting first exercises is to make sure that children's responses are firm by the end of the exercise. They are able to say the rule for bigger classes and are able to apply it to examples that you name. In step a, children say the rule for bigger classes—make sure that children are very firm on saying the rule before you move on to step b.

In step b, you name three classes—**children, girls, baby girls.** At different points in the exercise, you call on the children to name these three classes. If children tend to produce weak responses, tell them the three classes and go back to the beginning of step b and repeat until children's responses are firm.

Step d is the most critical step in the exercise. For children to understand how larger classes work, they must know that the larger classes have more kinds of things in them. If children's responses are particularly weak on this step, have the children repeat the descriptions for what is in each class and then tell the name for that class.

Make sure that by the time you have finished the exercise, the children's responses are reasonably firm on the contents of the three classes.

Through lesson 41, children continue to work on different variations of this exercise with different classes they have learned. By lesson 41, they have an understanding that the classes they have learned can be broken down into smaller classes. The class of vehicles, for instance, includes the class of cars, and the class of cars includes the class of red cars.

In lesson 42, children learn more about these nested classes. They learn that the smaller classes they have dealt with can be broken down into even smaller classes. And they learn a test for whether a class is bigger than another class. This test is "logical subtraction." We can show that the class of mashed potatoes is smaller than the class of potatoes by removing mashed potatoes from the class of potatoes. If nothing remains, the classes are the same size. But if other types of potatoes remain, the class of mashed potatoes is smaller than the class of potatoes.

Here's the exercise from lesson 42.

EXERCISE 1
CLASSIFICATION

a. We're going to talk about classes.
b. If we took all potatoes from the class of food, would there be any kinds of food left? (Signal.) *Yes.*

- Name some kinds of food that would be left. (Call on different children. Praise appropriate responses.)

c. The class of potatoes is made up of many kinds of potatoes. I'll name some kinds of potatoes in the class of potatoes. Listen: mashed potatoes, boiled potatoes.

- You name some kinds of potatoes in the class of potatoes. (Call on different children. Praise reasonable answers, such as: *fried potatoes, scalloped potatoes, baked potatoes.*)

d. Think about this. If we took all the mashed potatoes from the class of potatoes, would there be any potatoes left? (Signal.) *Yes.*

- Name some kinds of potatoes that would be left. (Call on different children. Praise all acceptable answers: that is, any kind of potato except mashed potatoes.)

e. Yes, if we took all the mashed potatoes from the class of potatoes, there would still be potatoes left. So which class is bigger, the class of mashed potatoes or the class of potatoes? (Signal.) *The class of potatoes.*

- How do you know? (Signal.) *The class of potatoes has more kinds of things in it.*

f. Think big. Which class is bigger, the class of potatoes or the class of food? (Signal.) *The class of food.*

- Think big. Which class is bigger, the class of potatoes or the class of mashed potatoes? (Signal.) *The class of potatoes.*

Teaching notes: The most crucial part of the exercise is step e. You ask children how they know the class of potatoes is bigger than the class of mashed potatoes. Children may not recite the exact answer shown *The class of potatoes has more kinds of things in it,* but children are to express this idea. You can lead them by asking additional questions. When we take all the mashed potatoes from the class of potatoes is there anything left? . . . What's left? . . . That tells why the class of potatoes is larger than the class of mashed potatoes. **Call on different children to tell how they know that the**

class of potatoes is bigger than the class of mashed potatoes. Praise children who give good answers. Prompt those who don't and call on them again.

Children do variations of this exercise and the basic exercise. They also do worksheet activities that involve larger–smaller classes starting with lesson 83. The work provides children with the basic rules about grouping things in different ways.

Word Skills

There are a number of specific things children can do with words if they have been taught the needed skills. The tracks in this group are **opposites, definitions, descriptions, synonyms,** and **contractions.** In these tracks, children learn the skills needed to

1. name and recognize pairs of words that are opposites;

2. define a word—first by naming a class for the things being defined, then by indicating characteristics of the things being defined that are true of only those things;

3. identify objects that are described through clues;

4. name and recognize synonyms;

5. form contractions using the correct pronoun and verb forms.

Opposites

The opposites track begins with a review of opposites taught in *Reading Mastery Plus,* Level K. These opposites are reviewed through lesson 22.

Starting at lesson 23, new opposite pairs are added to the set the children work with. First, each new opposite pair is presented in an introduction exercise. Next, an exercise gives the children practice in using opposites. Finally, the opposite pairs are reviewed.

Following is a list of the opposite pairs reviewed and taught in *Reading Mastery Plus,* Level 1.

Opposites	Lesson Introduced (or reviewed)
dry/wet, fat/skinny, small/big, young/old, full/empty, long/short	1
hotter/colder	3
short/tall	12
big/little	18
fast/slow	23
happy/sad	24
awake/asleep	25
narrow/wide	27
noisy/quiet	28
difficult/easy, winning/losing	43
crying/laughing	44
pushing/pulling, shiny/dull, dangerous/safe, raw/cooked	61
smooth/rough, shallow/deep	62
before/after, early/late, start/finish	65
under/over, wild/tame	68
shut/open	69
throwing/catching	73
in front of/in back of	74
feeling sick/feeling well	106
clean/dirty	108
far/near	111
quickly/slowly	117
bad/good	134
light/dark	139
strong/weak	144

Starting in lesson 1, children review the structure of opposites. **If something is wet, we know that it is not dry. If something is tall, we know that it is not short.**

Here's the review from lesson 1.

EXERCISE 2
OPPOSITES

a. Some words let you figure out things. Those are words like dry, skinny, full, young, long.
- If something is dry, it is not wet.
- If something is fat, it is not skinny.
- If something is small, it is not big.
- If something is young, it is not old.
- If something is full, it is not empty.
- If something is long, it is not short.

b. Your turn. If something is dry, what else do you know about it? (Signal.) *It is not wet.*
- If something is fat, what else do you know about it? (Signal.) *It is not skinny.*
- If something is small, what else do you know about it? (Signal.) *It is not big.*
- If something is young, what else do you know about it? (Signal.) *It is not old.*
- If something is full, what else do you know about it? (Signal.) *It is not empty.*
- If something is long, what else do you know about it? (Signal.) *It is not short.*

c. (Repeat step b until firm.)

d. Listen: I'm thinking of a chicken that is skinny. What else do you know about it? (Signal.) *It is not fat.*
- Listen: I'm thinking of a leaf that is wet. What else do you know about it? (Signal.) *It is not dry.*
- Listen: I'm thinking of a rope that is long. What else do you know about it? (Signal.) *It is not short.*
- Say the whole thing about the rope. Get ready. (Signal.) *The rope is not short.* Yes, the rope is not short.
- Listen: I'm thinking of a jug that is empty. What else do you know about it? Get ready. (Signal.) *It is not full.*
- Say the whole thing about the jug. Get ready. (Signal.) *The jug is not full.*

- Listen: I'm thinking of a duck that is young. What else do you know about it? (Signal.) *It is not old.*
- Say the whole thing about the duck. Get ready. (Signal.) *The duck is not old.*

Teaching notes: In step a, you review the relationship between pairs of different opposites. In step b, you test children on this relationship. In step d, you apply this relationship to concrete situations. Step b is the critical step in this exercise. Repeat the step if children's responses are not firm. Once they are firm on this step, children should have no trouble applying the rules to the concrete examples described in step d.

In lesson 18, children review the word *opposite* and identify pairs of opposites. Here's the exercise.

EXERCISE 7

OPPOSITES

a. Some words are opposites. Here are opposites: long and short. They are opposites because if something is long, you know it can't be short.
- You know the opposite of big. What's the opposite of big? (Signal.) *Small.*
- Here's another pair of opposites: big and little.
- From now on, what will you say for the opposite of big? (Signal.) *Little.*
- Here's another pair of opposites: young and old.
b. Your turn. What are young and old? (Signal.) *Opposites.*
- What are big and little? (Signal.) *Opposites.*
- What are long and short? (Signal.) *Opposites.*
- Who can name another pair of opposites? (Call on different children. Ideas: *wet and dry; fat and skinny; tall and short; full and empty.*)

---

c. I'll say words. You tell me the opposite.
- Listen: empty. What's the opposite of empty? (Signal.) *Full.*
- Yes, full is the opposite of . . . (Signal.) *empty.*
- Say the whole thing about full. Get ready. (Signal.) *Full is the opposite of empty.*
- Listen: old. What's the opposite of old? (Signal.) *Young.*
- Say the whole thing about young. Get ready. (Signal.) *Young is the opposite of old.*
- Listen: tall. What's the opposite of tall? (Signal.) *Short.*
- Say the whole thing about short. Get ready. (Signal.) *Short is the opposite of tall.*
d. (Repeat step c until firm.)

Teaching notes: Step c is the critical step. If children perform well on this step, you know that they understand that opposites occur in pairs and that they are called opposites. Make sure children's responses are firm on step c.

In later lessons, children respond to descriptions that use the word **opposite.** Here's the exercise from lesson 22.

EXERCISE 4

OPPOSITES

a. Get ready to tell me about opposites.
b. I'm thinking of an alligator that is the opposite of dry. So what do you know about it? (Signal.) *It's wet.*
- I'm thinking of an alligator that is the opposite of cold. So what do you know about it? (Signal.) *It's hot.*
- I'm thinking of an alligator that is the opposite of old. So what do you know about it? (Signal.) *It's young.*
- I'm thinking of an alligator that is the opposite of skinny. So what do you know about it? (Signal.) *It's fat.*
- I'm thinking of an alligator that is the opposite of empty. So what do you know about it? (Signal.) *It's full.*
c. (Repeat step b until firm.)

Teaching notes: This type of exercise is like some of the earlier review exercises except that it uses the word opposite. Instead of saying, for instance, I'm thinking of something that is not full, you say, I'm thinking of something that is the **opposite** of full.

New pairs of opposites are introduced beginning with lesson 23. Some of the children will know some of the opposites; however, even though the children may know some of the opposite words, they may not have a clear idea that the word is paired with another word and that the pair functions as opposites.

Here's the exercise from lesson 23.

EXERCISE 5
OPPOSITES

a. I'll tell you about some new opposites.
- Listen. The opposite of fast is slow. What's the opposite of fast? (Signal.) *Slow.*
- What's the opposite of slow? (Signal.) *Fast.*
b. Get ready to tell me about opposites.
- I'm thinking of a duck that is the opposite of dry. So what do you know about it? (Signal.) *It's wet.*
- I'm thinking of a duck that is the opposite of tall. So what do you know about it? (Signal.) *It's short.*
- I'm thinking of a duck that is the opposite of slow. So what do you know about it? (Signal.) *It's fast.*
- I'm thinking of a duck that is the opposite of cold. So what do you know about it? (Signal.) *It's hot.*
- I'm thinking of a duck that is the opposite of young. So what do you know about it? (Signal.) *It's old.*
- I'm thinking of a duck that is the opposite of skinny. So what do you know about it? (Signal.) *It's fat.*
c. (Repeat step b until firm.)

Teaching notes: In step a, you present the new pair of opposites. In step b, you review that pair in the context of familiar opposites.

You should be able to present this material quite fast, and the children should tend to not make any mistakes.

Starting with lesson 51, children say statements that use opposites.

Here's the exercise from lesson 51.

EXERCISE 6
OPPOSITES

a. Let's make up statements with the opposite word.
b. Listen. The boy is **laughing**. Say that statement. (Signal.) *The boy is laughing.*
c. Now say a statement with the opposite of **laughing**. Get ready. (Signal.) *The boy is crying.*
d. (Repeat steps b and c until firm.)
e. Listen. The door is **narrow**. Say that statement. Get ready. (Signal.) *The door is narrow.*
f. Now say a statement with the opposite of **narrow**. Get ready. (Signal.) *The door is wide.*
g. (Repeat steps e and f until firm.)

Teaching notes: Although the exercise is short, it presents important practice—creating a sentence that is parallel to the sentence you give but that has a specified opposite word, which gives the sentence the opposite meaning of the original. This extension of opposites to sentences seems very obvious but it is not always that obvious to the children. Make sure they are firm on saying the opposite sentences.

Definitions

Children receive some practice in constructing definitions, starting in lesson 45. The goal of the instruction is to acquaint children with how definitions give word meanings. They use a two-step operation. First, they identify a class for the word that is being defined. Next, they tell something about what is being defined that is true only of that object. For instance, to define gold, the class for the object is identified—metal. Then the definition says things about gold that cannot be said about other metals: it is a valuable, has a gold color, and does not rust or tarnish.

Here's the definitions exercise from lesson 45.

EXERCISE 1

DEFINITIONS

a. We're going to make up a definition for **corn.**
- First we name a class. Then we say something that is true of only corn. Remember, first we name a class. What do we do first when we make up a definition? (Signal.) *Name a class.*
- Next we say something that is true of only corn.
- What do we do next? (Signal.) *Say something that is true of only corn.*

b. (Repeat step a until firm.)

c. Once more. Everybody, what do we do first? (Signal.) *Name a class.*
- What do we do next? (Signal.) *Say something that is true of only corn.*

d. (Repeat step c until firm.)

e. Now let's make up a definition. Everybody, what do we do first? (Signal.) *Name a class.*
- Name a class for **corn.** (Call on different children. Accept reasonable responses but use: *food* or *plant.*)
  Yes, corn is a food or corn is a plant.

- We named a class. Now what do we do? (Signal.) *Say something that is true of only corn.*
- Yes, now say something that is true of only corn. (Call on one or two children. Accept all reasonable responses, but use: *It grows on ears.*)
  Yes, it grows on ears.

f. I'll say the definition for **corn:** Corn is food that grows on ears.

g. Your turn. Say the definition for **corn.** Get ready. (Signal.) *Corn is food that grows on ears.*
- (Repeat step g until firm.)

h. We're going to make up a definition for **tree.** Everybody, what do we do first? (Signal.) *Name a class.*
- Name a class for **tree.** Get ready. (Signal.) *Plants.*
  Yes, a tree is a plant.
- We named a class. Now what do we do? (Signal.) *Say something that is true of only a tree.*
- Yes, now say something that is true of only a tree. (Call on one or two children. Accept all reasonable responses, but use: *It has leaves, branches, and a trunk.*)
  Yes, it has leaves, branches, and a trunk.

i. Everybody, now say the definition for **tree.** Get ready. (Signal.) *A tree is a plant that has leaves, branches, and a trunk.*
- (Repeat step i until firm.)

j. Let's see if you remember these definitions.
- Everybody, say the definition for **corn.** Get ready. (Signal.) *Corn is food that grows on ears.*
- Everybody, say the definition for **tree.** Get ready. (Signal.) *A tree is a plant that has leaves, branches, and a trunk.*

Teaching notes: **Rehearse this exercise before you present it.** Make sure you know exactly what you expect the children to do at each step.

First you tell them the steps for creating a definition. In step c, you ask them What do we do first? and What do we do next? Make sure that children are very firm on their responses. In step e, they will apply this procedure to defining corn.

First, children name a class for corn. They may name a class that is too large, such as *object.* Tell them that they need a smaller class. Don't accept any classes unless they are true for all examples of corn. For instance, a child may say that *It's something in the kitchen.* Don't accept that class. A child may say that *It is a material.* Don't accept that class. A child may say *It grows on a farm.* That class is probably acceptable (even though there may be wild corn, which is not included in the class).

Children may also have trouble saying something that is true of only corn. They may say things like, *It's yellow; It grows; It's tall* or similar things that are true of other things besides corn. Acknowledge that what they say is true of corn, but that it is true of other things as well. For example, if children say that *Corn is yellow,* say, Yes, it's yellow. But it's not the only food that is yellow. Who can name some other foods that are yellow? . . . (*banana, squash*)

If children have a lot of trouble, tell them I'll say things that are true of corn. You'll tell me if they are true of only corn. It's food that grows on a farm . . . It's food that is tall . . . It's food that is good to eat . . . It's food that's yellow . . . It's food that grows on ears.

In step g, children say the definition for corn: *Corn is food that grows on ears.* Make sure that children are firm on saying the definition.

After children have completed the definition of corn, have them repeat the definition and possibly say the parts of the definition.

Say the part of the definition that tells the class for corn.

Say the part of the definition that tells something that is true of only corn. Repeat the definition until children's responses are firm.

In step h, children repeat the steps as they create a definition for tree.

In lessons 46 and 47, children practice making up definitions for other common objects (spider, elephant, bird, hammer).

Synonyms

Reading Mastery Plus, Level 1 teaches the following synonym pairs:

Synonyms	Lesson introduced
shut, close	85
skinny, thin	85
under, below	87
large, big	88
little, small	88
yell, shout	89
above, over	89
well, healthy	98
crying, weeping	99
fast, quick(ly)	107
near, close to	122
hard, difficult	122
bright, shiny	123
same, alike	127
end, finish	128

The work with synonyms begins in lesson 85 and continues to the end of the level. The only difference between "synonyms" and the funny words (such as zatch in lesson 85) that are presented through the description exercises is that synonyms are established words that mean the same thing (not a made up word that means the same thing as an established word). The work with descriptions sets the stage for synonyms.

Children sometimes have trouble distinguishing between opposites and synonyms. For this reason, synonyms are not introduced until the children have practiced opposites for many lessons.

The first synonyms are introduced as words that **mean the same thing.** Sentence tasks, reviews, and stories are part of each cycle.

The exercise in lesson 85 introduces the word *synonyms* and gives a definition. Here's the exercise.

EXERCISE 2

SYNONYMS

a. We're going to learn what **synonym** means.
b. Synonym. Say that. (Signal.) *Synonym.*
  • (Repeat until firm.)
c. Listen to the rule. A synonym is a word that means the same thing as another word.
d. Listen again: A synonym is a word that means the same thing as another word. Let's say that. Get ready. (Respond with the children.) *A synonym is a word that means the same thing as another word.*
e. All by yourselves. Say the rule. Get ready. (Signal.) *A synonym is a word that means the same thing as another word.*
f. (Repeat steps d and e until firm.)
g. What do we call a word that means the same thing as another word? (Signal.) *A synonym.*
  • Say the rule. Get ready. (Signal.) *A synonym is a word that means the same thing as another word.*

Teaching notes: Repeat step b until the children say **synonym** correctly. This is a difficult word for some children so you may have to repeat this step several times.

The rule in step d may require a number (four or more) of repetitions before the children can say it. To make it easier for the children to remember the rule, phrase it in a sing-song way, stressing the words **same thing.** A synonym is a word that means the **same thing** as another word.

• Use the individual tests as an indicator of whether the rule should be repeated. If more than one child has trouble, repeat the exercise from the beginning. Then repeat the individual tests.

To correct: If the children have trouble with the rule

1. Model the first part of the rule: A synonym is a word that means . . .

2. Say this part of the rule with the children. (Lead)

3. Have them say this part of the rule without help from you. (Test)

4. Model the entire rule: A synonym is a word that means the same thing as another word. If the children have trouble with any words in the second part of the rule, have them say the troublesome words before you repeat the entire rule.

In lesson 86, children apply what they have learned about synonyms by making up statements that mean the same thing. These statements have the same words except for the pair of synonyms. Because the synonyms mean the same thing, the sentences mean the same thing.

Here's the exercise from lesson 86.

EXERCISE 4
SYNONYMS

a. We're going to talk about synonyms.

b. Remember the rule: A synonym is a word that means the same thing as another word. Say that. Get ready. (Signal.) *A synonym is a word that means the same thing as another word.*

• (Repeat step b until firm.)

c. What's a word that means the same thing as another word? (Signal.) *A synonym.*

• Say the rule. Get ready. (Signal.) *A synonym is a word that means the same thing as another word.*

d. Let's make up statements that mean the same thing as other statements.

e. Listen. The book is thin. Say that. (Signal.) *The book is thin.*

f. Here's the statement that has a synonym: the book is skinny. Say that. (Signal.) *The book is skinny.*

g. I'll say one of the statements. You say the statement that has a synomym. My turn: The book is thin. Your turn. (Signal.) *The book is skinny.*

h. (Repeat steps e through g until firm.)

i. Here's another one.

j. Listen. Please close the window. Say that. (Signal.) *Please close the window.*

k. Here's a statement that has a synonym: Please shut the window. Say that. (Signal.) *Please shut the window.*

l. I'll say one of the statements. You say the statement that has a synonym. My turn: Please close the window. Your turn. (Signal.) *Please shut the window.*

m. (Repeat steps k and l until firm.)

Teaching notes: Present the activity as a game. Read as if you enjoy this activity. Make sure that children are firm in saying the sentences with the synonyms.

If children say opposites instead of synonyms, tell them what they did and repeat the task. Return to it later to make sure that children's responses are firm.

To correct: If children make up statements that contain opposites follow this correction:

1. You made up a statement with the synonym for **thin.** I want a statement with the synonym for **thin.** The synonym for **thin** is the word that means the same thing as **thin.** Everybody, what word is that? The children respond *Skinny.*

2. Repeat the step in which the mistake occurred.

The last type of synonym exercise begins in lesson 94. You present a story containing familiar words. The children name the synonyms for some of them. Then children say statements with the synonyms.

Here's the exercise from lesson 94.

EXERCISE 1
SYNONYMS

a. I'm going to make up a story. You're going to say the story too, but you are going to use synonyms.

b. There was a boy who was very thin.

• What's a synonym for **thin**? (Signal.) *Skinny.*

• So there was a boy who was very . . . (Signal.) *skinny.*

c. This boy really liked to shout.

• What's a synonym for **shout**? (Signal.) *Yell.*

• So this boy really liked to . . . (Signal.) *yell.*

d. One day he got in the closet and closed the door.

• What's the synonym for **closed**? (Signal.) *Shut.*

• So one day he got in the closet and . . . (Signal.) *shut the door.*

e. Let's do that story one more time and go a little faster.

f. There was a boy who was very thin. Say that. (Signal.) *There was a boy who was very thin.*

• Now say that statement with a synonym for **thin.** Get ready. (Signal.) *There was a boy who was very skinny.*

g. This boy really liked to shout. Say that. (Signal.) *This boy really liked to shout.*

• Now say that statement with a synonym for **shout.** Get ready. (Signal.) *This boy really liked to yell.*

h. One day he got in the closet and closed the door. Say that. (Signal.) *One day he got in the closet and closed the door.*

• Now say that statement with a synonym for **closed.** Get ready. (Signal.) *One day he got in the closet and shut the door.*

Teaching notes: The children have been making statements with opposites for some time. Expect them to make mistakes in steps b and c the first time this exercise appears. One way you can help them is to stress the word **synonym** in your directions and give the children thinking time before signaling them to respond.

Contractions

The objectives of this track are:

1. To teach subject-verb agreement.

2. To provide practice with the following contractions:

isn't   wasn't   doesn't   didn't

aren't   weren't   don't

Here's the exercise from Lesson 133.

EXERCISE 3
CONTRACTIONS

a. It's time for some statements.
b. I'll say a statement about a boy.
(Point to a boy.) He **does not** have wings. Now I'll say it a new way. He **doesn't** have wings.

c. Everybody, say the statement the **new** way. Get ready. (Signal.) *He doesn't have wings.*
  • (Repeat step c until firm.)
d. Listen: You do not have wings. Now I'll say it a new way. You **don't** have wings.
e. Everybody, say the statement the **new** way. Get ready. (Signal.) *You don't have wings.*
  • (Repeat step e until firm.)
f. Listen: She does not have wings. Now I'll say it a **new** way. She **doesn't** have wings.
g. Everybody, say the statement the **new** way. Get ready. (Signal.) *She doesn't have wings.*
  • (Repeat step g until firm.)
h. Listen: They **do not** have wings. Now I'll say it a **new** way. They **don't** have wings.
i. Everybody, say the statement the **new** way. Get ready. (Signal.) *They don't have wings.*
  • (Repeat step i until firm.)
j. Now let's see how fast you can go.
k. (Point to a boy.) Does he have wings? (Signal.) *No.*
  • Say the statement the new way. Get ready. (Signal.) *He doesn't have wings.*
l. (Point to two boys.) Do they have wings? (Signal.) *No.*
  • Say the statement the new way. Get ready. (Signal.) *They don't have wings.*
m. (Point to a girl.) Does she have wings? (Signal.) *No.*
  • Say the statement the new way. Get ready. (Signal.) *She doesn't have wings.*
n. (Repeat steps k through m until firm.)

Teaching notes: The exercise has two parts. In the first part (steps a–h), the teacher models four statements with **doesn't** and **don't.** In the last part of the exercise, the children produce statements with contractions after answering questions on which the statements are based.

Steps b and c, d and e, f and g, and h and i are paired statements. Each pair should be paced quickly, with a slight pause between pairs.

Listen carefully for mistakes—**doesn't** for **don't, has** for **have,** and the like.

To correct: If children say an inappropriate word or words in the statements like *He don't have wings* or *We doesn't has wings:*

1. Say the correct word or words: **Doesn't** or **Don't have.**

2. Everybody, say that.

3. Present a model of the statement again: He **doesn't** have wings.

4. Everybody, say that.

5. Return to the beginning of step c.

Use the same correction if children say the sentence without the contraction: He does not have wings.

You may have to repeat steps 3 and 4 of the correction quite a few times before all the children will be firm on the statements.

Later exercises introduce new contractions. These exercises present questions. As part of answering the questions, children use contractions.

Here's the exercise from lesson 134.

EXERCISE 4

CONTRACTIONS

a. (Point to a boy.)
• Everybody, is he a boy? (Signal.) *Yes.*
• My turn to say the statement the new way. **He's a boy.**
• Everybody, say the statement the new way. Get ready. (Signal.) *He's a boy.*
b. It's time for some questions and statements.
• (Point to a girl.)
• Everybody, does she have three arms? (Signal.) *No.*
• My turn to say the statement the new way. She **doesn't** have three arms.
• Everybody, say the statement the new way. Get ready. (Signal.) *She doesn't have three arms.*

c. (Point to several children.)
• Everybody, do they have three arms? (Signal.) *No.*
• My turn to say the statement the new way. They **don't** have three arms.
• Everybody, say the statement the new way. Get ready. (Signal.) *They don't have three arms.*
d. Now let's see how fast you can go.
• (Point to a girl.)
• Does she have three arms? (Signal.) *No.*
• Say the statement the new way. Get ready. (Signal.) *She doesn't have three arms.*
e. (Point to several children.)
• Do they have three arms? (Signal.) *No.*
• Say the statement the new way. Get ready. (Signal.) *They don't have three arms.*
f. (Point to a boy.)
• Does he have three arms? (Signal.) *No.*
• Say the statement the new way. Get ready. (Signal.) *He doesn't have three arms.*

Teaching notes: Expect children to make some mistakes when answering the questions about he or she. In step d, you ask, Does she have three arms? When children attempt to say the answer the new way, they may say, *She don't have three arms.*

To correct the mistake, stop the children as soon as you hear the word don't.

Call the children's attention to the word **does** in the question you ask. Listen: I ask about does. Does she have three arms? The answer is She doesn't have three arms.

Use a similar correction for the question, Do they have three arms? If children try to use the word doesn't, point out, I didn't ask about **does.** So you shouldn't tell me about **does.**

Practice the correction. Make sure that you correct the mistakes that children make. If they make persistent mistakes, review the entire exercise until their responses are firm. You may have to return to the exercise at the beginning of the next language period.

Sentence Skills

Four tracks comprise this group:

(1) Who–What–When–Where–Why

(2) Questioning Skills

(3) Verb Tense

(4) Statements

The common element of these tracks is that they deal with some of the properties of sentences and set the stage for grammatical analysis.

The first track in the group demonstrates that specific parts of sentences answer the questions **who, what, when, where,** or **why.** For example, the sentence "The dog sat on the fence" provides an answer to the questions "Where did the dog sit?" "Who sat on the fence?" and "What did the dog do?" The children's facility with these questions is a good indicator of how they will perform in reading comprehension.

The **questioning skills** track gives the children practice in asking questions, discriminating between the question and the answer and between the answer and the answer expressed as a complete statement. The track demonstrates the basic difference between two types of sentences—questions and statements.

The **verb tense** track provides practice in transforming statements in a given tense to statements in other tenses. For

example, given a present tense statement, the children transform it to either a past tense statement or a future tense statement.

One major purpose of the **statements** track is to demonstrate that a particular statement is limited in what it tells about an event.

Who–What–When–Where–Why

The track teaches sentence-analysis and question-answering skills that are basic to reading comprehension. Some children may find the exercise difficult. It is important to teach every exercise carefully and thoroughly.

The exercise in lesson 2 presents sentences that have a part that tells **where** and other sentences that do not tell **where.** The goal of this exercise is to acquaint children with the specific words in the sentence that answer the question where.

Here's the exercise from lesson 2.

EXERCISE 2
WHERE

a. Everybody, put two fingers on your elbow. Get ready. (Signal.) (Wait.) ✓
- Where are your fingers? (Signal.) *On my elbow.*
- Put two fingers on your wrist. Get ready. (Signal.) (Wait.) ✓
- Where are your fingers? (Signal.) *On my wrist.*
- Where were your fingers? (Signal.) *On my elbow.*
- Say the whole thing about where your fingers were. Get ready. (Signal.) *My fingers were on my elbow.*

b. Some statements tell **where.**

- Listen: My fingers were on my elbow. That statement tells where.
- Here are the words that tell where: on my elbow.
- Listen to the statement again: My fingers were on my elbow. Does that statement tell where? (Signal.) *Yes.*
- Say the words in the statement that tell where. Get ready. (Signal.) *On my elbow.*

c. Listen: The car was in the driveway. That statement tells where.
- Say the words in the statement that tell where. Get ready. (Signal.) *In the driveway.*
- Listen: The book was on the refrigerator. Does that statement tell where? (Signal.) *Yes.*
- Say the words in the statement that tell where. Get ready. (Signal.) *On the refrigerator.*
- Listen: The dog was under the tree. Does that statement tell where? (Signal.) *Yes.*
- Say the words in the statement that tell where. Get ready. (Signal.) *Under the tree.*
- Listen: The man was sad. Does that statement tell where? (Signal.) *No.*
- That statement does not tell where. There are no words in it that tell where something was.
- Listen: The dog was sleeping. Does that statement tell where? (Signal.) *No.*
- Listen: The cat was next to the garage. Does that statement tell where? (Signal.) *Yes.*
- Say the words in the statement that tell where. Get ready. (Signal.) *Next to the garage.*
- Listen: The penny was under the dresser. Does that statement tell where? (Signal.) *Yes.*
- Say the words in the statement that tell where. Get ready. (Signal.) *Under the dresser.*

d. Remember, a statement tells where if it has words that tell where.

Teaching notes: In step a, you ask familiar where questions. The children should have no problems in answering these questions. In step b you introduce the idea that some statements have a part that tells **where.**

In step c, you present sentences that have a part that tells where and other sentences that do not tell where. Children identify the parts that tell where.

Make sure that the group is able to answer all the questions correctly. You may have to repeat step c three or more times before all the children's responses are firm. One of the problems that some children have is that they omit some of the words that tell where. For example, instead of saying, *Under the tree,* they may say *The tree,* or *Under.* Correct the children by telling them the response and then have them repeat the task.

Also, children may not discriminate between sentences that tell where and those that do not. For the sentence, the man was sad, some children may say that it tells where. Show them how to test the sentence. Listen to the first part of the statement, The man. Does that tell where?

Listen to the last part of the statement. Was sad. Does that tell where? No part of the statement tells where, so the statement does not tell where.

Children review parts that tell **where** up through lesson 5. Then they learn about parts that tell **when** after they once more review parts that tell where. Here's the part of the exercise in lesson 5 that tells **when.**

c. Listen: Some statements tell **when.** Here are parts that tell when: yesterday, tomorrow, right now, in a minute, before school, at lunchtime.
- Here's a **statement** that tells when: We work very hard in the morning. Listen: **When** do we work hard? (Signal.) *In the morning.*
- Say the statement. Get ready. (Signal.) *We work very hard in the morning.*
- Say the words in the statement that tell when. Get ready. (Signal.) *In the morning.*

d. New statement: We take a break at lunch time. Listen: When do we take a break? (Signal.) *At lunch time.*

- Say the statement. Get ready. (Signal.) *We take a break at lunch time.*
- Say the words in that statement that tell when. Get ready. (Signal.) *At lunch time.*

e. New statement: The baby cried at four in the morning. Listen: When did the baby cry? (Signal.) *At four in the morning.*
- Say the statement. Get ready. (Signal.) *The baby cried at four in the morning.*
- Say the words in that statement that tell when. Get ready. (Signal.) *At four in the morning.*

f. New statement: I do a lot of things before school begins.
- Say the statement. Get ready. (Signal.) *I do a lot of things before school begins.*
- Say the words in that statement that tell when. Get ready. (Signal.) *Before school begins.*

Teaching notes: This exercise does not require the children to discriminate between parts that tell where and parts that tell when. However, they must identify the parts that tell when. Make sure that their responses are firm in steps d, e, and f.

In lesson 7, children discriminate between statements that tell where and statements that tell when. In this lesson, children first review statements that tell where. Then they review statements that tell when. Finally, they discriminate between the two types of the statements. Here's the part of the exercise that requires them to tell whether the statement tells where or when.

g. I'll say statements. Some will tell **when.** Some will tell **where.**
- Listen: The boat sailed under the bridge. Does that statement tell where or tell when? (Signal.) *Where.*
- Say the words that tell where. Get ready. (Signal.) *Under the bridge.*

h. Listen: The boat sailed in the evening. Does that statement tell where or tell when? (Signal.) *When.*

- Say the words that tell when. Get ready. (Signal.) *In the evening.*

i. Listen: The boat sailed near the shore. Does that statement tell where or tell when? (Signal.) *Where.*
- Say the words that tell where. Get ready. (Signal.) *Near the shore.*

j. Listen: The boat sailed for five days. Does that statement tell where or tell when? (Signal.) *When.*
- Say the words that tell when. Get ready. (Signal.) *For five days.*

k. Listen: The boat sailed during a terrible storm. Does that statement tell where or tell when? (Signal.) *When.*
- Say the words that tell when. Get ready. (Signal.) *During a terrible storm.*

l. Listen: The boat sailed over large waves. Does that statement tell where or tell when? (Signal.) *Where.*
- Say the words that tell where. Get ready. (Signal.) *Over large waves.*

Teaching notes: If children's responses are quite firm on where and on what they had learned about in lessons 5 through 7, they should not have serious problems with the discrimination. If their responses are not firm, however, they will have problems, particularly if they make mistakes on the preceding practice that lesson 7 provides with where and when statements. If the children start to make "guessing" mistakes on the part above, go on to the next part of the lesson and come back to this part later. Don't try to "drill" the children if they have been working on where and when for more than a few minutes.

Remember to come back to this part and firm responses, starting with the exercise that reviews where and correcting any mistakes students make. Also, if children had made mistakes on the part of the exercise shown above, first model the answers for each statement. Then present the statement to the children the way the script indicates.

In the following lessons, children review where and when. Starting in lesson 22, children are introduced to **who.** You present sentences that answer questions about when, where, and who. Here's the exercise.

WHO–WHERE–WHEN

a. I'm going to say sentences that answer a lot of questions. You'll answer the questions.
- Listen. The boys hiked near the river after school.
- Listen again. The boys hiked near the river after school.
- Your turn. Say the sentence. Get ready. (Signal.) *The boys hiked near the river after school.*
- That sentence has words that tell who, words that tell where, and words that tell when.

b. Listen. The boys hiked near the river after school.
- Everybody, say that sentence. Get ready. (Signal.) *The boys hiked near the river after school.*
- Who hiked? (Signal.) *The boys.*
- When did the boys hike? (Signal.) *After school.*
- Where did the boys hike? (Signal.) *Near the river.*

c. Everybody, say the whole sentence. Get ready. (Signal.) *The boys hiked near the river after school.*
- Which words tell who hiked? (Signal.) *The boys.*
- Which words tell where they hiked? (Signal.) *Near the river.*
- Which words tell when they hiked? (Signal.) *After school.*

d. (Repeat steps b and c until firm.)

e. New statement. Seven mice went in the barn last night.
- Everybody, say the sentence. Get ready. (Signal.) *Seven mice went in the barn last night.*
- Who was in the barn? (Signal.) *Seven mice.*

- Where did the seven mice go? (Signal.) *In the barn.*
- When did the mice go in the barn? (Signal.) *Last night.*

f. Everybody, say the whole sentence. Get ready. (Signal.) *Seven mice went in the barn last night.*
- Which words tell who went in the barn? (Signal.) *Seven mice.*
- Which words tell where they went? (Signal.) *In the barn.*
- Which words tell when they went in the barn? (Signal.) *Last night.*

g. (Repeat steps e and f until firm.)

Teaching notes: In step b children answer questions about who, where and when. Expect some children to make mistakes on the question Where did the boys hike? They will say, *Near the river after school.*

Tell them: You told me about where and about when. My turn: Where did they hike? Near the river.

When did they hike there? After school.

Your turn: Where did they hike?

When did they hike there?

Repeat until firm.

In step c, you ask the children to identify the words in the sentence that tell who, where, and when.

Children are often able to answer the questions about who, where, and when but are unable to say the words that tell who, where, or when. To correct mistakes follow these steps:

1. Repeat the sentence.

2. Ask the question about who, where, or when.

3. Tell students that the words they said to answer the questions are the words that tell who, where, or when.

For example, you present the statement, The boys hiked near the river after school. Then you ask, Which words tell where they hiked? and some of the children don't respond.

Correct by saying: Listen. The boys hiked near the river after school. Where did the boys hike? The children say *Near the river.*

Tell them, Those are the words that tell where.

Say the words that tell where.

Return to the beginning of step c and present the step.

In lesson 29 children answer questions about **what.**

Here's the exercise from lesson 29.

EXERCISE 4
WHO–WHERE–WHEN–WHAT

a. I'm going to say a sentence that answers questions about who, where, when, and what. You'll answer the questions.

b. Listen. Last night, two birds flew into the nest.

- Listen again. Last night, two birds flew into the nest.
- Your turn. Say the sentence. Get ready. (Signal.) *Last night, two birds flew into the nest.*
- Listen. Who flew into the nest? (Signal.) *Two birds.*
- Listen. What did the birds do? (Signal.) *Flew into the nest.*
- When did the birds do that? (Signal.) *Last night.*
- Where did the birds go? (Signal.) *Into the nest.*

c. Listen again. Last night, two birds flew into the nest.

- Everybody, say the whole sentence. Get ready. (Signal.) *Last night, two birds flew into the nest.*
- Which words tell who? (Signal.) *Two birds.*

- Which word tells what they did? (Signal.) *Flew.*
- Which words tell when? (Signal.) *Last night.*
- Which words tell where? (Signal.) *Into the nest.*

d. (Repeat step c until firm.)

Teaching notes: Children should not have serious problems with what questions. They have answered these as part of their action routines (What are you doing?) and as part of their picture-identification routines (What color is the dog? What kind of animal is next to the dog?).

Expect some children to have trouble with step c. Tell them the correct answers and repeat the step. Repeat the step at a later time if the children's responses are not perfectly firm when you leave the exercise.

In lesson 34, children are introduced to parts that tell **why.** Here's the exercise.

EXERCISE 4
WHO–WHEN–WHAT–WHY

a. I'm going to say a sentence that answers a lot of questions. One of the questions is why.

- Listen: Yesterday, the baby cried because she had a rash.
- Listen again: Yesterday, the baby cried because she had a rash.
- Your turn. Say the sentence. Get ready. (Signal.) *Yesterday, the baby cried because she had a rash.*

b. That sentence has words that tell why. Everybody, why did the baby cry? (Signal.) *Because she had a rash.*

c. Listen: Yesterday, the baby cried because she had a rash.

- Who cried? (Signal.) *The baby.*
- When did the baby cry? (Signal.) *Yesterday.*
- What did the baby do? (Signal.) *Cried.*
- Why did the baby cry? (Signal.) *Because she had a rash.*

d. (Repeat step c until firm.)

e. Everybody, say the whole sentence. Get ready. (Signal.) *Yesterday, the baby cried because she had a rash.*
- Which words tell who cried? (Signal.) *The baby.*
- Which word tells when? (Signal.) *Yesterday.*
- Which words tell why? (Signal.) *Because she had a rash.*
f. (Repeat step e until firm.)

Teaching notes: The children may make mistakes in step c when you ask What did the baby do? Some children may say, *Cried because she had a rash.*

To correct:

1. Tell the children The answer is cried.

2. Then ask Why did she cry?

3. Then ask What did she do?

This new order makes it easier for the children to identify the part that tells **why** and the part that tells **what** she did.

How questions are the final type presented in *Reading Mastery Plus,* Level 1. They are introduced in lesson 39. Here's the introduction.

EXERCISE 2
WHO—HOW—WHY

a. Some sentences have words that tell **how** somebody did things.
b. Listen: She ate slowly. How did she eat? (Signal.) *Slowly.*
- Listen: She ate without looking up. How did she eat? (Signal.) *Without looking up.*
c. Listen: The boys slept soundly because they had done a lot of work.
- Say the sentence. Get ready. (Signal.) *The boys slept soundly because they had done a lot of work.*
- How did the boys sleep? (Signal.) *Soundly.*
- Listen again: The boys slept soundly because they had done a lot of work.
- Who slept soundly? (Signal.) *The boys.*

- How did they sleep? (Signal.) *Soundly.*
- Why did they sleep soundly? (Signal.) *Because they had done a lot of work.*
d. (Repeat step c until firm.)
e. Everybody, say the whole sentence. Get ready. (Signal.) *The boys slept soundly because they had done a lot of work.*
- Which words tell who? (Signal.) *The boys.*
- Which two words tell what they did? (Signal.) *Slept soundly.*
- Which word tells how they slept? (Signal.) *Soundly.*
- Which words tell why? (Signal.) *Because they had done a lot of work.*
f. (Repeat step e until firm.)

Teaching notes: Some parts that tell how have only one word (quickly, well, etc.). Other parts that tell how have more than one word. In step c you present a sentence that answers questions about **who, how,** and **why.**

If children have trouble, tell them the answer to any question they miss, then repeat step c.

For the remainder of *Reading Mastery Plus,* Level 1 children review parts of sentences that answer who, what, when, where, and why. This work makes it easier for children to learn grammar. The questions that answer who are nouns or pronouns. The questions that answer what are verbs. The questions that answer what, where, and why are part of the sentence's predicate.

Questioning Skills

The questioning-skills track begins in lesson 19 on the worksheet and lesson 27 as an oral activity and continues through the end of the program. The track is designed to show children how to seek information through questions.

The track presents efficient ways for them to do this. In the first exercises you tell them that you're thinking of an object. Children ask specific questions that you answer. Then children identify the object.

Here's the oral exercise from lesson 27.

EXERCISE 1
QUESTIONING SKILLS

a. I'm thinking of an object. You'll ask questions to figure out what that object is. You'll ask these questions:
- What class is it in?
- What parts does it have?
- Where do you find it?

b. Listen to the questions again.
- What class is it in?
- What parts does it have?
- Where do you find it?

c. Everybody, say all three questions.
- Question 1. (Signal.) *What class is it in?*
- Question 2. (Signal.) *What parts does it have?*
- Question 3. (Signal.) *Where do you find it?*

d. Ask question 1. Get ready. (Signal.) *What class is it in?*
- It's in the class of furniture.

e. Ask question 2. Get ready. (Signal.) *What parts does it have?*
- It has a top and drawers.

f. Ask question 3. Get ready. (Signal.) *Where do you find it?*
- You find it in the bedroom.

g. Raise your hand when you know the object. ✓
- Everybody, what object was I thinking of? (Signal.) *A dresser.*

h. (Repeat steps d through g until firm.)

If children's responses are firm with the information presented in *Reading Mastery Plus,* Level K and *Reading Mastery Plus,* Level 1 they should have no trouble with this exercise.

The final exercise type of questioning skills starts in lesson 95. The exercise embeds question-asking in a story context. You start telling a story that contains words that not all children will know. The children tell you to stop when they hear such a word, and then they ask a question about the meaning of the word.

EXERCISE 6
QUESTIONING SKILLS

a. I'm going to tell a story. When you hear a word you don't know, say **stop.**

b. A boy was looking at an (pause) **illustration.** (Children should say *stop.*)
- Everybody, what word don't you know? (Signal.) *Illustration.*
- Ask the question about what the word illustration means. Get ready. (Signal.) *What does the word illustration mean?*
- I'll tell you what illustration means. Illustration is a synonym for **picture.** What is illustration a synonym for? (Signal.) *Picture.*
- If the boy was looking at an illustration, he was looking at a . . . (Signal.) *picture.*

c. Here's more of the story.
- The picture showed a large (pause) **feline.** (Children should say *stop.*)
- Everybody, what word don't you know? (Signal.) *Feline.*
- Ask the question about what the word feline means. Get ready. (Signal.) *What does the word feline mean?*
- I'll tell you what feline means. Feline is a synonym for cat. What is feline a synonym for? (Signal.) *Cat.*
- So if the boy was looking at an illustration of a feline, he was looking at a picture of a . . . (Signal.) *cat.*

d. Here's more of the story.
- The boy said: "That is a cat I (pause) **revere.**" (Children should say *stop.*)
- Everybody, what word don't you know? (Signal.) *Revere.*
- Ask the question about what the word revere means. Get ready. (Signal.) *What does the word revere mean?*

- I'll tell you what revere means. Revere means **adore.** What does revere mean? (Signal.) *Adore.*
- So if the boy revered the cat, he adored the cat.
- e. So then the boy took the illustration of the feline he revered and hung it on his wall. That's the end of the story.

Teaching notes:

- The pacing of this format should be quite rapid. Treat this task as a game.

- Remember to pause before saying each "new" word.

- If the children's responses are firm in steps a and b, you can simply tell them, Ask the question, after they tell you to *Stop.*

- Praise them for good performance.

Other Activities

The sentence skills track demonstrates how to ask questions about function, location, parts, class, and color. It also teaches children how to ask about the meaning of a word.

Here are suggestions for additional activities:

Start by showing the children a paper bag. Tell the group they have just ten questions to find out what's in the bag. Remind them of the strategies they've learned, such as asking about the class it's in, how it's used, where you find it, and what are its parts.

When you're explaining things outside the Language lessons remind the children, If you hear a word you don't understand, say *Stop.*

Finally, reinforce questions that children ask each other or you. If children ask a good question (one that will yield important information), praise them. That's a really good question.

Verb Tense

The verb tense track begins in lesson 47 with a review of the concepts **yesterday, today,** and **tomorrow.** After these are firm, children are taught to use the appropriate tense for each time. For example: Yesterday the man sat on his porch. Today the man sits on his porch. Tomorrow the man will sit on his porch. The pairing of time notation (yesterday, today, tomorrow) with words that indicate the tense (sat, sits, will sit) provides the children with framework for understanding some of the tense conventions.

The verb tense track presents both regular and progressive forms (sat, was sitting) in both singular and plural statements.

Here's the exercise from lesson 47.

EXERCISE 5

VERB TENSE

a. Listen. Tomorrow the cars **will be** on the street. Today the cars **are** on the street. Yesterday the cars **were** on the street.
b. I'll make the statement about the cars tomorrow. Tomorrow the cars will be on the street.
- Your turn. Make the statement about the cars tomorrow. Get ready. (Signal.) *Tomorrow the cars will be on the street.*
c. I'll make the statement about the cars today. Today the cars are on the street.

- Your turn. Make the statement about the cars today. Get ready. (Signal.) *Today the cars are on the street.*

d. I'll make the statement about the cars yesterday. Yesterday the cars were on the street.

- Your turn. Make the statement about the cars yesterday. Get ready. (Signal.) *Yesterday the cars were on the street.*

e. (Repeat steps b through d until firm.)

f. Listen to these statements.

- Today the car **is** on the street.
- Tomorrow the car **will be** on the street.
- Yesterday the car **was** on the street.

g. Make the statement about the car today. Get ready. (Signal.) *Today the car is on the street.*

h. Make the statement about the car tomorrow. Get ready. (Signal.) *Tomorrow the car will be on the street.*

i. Make the statement about the car yesterday. Get ready. (Signal.) *Yesterday the car was on the street.*

Teaching notes: The exercise seems simple, but some children have serious problems with tense because they practice saying things in a way that is different from formal English or school English. For instance, they may say, *Yesterday it's cold;* or *Yesterday it cold.*

Give the children enough practice in saying the statements the right way so they remember how to say them. Do not simply correct mistakes and assume that the corrections will make a difference in their performance on the next verb-tense exercise. Instead, repeat steps g, h, and i until the children's responses are very firm when saying the statements.

Through similar exercises, children review the use of the words **are** and **were.**

In lesson 108, children discriminate whether statements tell what somebody **did** or what somebody **will do.**

Here's the exercise from lesson 108.

VERB TENSE

a. It's time for some statements.

b. Listen. The baby will cry. Say that statement. Get ready. (Signal.) *The baby will cry.*

- Does that statement tell what the baby did or what the baby will do? (Signal.) *What the baby will do.*

c. Listen. The baby cried. Say that statement. Get ready. (Signal.) *The baby cried.*

- Does that statement tell what the baby did or what the baby will do? (Signal.) *What the baby did.*

Through similar exercises the children review tense and number (singular-plural) for different statement types that present problems for some children.

Statements

This track begins in lesson 65 and continues to the end of *Reading Mastery Plus,* Level 1. The major objectives of the track are to demonstrate what a simple statement tells about an event and what **it does not tell.**

Here's the exercise from lesson 65.

STATEMENTS

a. Listen to this statement. The girls are jumping rope.

- Everybody, say that statement. Get ready. (Signal.) *The girls are jumping rope.*

b. Does that statement tell what the girls are doing now? (Signal.) *Yes.*

- Does that statement tell what the girls did yesterday? (Signal.) *No.*
- Does that statement tell if the girls are happy? (Signal.) *No.*
- Does that statement tell if the girls are wearing shoes? (Signal.) *No.*

- Does that statement tell how many girls are jumping rope? (Signal.) *No.*

c. The girls are jumping rope.
   Everybody, say that statement again. Get ready. (Signal.) *The girls are jumping rope.*

d. Here's one thing that statement does not tell us. It doesn't tell how long the rope is. Your turn to name two more things the statement does not tell us. (Call on individual children. Repeat both correct responses.)

e. You named two things the statement does not tell us.
   - Everybody, name the first thing. Get ready. (Hold up one finger.) (Signal.) (The group repeats the first response.)
   - Everybody, name the second thing. Get ready. (Hold up two fingers.) (Signal.) (The group repeats the second response.)

f. (Repeat step e until firm.)

Teaching notes: If the children have trouble with step d, model a number of examples: The statement tells about the girls. But it doesn't tell what kind of girls. It doesn't tell whether they are young, fat, smart, whether they have long hair or short, brown eyes or blue. It doesn't tell what they are wearing.

The statement tells what the girls are doing—jumping rope. It doesn't tell where they are jumping rope. Are they in the park? On the sidewalk? Are they having a good time?

Before presenting the exercise in lesson 65 make sure that you can **name at least ten things that the statement doesn't tell.** Rehearse these responses so that you can act quickly when children have trouble naming things **not** addressed in the statement.

Reasoning Skills

The tracks in the reasoning skills group are: **same–different, true–false, can do,**

only, descriptions, analogies, and **if–then.** The common features of these tracks are:

1. These exercises deal with problem-solving. They involve relationships between objects and events rather than a single feature of an object or event. Here are some examples: Make up a statement that is true of only the boat. Why can't this be the man we're looking for? Tell me the clues that let you know I was thinking of a frog. I'll tell you where the person is. Then you have to describe that person. To correctly respond to these instructions, the children must understand and express relationships.

2. The instructions to the child are fairly complex. Instead of asking such questions as What color is this? or What class is this object in?, the teacher says, for example: Tell me if what I say is true of only the boat or if it is true of the boat and the car, or If a table has a girl on it, what is under it? The responses called for in these tasks usually consist of complete statements.

3. All the concepts used in these exercises have been taught. They are applied to figure out the answers to problems.

Same–Different

The same–different exercises in *Reading Mastery Plus,* Level 1 review and extend the skills that were taught in *Reading Mastery Plus,* Level K. These tracks reinforce the fact that **same** may mean that something about two or more things is identical, not necessarily that everything about these objects is identical. Things are "the same" because they have the same function, are found in the same place, have the same pattern, have the same parts, or they are in the same class.

The objectives of this track are:

1. To teach that **different** is the opposite of **same.**

2. To teach children to compare objects and make observations about how those objects are the same and how they are different.

The first same–different exercise appears in lesson 8.

EXERCISE 4
SAME–DIFFERENT

a. We're going to tell how things are the same and how they are different.
- Listen: a bird and an airplane. See if you can think of some ways they are the same. (Call on different children. Accept reasonable responses such as: *They both fly.*)
b. My turn. I'm going to name some ways they are **different.**
- Listen: A bird is an animal, but an airplane is not an animal. Everybody, say that. Get ready. (Signal.) *A bird is an animal, but an airplane is not an animal.*
- That's one way they are different.
- Listen: A bird has eyes, but an airplane does not have eyes. Everybody, say that. Get ready. (Signal.) *A bird has eyes, but an airplane does not have eyes.*
- That's another way they are different.
c. Now it's your turn.
- Name a way that a bird and an airplane are different. (Call on different children. For appropriate responses, say:) Everybody, say that. Get ready. (Signal.)

Teaching notes: This exercise reviews what children have learned in *Reading Mastery Plus,* Level K. You give children examples of how two objects are different, then they make observations of their own.

To correct: If the children do not produce any responses in steps c, repeat step b. Then present step c again. Praise the children even if they only repeat the responses you suggested. Then suggest another response. Keep prompting until the children originate responses.

Through the end of the level, different versions of this exercise are presented. You name two objects or events. Children name some ways they are the same and some ways they are different. You direct the group to repeat each acceptable response. This practice prepares children for later work when they are asked to compare things. The comparison involves doing what they have been practicing—naming important ways the things being compared are the same and different.

True–False

The **true–false** track sets the stage for the **only** and **description** tracks. Its goal is to demonstrate that a statement may report on what is observed or known (in which case the statement is **true**); the statement may contradict what is observed or known (in which case the statement is **false**); or the statement may refer to details that can't be confirmed/nor contradicted (in which case the statement **may be true** or **may be false.**)

The first exercise demonstrates that statements that are "right," or about which you can say yes, are true. Those that are not right are false.

Here's the exercise from lesson 15.

EXERCISE 5
TRUE–FALSE

a. I'm going to make statements about a truck.
- Say **yes** if I make a statement that is right. Say **no** if I make a statement that is not right.
- What are you going to say if I make a statement that is right? (Signal.) *Yes.*
- What are you going to say if I make a statement that is not right? (Signal.) *No.*

b. Listen. A truck is good to eat. Is that right? (Signal.) *No.*
- Listen. A truck can carry things. Is that right? (Signal.) *Yes.*
- Listen. A truck is a piece of furniture. Is that right? (Signal.) *No.*
- Listen. A truck has hands. Is that right? (Signal.) *No.*
- Listen. A truck has wheels. Is that right? (Signal.) *Yes.*

c. Listen again. This time say **true** if I make a statement that is right. Say **false** if I make a statement that is not right.
- What are you going to say if I make a statement that is right? (Signal.) *True.*
- What are you going to say if I make a statement that is not right? (Signal.) *False.*

d. Listen. A truck is good to eat. Is that true or false? (Signal.) *False.*
- Listen. A truck can carry things. Is that true or false? (Signal.) *True.*
- Listen. A truck is a piece of furniture. Is that true or false? (Signal.) *False.*
- Listen. A truck has hands. Is that true or false? (Signal.) *False.*
- Listen. A truck has wheels. Is that true or false? (Signal.) *True.*

e. (Repeat step d until firm.)

Teaching notes: In step b, the children respond to a series of statements by saying either **yes** or **no.** In step d the

same series is presented. This time the children respond with **true** or **false.**

Present the statements in steps b and d rapidly but pause before asking the questions so that the children will have time to consider their answer to each question.

A different type of exercise begins in lesson 46. In this exercise the children identify and make up statements that are true and false.

Here's the exercise from lesson 46.

EXERCISE 8
TRUE–FALSE

a. I'm going to make statements about beds. You'll say true or false.

b. Listen. You put blankets on beds. Is that true or false? (Signal.) *True.*
- Listen. You can sleep on a bed. True or false? (Signal.) *True.*
- Listen. Beds grow in the ground. True or false? (Signal.) *False.*
- Listen. You see a bed in a bedroom. True or false? (Signal.) *True.*
- Listen. Beds are covered with stone. True or false? (Signal.) *False.*
- (Repeat step b until firm.)

c. I'm going to say statements. Some of these statements are true and some are false. You tell me about each statement.

d. Cows lay eggs. True or false? (Signal.) *False.*
- Water is dry. True or false? (Signal.) *False.*
- Birds have feathers. True or false? (Signal.) *True.*
- A bottle is a container. True or false? (Signal.) *True.*
- Trees grow in the clouds. True or false? (Signal.) *False.*

e. My turn. I'm going to make up a statement about cows that is true. Listen. Cows sometimes live in barns. That statement is true.

f. Your turn. You make up a statement about cows that is true. (Call on one child. Praise an acceptable answer and have the group repeat it. Then say:) Everyone, that statement is . . . (Signal.) *true.*

g. Make up another statement about cows that is true. (Call on another child. Praise an acceptable answer and have the group repeat it. Then say:) Everyone, that statement is . . . (Signal.) *true.*

h. My turn. I'm going to make up statements about cows that are false. Listen. Cows say **meow.** Cows have feathers. Cows are plants. Those statements are false.

i. Your turn. You make up a statement about cows that is false. (Call on one child. Praise an acceptable answer and have the group repeat it. Then say:) Everyone, that statement is . . . (Signal.) *false.*

j. Make up another statement about cows that is false. (Call on another child. Praise an acceptable answer and have the group repeat it. Then say:) Everyone, that statement is . . . (Signal.) *false.*

Teaching notes: The children are not to make statements containing the word **not** in steps i and j. If they are allowed to do this, they will get the mistaken idea that all positive statements are true and that negative statements are false. This will lead to serious trouble later.

Children may make up a statement that is true but that contains the word not. For example, when trying to make up a false statement about cows, a child may say something like, *Cows are not birds.*

Tell the child, You said something that is true. Cows are not birds. You have to say something that is false.

If the child continues to have trouble constructing a false statement, identify some false statements. Listen to these false statements: Cows can fly. Cows give soda pop. Cows can talk. Cows read newspapers. Those statements are false. Your turn to make up a false statement.

Say something that is not true about cows.

Children may make up statements that are false but that have the word not. Tell them how to rephrase these statements so they do not have the word **not.** For example, a child may say, *Cows are not animals.*

Tell the child, Your statement is false because cows are animals. But can you name something they could be if they are not animals?

If the child starts to be confused, name some possible classes. You could say A cow is a plant, **or** A cow is a vehicle, **or** A cow is something made of bricks, **or** A cow is an appliance.

Remember, don't permit children to make up statements that have the word **not.**

Only

This track starts in lesson 19 and continues through lesson 44. In the only track children practice first identifying and then making up statements that are true either of only one object in a pair or of both objects. For example, when looking at a picture of a boat and a car, they identify (and later make up) statements about only the boat, only the car, and finally the boat **and** the car.

Only is treated as the opposite of the word **and.** The concept of **only** is somewhat tricky. For example, here is a statement that is true of a ball: It is a toy. That statement is true of a ball, but it is also true of some other things—dolls, blocks, and so forth. A statement that is true of **only** a ball would be true of a ball but of no other toys.

Here's the exercise from lesson 19.

EXERCISE 5

ONLY

a. I'm going to make statements that are true. Some of the statements will be true of **only** your eyes. Some statements will be true of **only** your teeth. Some statements will be true of **both** your eyes and your teeth.

b. Listen. You chew food with them. Is that true of only your eyes, only your teeth, or both your eyes and teeth? (Signal.) *Only your teeth.*

• Listen. You see things with them. Is that true of only your eyes, only your teeth, or both your eyes and teeth? (Signal.) *Only your eyes.*

• Listen. They are part of your head. Is that true of only your eyes, only your teeth, or both your eyes and teeth? (Signal.) *Both your eyes and teeth.*

• Listen. They are very hard. Is that true of only your eyes, only your teeth, or both your eyes and teeth? (Signal.) *Only your teeth.*

• Listen. The dentist fixes them when they have a problem. Is that true of only your eyes, only your teeth, or both your eyes and teeth? (Signal.) *Only your teeth.*

• Listen. They hurt if you hit them with a hard object. Is that true of only your eyes, only your teeth, or both your eyes and teeth? (Signal.) *Both your eyes and teeth.*

c. (Repeat step b until firm.)

Teaching notes: You make statements. Some are true of only teeth; some are true of only eyes; others are true of both teeth and eyes.

Children have worked on true–false since lesson 15, so they should be firm in their understanding that true means that the statement is right and false means that it is not right.

If children make mistakes in step b, correct the mistakes and then repeat step b until the children are able to go through the step without making any mistakes.

A variation of an only exercise appears in later lessons.

Here's the exercise from lesson 42.

EXERCISE 3

ONLY

a. I'm going to say a statement.
b. Listen. It is food. Say that. Get ready. (Signal.) *It is food.*
• Is that statement true of milk? (Signal.) *Yes.*
• Is that statement true of only milk? (Signal.) *No.*
• Name some other things it's true of. (Call on different children. Praise all reasonable responses.)
c. Listen. You can work with it. Say that. Get ready. (Signal.) *You can work with it.*
• Is that statement true of milk? (Signal.) *No.*
d. Listen. You can drink it. Say that. Get ready. (Signal.) *You can drink it.*
• Is that statement true of milk? (Signal.) *Yes.*
• Think about this. Is that statement true only of milk? (Signal.) *No.*
• Name some other things it's true of. (Call on different children. Praise all reasonable responses.)
e. Listen. You can drink it and it comes from cows. Say that. Get ready. (Signal.) *You can drink it and it comes from cows.*
• Is that statement true of milk? (Signal.) *Yes.*
• Think about this. Is that statement true only of milk? (Signal.) *Yes.*
• Yes, that statement is true of only milk.

Teaching notes: Children repeat statements that are true of milk. Then children tell whether the statement is true of only milk. If not, children name other things the statement tells about. If children make mistakes, name some things the statement is true of. If children tend to make more than one mistake in the exercise, repeat the exercise until responses are firm.

Can Do

This track begins in lesson 45 and teaches the relationship between what is being done and what **can** and **cannot** be done. For example: A boy is sitting. He **can** stand (that is, he is capable of standing); however, he **cannot** fly like a bird. The track also teaches the children to make observations about what objects can and cannot be used for. For example: A man can read a newspaper, but a man cannot cook soup in a newspaper. Work with can do clarifies what is possible and what is pretend.

The can do exercises require children to answer questions about what can and cannot be done with a given object. Then they make up complete statements that tell about can or cannot.

Here's the exercise from lesson 45.

EXERCISE 3
CAN DO

a. Get ready to answer some questions about a pair of scissors.
b. Can you use a pair of scissors to cut paper? (Signal.) *Yes.*
  • Can you use a pair of scissors to cut string? (Signal.) *Yes.*
  • Can you tear a pair of scissors into little pieces? (Signal.) *No.*
  • Can you drink from a pair of scissors? (Signal.) *No.*
c. (Repeat step b until firm.)
d. Here are some more questions about what you can do with a pair of scissors.

e. Can you put a pair of scissors into a box? (Signal.) *Yes.*
  • Can you cook hamburgers with a pair of scissors? (Signal.) *No.*
  • Can you step on a pair of scissors? (Signal.) *Yes.*
  • Can you hide inside a pair of scissors? (Signal.) *No.*
f. (Repeat step e until firm.)
g. I'm going to ask you about what a woman can do with a pair of scissors.
h. Can a woman cut paper with a pair of scissors? (Signal.) *Yes.*
  Say the whole thing about what a woman can do. Get ready. (Signal.) *A woman can cut paper with a pair of scissors.*
  • Can a woman write a letter with a pair of scissors? (Signal.) *No.*
  Say the whole thing. Get ready. (Signal.) *A woman cannot write a letter with a pair of scissors.*
i. (Repeat step h until firm.)

Teaching notes: In steps b and e children answer yes-no questions about what someone can do with a pair of scissors. In step h, they say complete sentences. If children make mistakes in any of these steps, repeat the step. If children make mistakes in more than one of these steps, repeat steps b through the end of the exercise.

In another variation, children make up statements about what someone can and cannot do with an object.

Here's the exercise from lesson 75.

EXERCISE 2
CAN DO

a. I'm going to ask questions about a woman and a paper bag.
b. Everybody, can a woman play music on a paper bag? (Signal.) *No.*
  • Say the statement. Get ready. (Signal.) *A woman cannot play music on a bag.*

c. Everybody, can a woman tear a paper bag? (Signal.) *Yes.*
• Say the statement. Get ready. (Signal.) *A woman can tear a paper bag.*
d. (Call on one child.)
Your turn. Make up another statement that tells something a woman can do with a paper bag. (After the child makes the statement, call on the group.)
• Say the statement about what a woman can do with a paper bag. Get ready. (Signal.) (The group repeats the child's statement.)
• (Repeat until firm.)
e. (Call on a different child.)
Your turn. Now make up a statement that tells something a woman cannot do with a paper bag. (After the child makes the statement, call on the group.)
• Say the statement about what a woman cannot do with a paper bag. (Signal.) (The group repeats the child's statement.)
• (Repeat until firm.)
f. (Repeat steps d and e until firm.)

Teaching notes: Steps d and e are the critical steps. All statements that children compose should begin with the words *A woman . . .* and should tell about something the woman can or cannot do with a paper bag.

Make sure that children repeat each acceptable statement. If children are weak on either step d or e call on different children to make up statements that the group repeats.

Children sometimes treat the word can as if it refers to what is allowed, not what is possible. For example: Can you tear a paper bag into little bits and scatter them all over the rug? Yes, you can. **Should** you do this? No. The confusion of **can** with **should** sometimes becomes apparent in step e. Children sometimes name things they **should** not do with a paper bag, for example: *You can't hit your brother with a paper bag.*

To correct the confusion of can not and should not:

• Tell the children, You're telling me about what you **should** do.

• Firm their responses on a series of paired **should-can** statements, such as:

Should you write on the walls with crayons?

Can you write on the walls with crayons?

Should you spill your juice?

Can you spill your juice?

• Repeat step e. When necessary, remind the children, Don't tell me what you should or should not do with a paper bag. Tell me what you can or can not do.

Description

The description track starts in lesson 52. The exercises in this track provide children with facts that function as clues for figuring out what object you are referring to. The first clue that you present does not identify a particular object. Rather, the first clue refers to a lot of possible objects. The next clue narrows the possibilities. The final clue limits the possibilities to one. The content that is presented in the description track dovetails with information that children have learned about only and about can do.

Here's the exercise from lesson 52.

DESCRIPTION

a. I'm thinking of an object. See if you can figure out what object I'm thinking of. I'll tell you something about the object.

b. Listen. It's made of metal. Everybody, what do you know about the object? (Signal.) *It's made of metal.*

c. Is a can made of metal? (Signal.) *Yes.*
So could I be thinking of a can?
(Signal.) *Yes.*

d. Is a fish made of metal? (Signal.) *No.*
So could I be thinking of a fish?
(Signal.) *No.*

e. Is a baseball made of metal? (Signal.) *No.*
So could I be thinking of a baseball?
(Signal.) *No.*

f. Is a spoon made of metal? (Signal.) *Yes.*
So could I be thinking of a spoon?
(Signal.) *Yes.*

g. Listen. The object I'm thinking of is (hold up one finger) made of metal and (hold up two fingers) it's round.

h. Everybody, what is the first thing you know about the object?
(Hold up one finger.) (Signal.) *It's made of metal* and (hold up two fingers) *it's round.*

i. (Repeat step h until firm.)

j. Is a rubber ball made of metal and is it round? (Signal.) *No.*
So could I be thinking of a rubber ball?
(Signal.) *No.*
• Why not? (Signal.) *It's not made of metal.*

k. (Repeat step j until firm.)

l. Is a coin made of metal and is it round?
(Signal.) *Yes.*
So could I be thinking of a coin?
(Signal.) *Yes.*

m. (Repeat step l until firm.)

n. Is a can made of metal and is it round?
(Signal.) *Yes.*
So could I be thinking of a can?
(Signal.) *Yes.*

o. (Repeat step n until firm.)

p. Listen. The object I'm thinking of is (hold up one finger) made of metal and (hold up two fingers) it's round and (hold up three fingers) you can use it to buy things in a store.

q. Everybody, name the object I am thinking of.
(Pause two seconds.) Get ready. (Signal.)
A coin.
Yes, a coin.

r. How do you know I'm thinking of a coin? (Hold up one finger.) (Signal.) *It's made of metal* and (hold up two fingers) *it's round* and (hold up three fingers) *you can use it to buy things in a store.*

s. (Repeat step r until firm.)

Teaching notes: In steps a and b, you tell the children that the object you are thinking of is made of metal. You then name different objects (steps c through f) and have the children test each one—is it made of metal? In step g you tell the children that the object is round, and in step p you tell them that you use it to buy things in the store.

• Each step should be presented quickly.

• Pay particular attention to step j. The answer to Why not? is very specific. *It's not made of metal.*

• Follow the instructions for holding up fingers. The task of remembering the information is easier for the children if it is associated with finger cues.

Starting in lesson 64, children play detective. They listen to descriptions that provide clues about the identity of an object.

Here's the exercise from lesson 64.

DESCRIPTION

a. Get ready to play detective and find out what object I'm thinking of. I'll give you two clues.

b. (Hold up one finger.) It's a building.
(Hold up two fingers.) It has a lot of seats.

c. Say the two things we know about the object. Get ready.
(Hold up one finger.) (Signal.) *It's a building.*
(Hold up two fingers.) *It has a lot of seats.*
d. (Repeat step c until firm.)
e. Those clues don't tell you enough to find the right building. They could tell you about a lot of buildings. See how many buildings you can name that have a lot of seats.
(Call on different children. The group is to name at least three buildings that have a lot of seats, such as *a school, a theater,* and *a temple.*)
f. Here's another clue for finding the right object. Listen. Children go there to learn.
Everybody, say that. Get ready. (Signal.)
Children go there to learn.
g. Now here are the three things we know about the object.
(Hold up one finger.) *It's a building.*
(Hold up two fingers.) *It has a lot of seats.*
(Hold up three fingers.) *Children go there to learn.*
h. Everybody, say all the things we know.
(Hold up one finger.) (Signal.) *It's a building.*
(Hold up two fingers.) *It has a lot of seats.*
(Hold up three fingers.) *Children go there to learn.*
i. Everybody, tell me what I'm thinking of.
(Pause.) Get ready. (Signal.) *A school.*
Yes, a school.

Teaching notes: You provide two clues about the object in step b. In step c, children repeat the clues as you signal.

The clues could describe various buildings. In step e, children identify buildings that have a lot of seats. If children have trouble lead them by asking about different buildings. Does a church have lots of seats? Does a barn have lots of seats? Does a theater have lots of seats? . . . Then repeat step e.

You give the children another clue in step f and review the clues in step g. In step h the children review the clues and in step i they identify the building.

Children may be able to identify the building before you present step h. Do not skip step h. Make sure that children's responses are firm when saying the three clues before you direct them to name the object you've been describing.

In lesson 74, a new kind of description exercise presents a nonsense word. This type is particularly important for children because it shows them the difference between words and meaning. Often children have trouble separating names from meanings. The type of exercise that begins in lesson 74 helps children by showing them that information about an object's characteristics doesn't come from the name of the object but from information about the object. (A rose by any other name . . .)

Here's the exercise from lesson 74.

EXERCISE 2

DESCRIPTION

Note: The children are not to memorize the "funny" name in this task.

a. I'm going to tell you about an object you know. But I'm going to call it a funny name. See if you can figure out what object I'm thinking about.
b. (Hold up one finger.)
A tunk is a tool. Say that. (Signal.) *A tunk is a tool.*
• (Hold up two fingers.)
A tunk is used to pound nails. Say that. (Signal.) *A tunk is used to pound nails.*
c. Everybody, say the things you know about a tunk. Get ready.
• (Hold up one finger.) (Signal.) *A tunk is a tool.*
• (Hold up two fingers.) (Signal.) *A tunk is used to pound nails.*
d. (Repeat steps b and c until firm.)

e. Everybody, tell me the kind of tool I am calling a tunk. (Pause.) Get ready. (Signal.) *A hammer.*

f. I couldn't fool you. It's really a hammer. How do you know a tunk is a hammer? (Call on a child. Idea: *It's a tool. It's used to pound nails.*)

g. How would you like to eat with a tunk? (Children respond.)

Teaching notes: Treat this exercise as a game. Smile, and act as if you enjoy presenting it.

Note how you first signal with one finger, then two, in steps b and c.

Don't allow the children to identify the object at the end of step b. Tell them, Don't say the answer yet. Then repeat step b.

Don't leave step c until the children are saying both statements correctly.

If the children give the wrong answer in step e, correct as follows:

1. Say the things you know about a tunk.

2. Ask What tool do you use to pound nails?

The work with descriptions provides children with the mind set that words are simply tools that tell about objects and events. If a new word describes the same thing that familiar words describe, the words mean the same thing. They are synonyms. The work with synonyms begins in lesson 85, after children have worked extensively with description exercises.

Analogies

Worksheet analogies begin in lesson 54. The oral work on the analogies track begins in lesson 72. The track is designed to give children practice in applying what has been taught about classification and sameness. It provides children with practice in expressing different analogous relationships. Analogy skills are important because they form one of the basic reasoning strategies for generalizing to new experiences or they organize new facts. The children learn to:

1. Complete analogies. (Red is to stop as green is to . . .)

2. Construct analogies that follow a specific rule. (Make up an analogy that tells how a bird and a fish move. *A bird is to flying as a fish is to swimming.*)

3. Tell what analogies are about. (A baseball is to throwing as a banana is to eating. What does that analogy tell about the objects? *What you do with them.*)

The first exercises in the track introduce children to the statements that are used in analogies. Instead of saying *A bird is like an airplane,* children say, *A bird is an airplane.*

Here's the exercise from lesson 72.

EXERCISE 6

ANALOGIES

a. You're going to make up sentences that are like the sentence I start with.

b. Listen: Your shoe is for some part of your body. What part? (Signal.) *Your foot.* Yes, your shoe is for your foot.
• Everybody, say that. Get ready. (Signal.) *Your shoe is for your foot.*

c. Your glove is for . . . (Signal.) *your hand.*
• Say the statement about your glove. Get ready. (Signal.) *Your glove is for your hand.*

d. Your shoe is for . . . (Signal.) *your foot.*
• Say the statement about your shoe. Get ready. (Signal.) *Your shoe is for your foot.*

e. Your hat is for . . . (Signal.) *your head.*

- Say the statement about your hat. Get ready. (Signal.) *Your hat is for your head.*
f. Your belt is for . . . (Signal.) *your waist.*
- Say the statement about your belt. Get ready. (Signal.) *Your belt is for your waist.*

In this exercise, children are presented with statements of the form, Your shoe is for your foot.

The work that children will do later in the program assumes that their responses are firm when making these statements. If you are in doubt, give the children individual turns.

In lesson 75, children do tasks similar to those from lesson 72 except that they also say the statement a different way.

Here's the exercise from lesson 75.

| EXERCISE 5 |
ANALOGIES

a. You're going to make up sentences that are like the sentence I start with.
b. Listen: A magazine is made of some material. What material? (Signal.) *Paper.*
   Yes, a magazine is made of paper.
   - Everybody, say the statement. Get ready. (Signal.) *A magazine is made of paper.*
c. What material is a window made of? (Signal.) *Glass.*
   - Say the statement about a window. Get ready. (Signal.) *A window is made of glass.*
d. What material is a towel made of? (Signal.) *Cloth.*
   - Say the statement about a towel. Get ready. (Signal.) *A towel is made of cloth.*
e. What material is a coin made of? (Signal.) *Metal.*
   - Say the statement about a coin. Get ready. (Signal.) *A coin is made of metal.*
f. What material is a board made of? (Signal.) *Wood.*
   - Say the statement about a board. Get ready. (Signal.) *A board is made of wood.*

g. We'll talk about the same things, but we'll use a different type of statement.
h. Listen: A window is to glass. Say the statement. Get ready. (Signal.) *A window is to glass.*
i. Listen: A coin is to metal. Say the statement. Get ready. (Signal.) *A coin is to metal.*
j. Listen: A towel is to cloth. Say the statement. Get ready. (Signal.) *A towel is to cloth.*
k. Listen: A magazine is to paper. Say the statement. Get ready. (Signal.) *A magazine is to paper.*

Teaching notes: Through step f children make statements that tell what the objects are made of. In step g you tell the children that you're talking about the same things, but you're using a different type of statement. Starting with step h, they use the statement form **window is to glass.**

The exercise does not call for individual turns, but if you're in doubt about whether children are saying the statements properly, present individual turns.

After children have practiced saying the statements that are used in analogies for several lessons, children make up their first analogy.

Here's the exercise from lesson 76.

| EXERCISE 6 |
ANALOGIES

a. We're going to make up an **analogy.** What are we going to make up? (Signal.) *An analogy.*
   - An analogy tells the way things are the same and the way they're different.
b. We're going to make up an **analogy** that tells how animals move.
   - What is the analogy going to tell? (Signal.) *How animals move.*
c. Here are the animals we're going to use in the analogy: A bird and a fish.
   Which animals? (Signal.) *A bird and a fish.*

d. Name the first animal. Get ready. (Signal.) *A bird.*
  - Yes, a bird. Tell me how that animal moves. Get ready. (Signal.) *It flies.*
e. Here's the first part of the analogy. Listen. A bird is to flying. Say the first part of the analogy. Get ready. (Signal.) *A bird is to flying.*
  Yes, a bird is to flying.
f. The second animal is a fish.
  - Tell me how that animal moves. Get ready. (Signal.) *It swims.*
g. Here's the second part of the analogy. Listen. A fish is to swimming. Say the second part of the analogy. Get ready. (Signal.) *A fish is to swimming.*
  Yes, a fish is to swimming.
h. (Repeat steps c through g until firm.)
i. My turn. I'm going to say the whole analogy. First I'm going to tell how a bird moves, and then I'm going to tell how a fish moves. Listen. A bird is to flying **as** a fish is to swimming.
j. Let's say the analogy together. Get ready. *A bird is to flying **as** a fish is to swimming.*
k. All by yourselves. Say the analogy that tells how a bird moves and how a fish moves. Get ready. (Signal.) *A bird is to flying **as** a fish is to swimming.*
l. (Repeat step k until firm.)

Teaching notes: In step a, you introduce the word analogy, and in step b you tell the children about the analogy they are going to make up.

After you lead the children through the analogy, you say the whole analogy in step i. Make sure you have good rhythm when you present the analogy, and be sure to stress the word **as.** You may want to say the word **as** so it clearly divides between the parts of the analogy.

A bird is to flying (Pause) **as** (Pause) a fish is to swimming.

Make sure you say the analogy the same way when you say it with the children.

In step k, the children say the analogy by themselves. Make sure they say all the words clearly. If you're in doubt present individual turns, then repeat step k. If children learn to say the analogy correctly, they will find the following analogy exercises much easier than they would if their responses were not firm with the wording.

In lesson 83, children make up two analogies that involve the same categories. The categories are a deer and a fish. Children first make up an analogy to tell how the animals move. Next they make up an analogy that tells where you find the animals.

Here's the exercise from lesson 83.

EXERCISE 1

ANALOGIES

a. We're going to make up **two** analogies.
  - We're going to make up analogies about a deer and a fish. Which animals? (Signal.) *A deer and a fish.*
b. The first analogy tells how the animals move.
  - How does a deer move? (Call on a child. Accept all reasonable answers, but use: *Runs.*)
  - How does a fish move? (Signal.) *Swims.*
c. So a deer is to running as a fish is to . . . (Signal.) *swimming.*
  - Say that analogy about a deer and a fish. Get ready. (Signal.) *A deer is to running as a fish is to swimming.*
d. Listen: A deer is to running as a fish is to swimming. Does that analogy tell **where** you **find** the animals? (Signal.) *No.*
e. Listen: A deer is to running as a fish is to swimming. Does that analogy tell how the animals move? (Signal.) *Yes.*
f. Listen: A deer is to running as a fish is to swimming. Does that analogy tell what parts the animals have? (Signal.) *No.*
g. (Repeat steps d through f until firm.)

h. We made up an analogy that tells how the animals move. The next analogy tells where you find the animals.
- Where do you find a deer? (Call on a child. Accept all reasonable answers, but use: *in the forest.*)
- Where do you find a fish? (Call on a child. Accept all reasonable answers, but use: *in the water.*)

i. A deer is to the forest as a fish is to the . . . (Signal.) *water.*
- Say that analogy about a deer and a fish. Get ready. (Signal.) *A deer is to the forest as a fish is to the water.*

j. We made up an analogy that tells how the animals move. Then we made up an analogy that tells where you find the animals. Let's see if you can say both those analogies.

k. Think. Say the analogy that tells how the animals move. (Pause.) Get ready. (Signal.) *A deer is to running as a fish is to swimming.*
- Think. Say the analogy that tells where you find the animals. (Pause.) Get ready. (Signal.) *A deer is to the forest as a fish is to the water.*

l. (Repeat step k until firm.)

Teaching notes: Make sure that children's responses are firm in the steps through i. In step k children say both the analogies. If children make mistakes on step j repeat the step but not always with the tasks in the same order. For example, tell them: Say the analogy that tells how they move . . . Say the analogy that tells how they move . . . Say the analogy that tells where you find the animals . . . Say the analogy that tells how they move.

Try to make sure that the children's responses are firm for the pair of analogies before leaving the lesson.

Children work on similar analogy pairs through lesson 90. In lesson 91 children use what they have learned about analogies to identify what an analogy is about.

Here's the exercise from lesson 91.

ANALOGIES

a. You're going to figure out what an analogy is about.

b. Listen to this: A boat is to water as an airplane is to . . . (Signal.) *air.*

c. What class are a boat and an airplane in? (Signal.) *Vehicles.*
- Yes, vehicles. Our analogy tells something about vehicles.

d. A boat is to water as an airplane is to air.
- Does our analogy tell where you find the vehicles? (Signal.) *Yes.*
- Does our analogy tell what parts they have? (Signal.) *No.*
- Does our analogy tell what they are made of? (Signal.) *No.*
- Does our analogy tell what color they are? (Signal.) *No.*
- Our analogy tells where you find them.
- (Repeat step d until firm.)

e. Where do you find a boat? (Signal.) *In water.*
- Say the **first** part of the analogy. Get ready. (Signal.) *A boat is to water.*

f. Where do you find an airplane? (Signal.) *In air.*
- Say the **next** part of the analogy. Get ready. (Signal.) *An airplane is to air.*

g. Tell me what the analogy tells about the vehicles. Get ready. (Signal.) *Where you find them.*

h. Everybody, say the whole analogy. Get ready. (Signal.) *A boat is to water as an airplane is to air.*

i. (Repeat steps g and h until firm.)

Teaching notes: Make sure that children are correct when identifying what the analogy is about in step d. Also make sure that responses are firm in steps g and h. If children make mistakes on exercises of this type, firm them. Then repeat the same exercise at the beginning of the next Language lesson.

Later exercises in the track are like the exercise in lesson 91 except that you present more than one analogy that refers to the same objects. For instance, in lesson 122 children analyze two analogies that involve a paint brush and a hammer.

- A paint brush is to painting as a hammer is to . . .

- A paint brush is to bristles as a hammer is to . . .

Children complete the analogies and indicate what each tells about the tools.

The work with analogies reinforces what children have learned about descriptions and classification. The work provides children with a useful mental framework for telling how things are the same.

If–Then

The if–then track starts in lesson 128. The children practice expressing causal statements that start with **if**; for example, *If you drop raw eggs, they will break.*

Here's the exercise from lesson 132.

EXERCISE 6

IF–THEN

a. You're going to make up if-then statements.
b. Listen: Which ice would melt, ice that is in a freezer or ice that is on a table? (Signal.) *Ice that is on a table.*
c. Start with the words "If ice is," and say the whole statement. Get ready. (Signal.) *If ice is on the table, it will melt.*
d. (Repeat steps b and c until firm.)
e. Listen: Which door will not open, a door that is locked or a door that is unlocked? (Signal.) *A door that is locked.*
f. Start with the words, "If a door is locked," and say the whole statement. Get ready. (Signal.) *If a door is locked, it will not open.*
g. (Repeat steps e and f until firm.)
h. Let's do those statements again.

i. Say the statement that tells about ice that is on the table. Get ready. (Signal.) *If ice is on the table, it will melt.*
j. Say the statement that tells about a door that is locked. Get ready. (Signal.) *If a door is locked, it will not open.*
k. (Repeat steps i and j until firm.)

Teaching notes: The if–then track is fairly short, but you should make sure that the children learn how to say if–then statements. Often children understand the logic of if–then, but they may phrase the statements quite differently. *You do that and you get in trouble.* (If you do that, you'll get in trouble.)

If you don't feel that the program provides children with enough practice with if–then statements, have the children construct additional examples. Here's an example: If you're hungry, what do you want to do? Say the whole statement . . . If you're thirsty, what do you want to do? . . . Say the whole statement. If you're tired, what do you want to do? . . . Say the whole statement.

Directional Skills

Many teaching demonstrations and worksheet instructions used in the primary grades assume that children understand the meaning of such terms as **from** and **left.** Children are also expected to be able to read and understand simple maps.

The exercises in the directional skills track are designed to teach these basic concepts. The specific objectives are:

1. To teach the meaning of the words **from, to; north, south, east,** and **west.**

2. To provide adequate practice in making statements that contain these words.

From–To

The introduction of from–to is provided through a worksheet exercise in lesson 35. Here's the student material and the exercise:

 **Worksheet** 35

EXERCISE 7

FROM–TO

a. (Hold up worksheet.) Find the black dog. ✓
- The **black dog** is moving **from** the circle to the triangle. What is the dog moving **from**? (Signal.) *The circle.*
- What is the dog moving **to**? (Signal.) *The triangle.*
b. (Repeat step a until firm.)
c. Touch the thing the dog is moving **from**. ✓ Everybody, what are you touching? (Signal.) *The circle.*
- Touch the thing the dog is moving **to**. ✓ Everybody, what are you touching? (Signal.) *The triangle.*
d. Here's the rule about the thing the dog is moving **to**. It should be yellow. Name the thing you are going to color yellow. Get ready. (Signal.) *The triangle.*
- Make a yellow mark on the thing the dog is moving **to**. (Observe children and give feedback.)
- Here's a rule about the thing the dog is moving **from**. It should be blue. Name the thing you are going to color blue. Get ready. (Signal.) *The circle.*

- Make a blue mark on the thing the dog is moving **from**. (Observe children and give feedback.)
e. Touch the **spotted dog**. ✓
- That dog is moving **from** something to something else. Touch the thing the dog is moving **from**. ✓
- Everybody, what is the dog moving **from**? (Signal.) *The circle.*
- Touch the thing the dog is moving **to**. ✓
- Everybody, what is the dog moving **to**? (Signal.) *The triangle.*
f. The rule is the same for **all** the dogs. The thing the dog is moving **to** should be yellow. Name the thing you are going to color yellow. (Signal.) *The triangle.*
- Make a yellow mark on the thing the spotted dog is moving **to**. (Observe children and give feedback.) The thing the dog is moving **from** should be blue. Name the thing you are going to color blue. (Signal.) *The circle.*
- Make a blue mark on the thing the spotted dog is moving **from**. (Observe children and give feedback.)
g. Now make marks for a **white dog**. Make a yellow mark on the thing that dog is moving **to**. ✓
- Make a blue mark on the thing that the dog is moving **from**. ✓
h. Later you'll fix the other white dog.

Teaching notes: By introducing from–to in worksheet activities, you provide children with the concrete information they need to appreciate how from–to actually works.

In step a, you tell the children what the black dog is doing—moving from the circle to the triangle. You ask what the dog is moving from and to.

In step c, children touch the thing the dog is moving from. Make sure they are touching the circle. If they are not, repeat steps a and b.

Use the same strategy for mistakes in step c.

Starting with step e, the children identify what the spotted dog is moving from and what it is moving to. You do not first model the responses the children are to make. They are to figure out the responses from looking at the picture. Children should not have serious problems with this exercise.

Through lesson 40, children work with similar coloring rules that involve from–to. In lesson 41, you present actual instances of something moving from one place to another. These exercises require children to observe the movement and figure out where the movement went from and where it went to.

Here's the exercise from lesson 41.

EXERCISE 2

FROM–TO

a. (Draw a small circle on the chalkboard.)
- Get ready to tell me if I move my finger **from** the circle.
b. (Place your finger to the left of the circle.) Watch. (Move it toward the circle.)
- Did I move from the circle? (Signal.) *No.*
c. (Place your finger inside the circle. Move it straight up from the circle.)
- Did I move from the circle? (Signal.) *Yes.*
d. (Place your finger inside the circle.) Watch. (Move it from the circle to the left.)
- Did I move from the circle? (Signal.) *Yes.*
e. (Place your finger above the circle.) Watch. (Move it straight down to the circle.)
- Did I move from the circle? (Signal.) *No.*
f. (Place your finger inside the circle.) Watch. (Move it from the circle to the right.)
- Did I move from the circle? (Signal.) *Yes.*
g. (Place your finger below the circle.) Watch. (Move it straight up to the circle.)
- Did I move from the circle? (Signal.) *No.*
h. (Repeat steps b through g until firm.)
i. (Place your finger inside the circle.) Watch. (Move it below the circle.)

- Did I move from the circle? (Signal.) *Yes.*
- How did I move my finger? (Signal.) *From the circle.*
- Say the whole thing about how I moved my finger. Get ready. (Signal.) *You moved your finger from the circle.*
j. (Repeat step i until firm.)

Teaching notes: For this exercise, you draw a circle on the chalkboard. You move your finger from the circle or toward the circle. After each move, you ask the children, Did I move **from** the circle?

If children make mistakes repeat steps a through g until responses are firm.

The development of from–to continues largely throughout worksheet activities that are similar to the one presented in lesson 35. These activities provide the children with practice in linking their knowledge of from–to with rules for coloring different objects.

Map Reading

The map reading exercises begin in lesson 51. They teach the children the names of the four directions–**north, south, east,** and **west.** They also teach decoding simple maps, facing different directions, and moving in different directions. These exercises also make use of the previously taught concepts from and to.

The introduction of the four directions require you to make small signs and place them on the appropriate walls of the room. You then show the children that the name on the wall you face tells the direction you are facing.

Here's the exercise from lesson 51.

MAP READING

Note: Make sure **north, south, east,** and **west** cards are placed on the appropriate walls.

a. Everybody, we're going to learn about directions. What are we going to learn about? (Signal.) *Directions.*

b. (Point north.) The signs on the walls show the four directions. (Point to each sign and read them in this order:) North, south, east, west.

c. Your turn. I'll point in different directions. You tell me the directions.
   • (Point north.) Everybody, which direction is this? (Signal.) *North.*
   • (Point south.) Everybody, which direction is this? (Signal.) *South.*
   • (Point east.) Everybody, which direction is this? (Signal.) *East.*
   • (Point west.) Everybody, which direction is this? (Signal.) *West.*

d. (Repeat step c until firm.)

e. (Move to the middle of the room.) Look at me. I'm going to walk. You point to the wall I'm walking to. That's the **direction** I'm walking.

f. Watch. (Walk toward the south wall.) Everybody, which direction? (Signal.) *South.* Yes, I walked south.
   • (Return to the middle of the room.)

Error

The children don't say *south.*

Correction

1. (Point to the south wall.)
   Which wall am I pointing to? (Signal.) *The south wall.*
2. So which direction am I pointing? (Signal.) *South.*
3. (Repeat step f.)

---

g. Watch. (Walk toward the north wall.) Everybody, which direction? (Signal.) *North.* Yes, I walked north.
   • (Return to the middle of the room.)

h. (Repeat steps f and g until firm.)

Teaching notes:

• Arrange the signs before the Language period so that you don't lose time with the children.

• Place the signs so that you will be walking in the appropriate direction when you move from your starting position to the signs. You should actually walk south to reach the **south** sign.

• In step e, make sure that children are pointing to the sign on the south wall.

• If children make mistakes or produce weak responses in the later steps of the exercise, direct them to point to the wall you are walking to.

In the following lessons, you present variations of the basic exercise. You walk in different directions. Children name the directions. The signs continue to be on the wall and children refer to the signs when figuring out the directions.

In lesson 55, you introduce a variation that requires children to face different directions and make statements about the directions they face. The signs should still be on the appropriate walls.

Here's the exercise from lesson 55.

MAP READING

a. Let's all stand up. (Signal.) (All stand.)

b. I'm going to face east. Watch. (Face the east wall.)
   • What am I doing? (Signal.) *Facing east.*
   • Say the statement. (Signal.) *You are facing east.*

c. Everybody, now you're going to face east. (Pause.) Get ready. (Signal.) (The children face east.)
 • What are you doing? (Signal.) *Facing east.*
 • Say the statement. (Signal.) *I am facing east.*
d. Everybody, you're going to face north. (Pause.) Get ready. (Signal.) (The children face north.)
 • What are you doing? (Signal.) *Facing north.*
 • Say the statement. (Signal.) *I am facing north.*
e. Everybody, you're going to face south. (Pause.) Get ready. (Signal.) (The children face south.)
 • What are you doing? (Signal.) *Facing south.*
 • Say the statement. (Signal.) *I am facing south.*
f. (Repeat steps b through e until firm.)
g. Let's sit. (Signal.) (All sit.)
h. (Point east.) Tell me the direction I'm pointing. Get ready. (Signal.) *East.*
 • Say the statement. Get ready. (Signal.) *You are pointing east.*
 • Yes, if I walked all day in this direction, I would be going east.
i. (Point north.) Tell me the direction I'm pointing. Get ready. (Signal.) *North.*
 • Say the statement. Get ready. (Signal.) *You are pointing north.*
 • Yes, if I walked for an hour in this direction, I would be going north.
j. (Repeat steps h and i until firm.)

Teaching notes: Make sure that children face the correct directions. They should not simply face the sign unless they face the correct direction when they face the sign.

Do not hurry the children. Pause for several seconds before saying Get ready, particularly if children do not respond on signals.

If children do have problems, repeat the exercise. Make sure that children are not copying the responses of others. If children are slow at responding, present individual turns.

Starting in lesson 57, children learn the conventions for how directions are indicated on the map.

Here's the exercise from lesson 57.

EXERCISE 6

MAP READING

a. (Draw a large rectangle on the board. Label as indicated:)

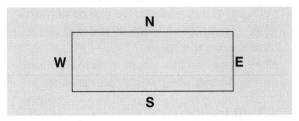

b. We're going to learn a rule about reading maps.
c. Here's the rule about maps. (Touch each letter as you say:) **North** is on the top; **south** is on the bottom; **east** is on this side; **west** is on this side.
d. (Repeat step c.)
e. See if you can say the rule with me. Get ready. (Touch each letter as you and the children say the rule.)
North is on the top; south is on the bottom; east is on this side; west is on this side.
f. Listen. North is on the top; south is on the bottom. Say that.
(Touch each letter as the children respond. Do **not** respond with the children.)
North is on the top; south is on the bottom.
g. (Repeat step f until firm.)
h. Listen. East is on this side; west is on this side. Say that. (Touch each letter as the children respond without you.) *East is on this side; west is on this side.*
i. (Repeat step h until firm.)
j. Now say the whole rule. (Touch each letter as the children respond. Do **not** respond with the children.)
North is on the top; south is on the bottom; east is on this side; west is on this side.
k. (Repeat steps f through j until firm.)
l. I'm going to move my finger. Tell me the direction I go.

m. (Touch the middle of the rectangle.) Watch. (Move toward the north.) Everybody, which direction did I go? (Touch.) *North.* Yes, north. I went north.

n. (Touch the middle of the rectangle.) Watch. (Move toward the south.) Everybody, which direction did I go? (Touch.) *South.* Yes, south. I went south.

o. (Touch the middle of the rectangle.) Watch. (Move toward the west.) Everybody, which direction did I go? (Touch.) *West.* Yes, west. I went west.

p. (Repeat steps m through o until firm.)

q. Let's say the rule about the map one more time. (Touch each letter as you and the children say the rule.)
North is on the top; south is on the bottom; east is on this side; west is on this side.

Teaching notes: You start by drawing a large rectangle on the board and lettering the sides to show the four directions.

Practice saying the rule about the map in step c rhythmically and expressively. Some children will require a lot of repetition before they can say the rule. The practice will be far more pleasant if what they are trying to say sounds like a lively poem.

When practicing the rule, touch each side of the map as you say the appropriate direction.

- If children are unable to say the entire rule of step f after six or more trials, let them know that they are doing a good job, acknowledge that the rule is very hard, and tell them that you will return to the rule later. Before the end of the lesson, try to get in a few more practice trials.

- If the children have trouble saying the rule, follow the model, lead, and test procedure. Say the part of the rule they are having trouble with. Have them say

that part with you, then test them on that part. Then add another part and repeat the model, lead, and test procedure.

- Some students may have trouble with steps l through o particularly if the map is not drawn on the north wall. (If it is drawn on the south wall, for example, a movement to the right is moving east on the map, but toward the west wall of the room.)

- Point out the difference between the map and the room. You're telling me about the directions in **this room.** But that's not the rule for the map. You have to look at the side of the map I'm moving to.

- Give a few examples. Start at the middle of the map and move your finger north. Ask, Which side of the map did I move to? Then ask, So which direction did I go? Repeat with south, then do east and west.

- When children respond correctly to the examples, repeat steps l through o until responses are firm.

The basic exercise above is repeated on the next lesson. At the end of that lesson, children's responses should be firm on the rule for maps. In lesson 59, children do their first worksheet exercise involving maps (north on the top, south on the bottom). The early exercises show arrows facing different directions. Children identify arrows that face north, for example, and make them a particular color. (See pages 186–187 for more detail on the worksheet sequence.)

The development of the map skills provides children with a solid foundation for understanding how to interpret maps and how to make them.

Information

The two main information tracks present calendar information and information about materials (concrete, plastic, wood, etc.). Additional information is provided through worksheet activities where children learn about the features of particular locations (such as the doctor's office or a forest) and about the parts of common objects.

Days, Months, and Seasons

This track starts in lesson 2 and continues throughout the level. It teaches the children the following information:

1. The names of the days of the week, the months, and the seasons.

2. The number of days in a week, a month, and seasons in a year; the number of days and weeks in a year.

3. The meaning of yesterday, today, and tomorrow.

4. How to locate and interpret dates on a calendar.

This track begins with exercises that review what the children were taught in *Reading Mastery Plus,* Level K.

Here's a review exercise from lesson 2.

EXERCISE 3

CALENDAR FACTS

a. Here are facts about days and dates.

- Listen: There are seven days in a week. Say the fact. Get ready. (Signal.) *There are seven days in a week.*

- When you name the days of the week you start with Sunday. Listen: Sunday, Monday, Tuesday, Wednesday, Thursday, Friday, Saturday.

- Your turn. Start with Sunday and say the seven days of the week. Get ready. (Signal.) *Sunday, Monday, Tuesday, Wednesday, Thursday, Friday, Saturday.*

b. New fact: There are four seasons in a year.

- Everybody, say the fact. Get ready. (Signal.) *There are four seasons in a year.*

c. (Repeat step b until firm.)

d. When you name the seasons, you start with the first season of the year. That's winter. Listen: winter, spring, summer, fall.

- Your turn. Name the four seasons of the year. Get ready. (Signal.) *Winter, spring, summer, fall.*

Teaching notes: The children who have gone through *Reading Mastery Plus,* Level K should know this material. A goal of the program is to make sure that the children learn this information thoroughly enough for it to become automatic. If children's responses are firm, go through the exercise quickly.

Also in lesson 2, children are introduced to the calendar. Here's the exercise:

EXERCISE 6

CALENDAR

Note: You will need a current calendar for steps c through f.

a. Everybody, how many days are in a week? (Signal.) *Seven.*

- Start with Sunday and say the days. Get ready. (Signal.) *Sunday, Monday, Tuesday, Wednesday, Thursday, Friday, Saturday.*

b. (Repeat step a until firm.)

c. (Present calendar. Point to the month.) Listen: This month is _____. What's this month? (Signal.)
- This is a calendar. It shows the dates. Those are the numbers of the days for this month.
- The calendar shows days of the week. The first column shows Sunday. (Point to Sunday column.) The next column shows Monday. (Point to Monday column.) The next column shows Tuesday. (Point to Tuesday column.)

d. I'll touch columns. You tell me if I'm touching numbers for Sunday, Monday, or Tuesday.
- (Touch a number for Sunday.) What day? (Signal.) *Sunday.*
- (Touch another number for Sunday.) What day? (Signal.) *Sunday.*
- (Touch a number for Monday.) What day? (Signal.) *Monday.*
- (Touch another number for Monday.) What day? (Signal.) *Monday.*
- (Touch a number for Sunday.) What day? (Signal.) *Sunday.*
- (Touch a number for Monday.) What day? (Signal.) *Monday.*
- (Touch a number for Tuesday.) What day? (Signal.) *Tuesday.*
- (Touch a number for Monday.) What day? (Signal.) *Monday.*
- (Touch a number for Tuesday.) What day? (Signal.) *Tuesday.*
- (Touch another number for Tuesday.) What day? (Signal.) *Tuesday.*

e. I'll show you the number for today. (Touch number. Say date: day, month, number; e.g: Today is Wednesday, September 15th.)
- Your turn. Say the date. (Signal.)

f. (Repeat step e until firm.)

Teaching notes: You will need a calendar, ideally a large one that shows the entire month. A reproducible blank calendar appears at the end of this guide in Appendix C. This calendar provides cells for up to 6 weeks.

This exercise acquaints children with the conventions of the calendar. Each column shows a particular day. All the dates shown in the column are the same day, shown during different weeks.

In the steps that precede c, you show children how the columns work. Practice this routine before presenting to the children so that you don't have to keep referring to the script. Remember, you're going to show children that everything in the first column is a Sunday and everything in the next column is a Monday. You'll go back and forth from column to column so that children will learn to distinguish between the columns.

In step e, you show children the number for the current date. When you tell them the date, remember to say, for example, Today is Thursday, September 14th. (You may add the year if you wish; however, the information that is relevant to the calendar is the day of the week and the number for the day.)

On later lessons, children learn new calendar information. It is integrated with the information they have already learned and reviewed regularly.

From Lesson 33 until the end of the program, children are asked to say the date that is one week from today. Fill in the first part of the upcoming month when this information is called for in the lesson.

September

Sunday	Monday	Tuesday	Wednesday	Thursday	Friday	Saturday
					1	2
3	4	5	6	7	8	9
10	11	12	13	14	15	16
17	18	19	20	21	22	23
24	25	26	27	28	29	30

October

1	2	3	4	5	6	7

Materials

The list below shows the materials that are taught or reviewed in *Reading Mastery Plus,* Level 1 and shows the lesson in which the material first appears.

Materials	Lesson
Plastic	17
Cloth	17
Paper	17
Wood	19
Graphite	19
Rubber	19
Leather	22
Glass	33
Concrete	39
Metal	39

The materials track starts in lesson 17 and continues through lesson 126. Children review the materials information they learned in *Reading Mastery Plus,* Level K; throughout the level, they learn new information about materials.

Here's part of the review from lesson 17.

EXERCISE 5

MATERIALS

a. (Present the three circles.)
- We're going to learn what things are made of.
- (Point to the circles.) Everybody, what are these? (Signal.) *Circles.*
  Yes, circles.

b. (Point to the paper circle.)
  This circle is made of paper. What is it made of? (Signal.) *Paper.*
- (Point to the cloth circle.)
  This circle is made of cloth. What is it made of? (Signal.) *Cloth.*
- (Point to the plastic circle.)
  This circle is made of plastic. What is it made of? (Signal.) *Plastic.*

c. I'll point to each circle. You tell me what it is made of.

d. (Point to the plastic circle.) What is this circle made of? (Signal.) *Plastic.*
- (Point to the cloth circle.) What is this circle made of? (Signal.) *Cloth.*
- (Point to the paper circle.) What is this circle made of? (Signal.) *Paper.*

e. (Repeat step d until firm.)

Teaching notes: For this exercise, you will need circles made of plastic, cloth, and paper. Children should be familiar with these materials; however, in the introductory exercise you name the materials before asking children to identify them.

The critical step of the exercise is step d. Make sure that children's responses are firm in step e before you leave the exercise.

In some of the later exercises, children integrate information they have learned about part–whole and materials.

Here's the exercise from lesson 26.

EXERCISE 1

MATERIALS

Note: You will need a wooden pencil with an eraser and a point.

a. (Touch the eraser.)
- Everybody, what is the name of this part? (Signal.) *The eraser.*
- (Touch the point.)
- Everybody, what is the name of this part? (Signal.) *The point.*
- (Touch the shaft.)
- Everybody, what is the name of this part? (Signal.) *The shaft.*

b. (Repeat step a until firm.)

c. (Touch the eraser.)
  - What is the name of this part? (Signal.) *The eraser.*
  - What is this part made of? (Signal.) *Rubber.*
  - (Touch the point.)
  - What is the name of this part? (Signal.) *The point.*
  - What is this part made of? (Signal.) *Graphite.*
  - (Touch the shaft.)
  - What is the name of this part? (Signal.) *The shaft.*
  - What is this part made of? (Signal.) *Wood.*
d. (Repeat step c until firm.)
e. (Ask different children the following questions. Accept reasonable responses.)
  - Why do you think the eraser is made of rubber?
  - Why do you think the shaft is made of wood?
  - Why do you think the point is made of graphite?

Teaching notes: You present a wooden pencil with a visible eraser and point. Children identify the parts of the pencil (which information has been taught in *Reading Mastery Plus,* Level K and has been reviewed throughout worksheet exercises) and then identify the material that each part is made of. Children who are placed appropriately in the program should have no trouble with this type of application.

A common review exercise directs children to name objects that are made of different materials.

Here's the exercise from lesson 39.

EXERCISE 5

MATERIALS

a. Think of things that are made of leather.
b. Let's see who can name at least three things made of leather. (Call on different children to name objects made of leather. Each child should name at least three things.)
c. Think of things that are made of metal.
d. Let's see who can name at least three things made of metal. (Call on different children to name objects made of metal. Each child should name at least three things.)
e. Think of things that are made of concrete.
f. Let's see who can name at least three things made of concrete. (Call on different children to name objects made of concrete. Each child should name at least three things.)

Teaching notes: In step b children name things that are made of leather. If children do not readily name things that are made of leather, name some things that are made of leather. You could also ask questions, such as, Do you ever wear something made of leather around your waist? What do you wear? Do you ever wear anything made of leather on your feet? What do you wear? Did you ever sit on anything made of leather? What did you sit on?

Sometimes, children give suspicious responses. For instance, they may say that pants are made of leather. The best way to clarify whether the children are knowledgeable about leather pants is to say something like this:

Is anyone in this room wearing pants made of leather?

When would a person wear pants that are made of leather?

The exercise that requires children to name things that are made of a specified material recur throughout the program. It is important for children to be facile with this type of information. From time to time, call on a child and direct her to name four or five things that are made of a particular material.

Applications

Two tracks apply rules to different situations. They are absurdities and temporal sequencing. In the absurdities track, children are presented with situations that have a serious incongruity or inconsistency. Children identify what is absurd and tell why it is absurd. In the temporal sequencing track, children identify a sequence of events or perform a sequence of events according to verbal directions.

Absurdities

This track begins in lesson 9. The early exercises are similar to those that children had worked with in *Reading Mastery Plus,* Level K. The exercise in lesson 9 reviews the meaning of absurdity and presents examples of it. Here's the exercise.

EXERCISE 7

ABSURDITY

a. Listen: Things that are very silly are **absurd.** What's another word for very silly? (Signal.) *Absurd.*
b. Why do we need hats? (Call on a child. Praise good answers such as: *to protect our heads; to keep our heads warm.*)
c. Why do we need shoes? (Call on a child. Praise good answers such as: *to protect our feet; to keep our feet warm.*)
d. Would you wear a hat on your arm? (Signal.) *No.*
   That would be absurd.
 • Would you wear a hat on your head? (Signal.) *Yes.*
 • Would you use a hat to hammer a nail? (Signal.) *No.*
   That would be absurd.
e. Remember, things that are very silly are **absurd.**

Teaching notes: Children should not have any trouble with this exercise. They tend to like the absurdity track. If you respond to the absurdities as if they are funny, children will tend to respond in the same way.

If children are new to the program, however, they may not receive enough practice with the word absurd. For these children you could present the following task at the beginning of the next few lessons:

You learned another word for very silly. What word is that?

The absurdity track presents different types of absurdity, and these relate to the different tracks in *Reading Mastery Plus,* Level 1—parts that are absurd, actions that are absurd, materials that are absurd, absurd sequences of events, objects that are in an absurd location, and objects that are put to absurd uses.

Temporal Sequencing

This track begins in lesson 15 and continues through lesson 32. Its goal is to sharpen the children's understanding of how to sequence events. This skill is very important for reading comprehension and retelling. In *Reading Mastery Plus,* Level 1 the work with temporal sequencing also provides children with skills that they use in worksheet applications of temporal sequencing.

Here's the exercise from lesson 15.

SEQUENCE

a. I'll tell you four things that happened. Listen.
- First, the man put on ice skates.
- Next, the man went out on the ice.
- Next, the man skated.
- Last, the ice cracked.

b. Listen again.
- First, the man put on ice skates.
- Next, the man went out on the ice.
- Next, the man skated.
- Last, the ice cracked.

c. Tell me the four things that happened.
- What happened first? (Signal.) *The man put on ice skates.*
- What happened next? (Signal.) *The man went out on the ice.*
- What happened next? (Signal.) *The man skated.*
- What happened last? (Signal.) *The ice cracked.*
- (Repeat step c until firm.)

d. I'll say the four things, but I'm going to make mistakes. As soon as you hear a mistake, say **stop,** then tell me the right thing that happened.
- Listen. First the man put on skates. Next, the man skated. (Children say *stop.*)
- What happened just after the man put on ice skates? (Signal.) *He went out on the ice.*

e. Listen again. First, the man put on ice skates. Next, the man went out on the ice. Next, the ice cracked. (Children say *stop.*)
- What happened just after the man went out on the ice? (Signal.) *The man skated.*

f. Everybody, say all four things in the right order. Get ready. (Signal.) *First, the man put on skates. Next, the man went out on the ice. Next, the man skated. Last, the ice cracked.*

Teaching notes: If the children have trouble remembering all the events in step c, repeat step b but hold up a finger for each event. If children continue to make mistakes, correct it and point out the number. Listen: The man skated. That's the third thing that happened. Remember, three fingers for the man skated.

After children respond correctly in step c, repeat step c without using the finger prompt.

The main thing you should tell children who don't remember the events is that everything that is done is in a sensible order. The ice won't crack unless something makes it crack. So the man must skate before the ice cracks.

In step d, the children should respond immediately to your mistakes. If children take more than a second to respond, they are not sufficiently firm on the sequence. Repeat step c.

Language Worksheets

One worksheet accompanies each Language lesson, 1 through 145. For most lessons, the worksheet presents two activities. Some of the worksheet activities are fairly structured; others are more independent.

The worksheets extend what the children are being taught during the other parts of the lessons. In some cases, the worksheets provide the primary teaching. This situation occurs when the skill or concept being taught must be illustrated, as it is with some sequencing and map reading skills.

Below is a list of the primary categories of activities that appear on the worksheets. The lesson of the first appearance of each category is indicated.

Category	First Appearance
Classification	Lesson 1
Part–Whole	*Lesson 1*
Locations	*Lesson 9*
Questioning Skills	**Lesson 19**
From–To	**Lesson 35**
Materials	Lesson 42
Analogies	Lesson 54
Map Reading (writing directions)	**Lesson 59**
Story-Related Activities (what characters say, sequencing events, data collection)	Lesson 16
Writing Opposites	Lesson 124

Italicized categories are reviews of material taught in *Reading Mastery Plus,* Level K. Part–whole and locations are largely review; however, some of the information children respond to is taught for the first time in *Reading Mastery Plus,* Level 1.

Boldfaced categories indicate that the primary instruction occurs through worksheets.

Categories that are neither italicized nor boldfaced are extensions of what is taught in *Reading Mastery Plus,* Level 1.

General Response Exercises

The purpose of the worksheets is to strengthen what children learn. The goal is for children to produce responses that clearly indicate that they know important facts and relationships. *Reading Mastery Plus,* Level 1 uses several response formats that are capable of yielding clear indications of the children's knowledge and possibly of the problems they have with specific skills or information.

One format involves coloring rules. You give the children directions to color all the examples of a certain type of color. In classification exercises, for instance, you might direct them to color all the appliances green. For part-whole, you might direct children to color the handle of the object blue.

Another generic format requires children to draw lines to connect or categorize things that go together. For instance, for an analogy that tells about things and the parts they have, you direct children to draw lines from objects to their parts (from a boy to an arm and from a tree to a branch).

A third generic format requires children to write. A classification exercise may direct children to write the name of the furniture or container under each of the illustrated objects.

Here's a brief summary of the various worksheet categories.

Classification

Most of the early classification exercises present coloring rules.

Here's the worksheet from lesson 15.

The coloring rules are: color the animals orange; color the food purple. Children do not do the coloring at this time. Instead

they make a colored mark on one of the objects. For instance, they mark one of the animals orange. That mark indicates that they are to color all the animals orange.

Some of the later coloring rules are more complicated. They contain the words **some, or,** and **and.**

Here's the exercise from lesson 30 that presents directions that refer to **all** and **some.**

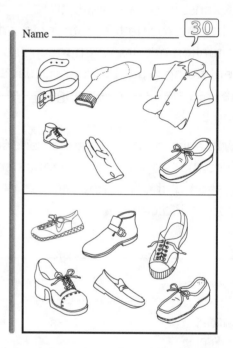

Name _____ 30

EXERCISE 2

CLASSIFICATION

a. (Hold up worksheet. Point to second half.) The box shows two pictures. Some of the things in one picture are shoes. All of the things in the other picture are shoes.

b. Touch the picture where some of the things are shoes. ✓

• Here's the rule about the picture where **some** of the things are shoes. The shoes should be green. What's the rule? (Signal.) *The shoes should be green.*

• Fix up the picture where **some** of the things are shoes. ✓

c. Here's the rule about the picture where **all** of the things are shoes. The shoes should be

yellow or black. What's the rule? (Signal.)
The shoes should be yellow or black.

- Make a yellow mark on one shoe and a black mark on another shoe. ✓

One picture shows some things that are shoes. The rule for that picture is: the shoes should be **green.**

The other picture shows only shoes. The rule for that picture is: the shoes should be **yellow** or **black.** (Children make a black mark on one shoe and a yellow mark on another shoe in this picture. The mark shows that the shoes may be either yellow or black.)

Some classification worksheets require children to write the class names for objects in the picture.

Here's the student material from lesson 97.

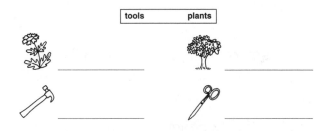

Children write the name **tool** next to each tool and the name **plant** next to each plant.

Some of the later classification activities present two pictures, one showing a smaller class and the other showing a larger class.

In lesson 104, children identify the smaller class (frying pans) and the larger class (containers) and then follow a coloring rule for the frying pans in each picture.

Here's the student material from lesson 104.

Part–Whole

Children review part-whole nomenclature at the beginning of *Reading Mastery Plus,* Level 1. Part-whole worksheet activities occur throughout the level.

Here's an early part-whole activity from lesson 4.

Worksheet 4

EXERCISE 7

PART—WHOLE

a. (Hold up worksheet.) Find the picture of the pencil. ✓
b. Here's a coloring rule for the pencil. Listen. Color the eraser green. What's the rule? (Signal.) *Color the eraser green.*
 • Mark the eraser. ✓
c. Here's another coloring rule for the pencil. Listen. Color the shaft blue. What's the rule? (Signal.) *Color the shaft blue.*
 • Mark the shaft. ✓
d. Part of the pencil is missing. What part is missing? (Signal.) *The point.*
 • Yes, the point. Before you color the pencil, you're going to follow the dots with your pencil to make the point.
e. Here's the coloring rule for the point. Listen. Color the point yellow. What's the rule? (Signal.) *Color the point yellow.*
 • Mark the point. ✓

You review the parts of a pencil. Then children complete the picture of the pencil (identifying and drawing the missing part). Then children follow coloring rules: Color the eraser green; color the shaft blue; color the point yellow.

The color designations are sometimes not what one would commonly observe. This feature of the coloring rules is purposeful. Children must attend to the details of the rule to perform the task correctly. They can't simply rely on what they know to be true of pencils—black point, yellow shaft, red eraser.

Later part-whole activities have less structure but require children to apply various coloring rules and drawing rules.

Locations

Here's a list of the various locations and when they first appear on worksheets in *Reading Mastery Plus,* Level 1.

Location	Lesson
doctor office	9
farm	10
garage	12
airport	13
playground	15
dentist office	17
city	19
jungle	25
beach	27
restaurant	29
fire station	35
gas station	40
bus station	49
beauty parlor	54
pet store	62
hospital	64

For these activities, children identify the location shown in the picture and then follow coloring rules.

Here's a location picture from lesson 10.

One coloring rule is: Color some of the farm animals black and color some of the farm animals brown.

Another rule is: Color the buildings red.

Questioning Skills

Some primary teaching for questioning skills is presented throughout the worksheet activities. The first questioning-skills exercise appears in lesson 19.

Here's the student material and the activity from lesson 20.

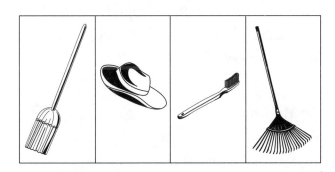

 **Worksheet**

EXERCISE 1
QUESTIONING SKILLS

a. (Hold up worksheet. Point to the boxes.) I'm thinking about one of these pictures. It's either a broom, a hat, a toothbrush, or a rake. You'll ask questions to find out what object I'm thinking of.
- Everybody, ask the question about the parts it has. Get ready. (Signal.) *What parts does it have?*

- Everybody, ask a question about where you find it. Get ready. (Signal.) *Where do you find it?*
b. Let's ask those questions again.
c. Everybody, ask the question about the parts it has. Get ready. (Signal.) *What parts does it have?*
- Everybody, ask the question about where you find it. Get ready. (Signal.) *Where do you find it?*
d. (Repeat step c until firm.)
e. Ask those questions again, and I'll tell you the answers.
f. Everybody, ask the question about the parts it has. Get ready. (Signal.) *What parts does it have?*
- Here's the answer. A handle and bristles. What parts? (Signal.) *A handle and bristles.*
- Could it be a broom? (Signal.) *Yes.*
- Could it be a hat? (Signal.) *No.*
- Could it be a toothbrush? (Signal.) *Yes.*
- Could it be a rake? (Signal.) *No.*
g. Everybody, ask the question about where you find it. Get ready. (Signal.) *Where do you find it?*
- Here's the answer. In the bathroom. Where do you find it? (Signal.) *In the bathroom.*
h. Everybody, make a yellow mark on the thing I'm thinking of. ✓
- Everybody, what was I thinking of? (Signal.) *A toothbrush.*

First children repeat the questions they will ask to identify the object. Then they ask the questions and you answer them.

You do not ask the children to identify the object before they follow a coloring rule and mark the correct object yellow (step h).

Through similar exercises, children become facile at asking questions to secure information.

From–To

For these activities, an illustration shows something moving from one thing to another thing.

Here's an example from lesson 35.

Children follow two coloring rules for each arrow. **Color the thing the dog is moving to yellow. Color the thing the dog is moving from blue.** By following the rule, the children become firm in the idea that the dog may move in any direction.

Materials

Here's the student worksheet from lesson 42.

For most activities, children follow a coloring rule that directs them to color objects made of a particular material a specific color.

You present children with if–then rules: If an object is made of paper, color it green. If an object is made of metal, color it black.

Later material exercises are similar, except that some of them have more complicated rules and at least one of the objects may have a missing part. In lesson 105, for instance, children are to color things made of wood either black or brown, and things made of cloth orange. Children also draw the part that is missing from the shirt (a sleeve).

Analogies

The worksheet exercises that involve analogies parallel the oral work that children do. The first analogy worksheet exercise appears in lesson 54.

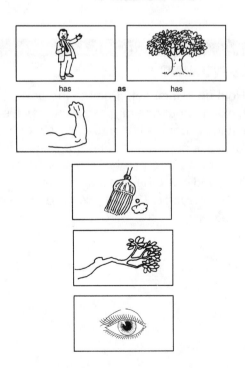

Worksheet 54

EXERCISE 9

ANALOGIES

a. (Hold up worksheet. Point to first half.)
- The pictures show something and part of the thing.

b. Touch the man. ✓

c. Now touch the picture that's right below the man. It shows part of the man. Everybody, what part? (Signal.) *An arm.*
- Yes, those pictures show that a man has an arm.

d. Touch the tree. ✓
- One of the pictures below the tree shows the part it has. Touch the picture that shows the part a tree has. ✓
- Everybody, what part does a tree have? (Signal.) *A branch.*

e. Listen: A man has an arm **as** a tree has a branch.
- Tell me about a man. Get ready. (Signal.) *A man has an arm.*
- Tell me about a tree. Get ready. (Signal.) *A tree has a branch.*

f. Draw a line from the tree to the part it has. (Observe children and give feedback.)

Children show the analogous relationship between "the man has an arm" and "the tree has a branch" by drawing a line from the tree to the branch.

The worksheet activities present a full range of analogy types. Here are three different types:

Lesson 116

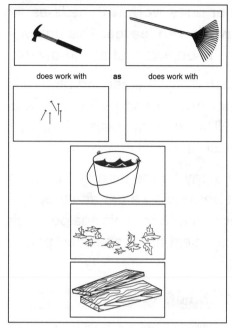

Lesson 127

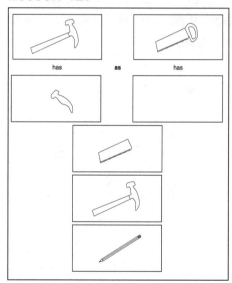

Lesson 134

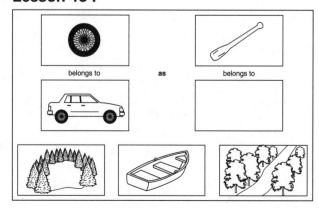

The analogy for the first picture is: **A hammer does work with nails as a rake does work with leaves.** This analogy deals with objects that accompany tools.

The analogy for the second picture is: **A hammer has a head as a saw has a blade.** This analogy deals with the parts an object has.

The analogy for the third picture is: **A wheel belongs to a car as an oar belongs to a boat.** This analogy indicates that the object has a specified part.

Map Reading

Map reading activities begin in lesson 59. For some activities, children color arrows that show a particular direction. Here's the first exercise.

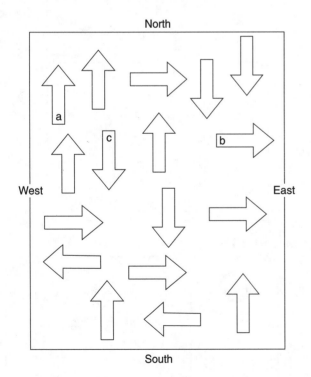

 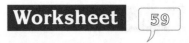
EXERCISE 5

MAP READING

a. (Hold up worksheet. Point to first half.)
- Some of the arrows have letters on them. Find the arrow with the letter **A.** ✓
- That arrow is pointing **north.** Which direction? (Signal.) *North.*

b. Find the arrow with the letter **B.** ✓
- That arrow is pointing **east.** Which direction? (Signal.) *East.*

c. Find the arrow with the letter **C.** ✓
- That arrow is pointing **south.** Which direction? (Signal.) *South.*

d. Touch **A.** ✓
- Everybody, which direction is that arrow pointing? (Signal.) *North.*
- Touch **B.** ✓
- Everybody, which direction is that arrow pointing? (Signal.) *East.*
- Touch **C.** ✓
- Everybody, which direction is that arrow pointing? (Signal.) *South.*

e. Listen: Here's a rule about the arrows that are pointing **north.** All arrows that are pointing **north** should be blue. What color? (Signal.) *Blue.*
- There are six arrows that are pointing **north.** Put a blue mark on each arrow that is pointing **north.**
  (Observe children and give feedback.)

f. Here's a rule about the arrows that are pointing **east.** All the arrows that are pointing **east** should be red. What color? (Signal.) *Red.*
- There are five arrows pointing **east.** Put a red mark on each of them.
  (Observe children and give feedback.)

g. Later you can color the arrows that are pointing **north** and the arrows that are pointing **east.**

Children have received some instructions about the directions on a map. They have just learned the directions for the four sides of the map. Children first find an arrow with a particular letter. Children then follow coloring rules such as, All the arrows that are pointing east should be red.

For some of the later map reading, children write letters that show directions.

Here's the student material from lesson 68.

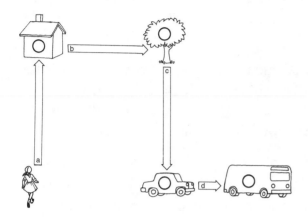

The arrows show the route the girl took to reach each object. Children write the letter of the direction the girl had to go. For instance, they write **N** in the house to show that the girl went north to reach the house.

Writing Opposites

The worksheets for opposites begin in lesson 124 and continue to the end of the level. Unlike many of the earlier tasks, the work with opposites is written.

Here's the student and teacher material from lesson 124.

rough	tall	old	pull

1. push _____

2. young _____

3. smooth _____

4. short _____

Worksheet 124

EXERCISE 6

OPPOSITES

a. (Hold up worksheet. Point to top half.) Find the words in the box at the top of your worksheet. ✓
- I'll read those words. Touch and follow along: **rough, tall, old, pull.** ✓

b. Your turn. Touch the first word. ✓
What word? (Signal.) *Rough.*
- Next word. ✓
What word? (Signal.) *Tall.*
- Next word. ✓
What word? (Signal.) *Old.*
- Last word. ✓
What word? (Signal.) *Pull.*
- (Repeat step b until firm.)

c. You're going to write words that tell the opposite.
- Touch number 1. ✓
- That word is **push.** What word? (Signal.) *Push.*
- Everybody, what's the opposite of **push?** (Signal.) *Pull.*

d. The word **pull** is in the word box. Copy that word right after the word **push.**
(Observe children and give feedback.)

e. Touch number 2. ✓

- That word is **young.** What word? (Signal.) *Young.*
- Everybody, what's the opposite of **young?** (Signal.) *Old.*

f. The word **old** is in the word box. Copy that word right after the word **young.** (Observe children and give feedback.)

g. Touch number 3. ✓
- That word is **smooth.** What word? (Signal.) *Smooth.*
- Everybody, what's the opposite of **smooth?** (Signal.) *Rough.*

h. The word **rough** is in the word box. Copy that word right after the word **smooth.** (Observe children and give feedback.)

i. Touch number 4. ✓
- That word is **short.** What word? (Signal.) *Short.*
- Everybody, which word in the box is the opposite of **short?** (Signal.) *Tall.*

j. Copy the word **tall** right after the word **short.**

Children read the words. The first word is **push.** They find the word that is the opposite of **push.** Then they copy the word right after the word push.

Similar exercises review the various opposites that children have learned.

Story-Related Activities

In Language lessons 6–141, every lesson whose number ends in 1 or 6 presents activities that are related to stories. These activities are coordinated with the stories that the children read. Many of the stories they hear in *Reading Mastery Plus,* Level K and Level 1 are stories they will read in *Reading Mastery Plus,* Level 2.

The activities that occur in the story activities track are: **Extrapolation (What Characters Say), Data Collection, Sequencing Events, Storytelling** and **Putting on a Play.**

Not all of the activities involve stories. Some involve the story characters children know. The activities are topically or thematically related to the stories. For instance, children sequence story events or analyze a picture to find out the answer to a data question.

Characters and Story Grammars

Each character that children hear about in *Reading Mastery Plus,* Level 1 stories is unique. Each character has predictable behaviors and preferences. Here's a summary of the various characters and their story grammars.

Paul—Lessons 6, 71

Paul loves to paint—but in only two colors, pink and purple.

Paul speaks in p-starting words: "Purple plums would be perfectly pleasing."

He has a predictable solution to problems of spilled paint. If paint plops onto the porch while Paul is painting a pretty picture of purple plums, Paul says something like, "That porch looks poor with puddles of purple paint on it, but I can fix it." His solution: Paint the whole porch purple.

In the first story, purple paint gets on the pane of a window, the porch, and other places. Then his brother comes out and gets paint on his pants. Paul says, "But brother, don't worry. I can fix it." The story doesn't tell how he does that, but the children know because the story grammar is very strong.

The Bragging Rats— Lessons 11, 76, 111, 126

Two rats constantly argue about who is best at doing something. When describing how good they are, they go beyond exaggeration to incredible lies. After it becomes apparent to all the rats that the Bragging Rats do not know how to settle their argument, the wise old rat intervenes and shows them how to stage a contest to determine which Bragging Rat is the best.

In the first Bragging Rats story, the rats argue about who is the fastest runner. The wise old rat sets up a course that goes to the edge of the pond and then back to the starting line. The two Bragging Rats get tangled up just before they turn around, tumble into the pond and don't finish the race. The little black rat wins. But the contest is for naught because the Bragging Rats are now arguing about who is the fastest swimmer. "I may not be the fastest **runner** in this bunch, but there is no rat in the world that can **swim** as fast as I can."

Roxie—Lessons 16, 21, 96

Roxie's story grammar is fairly simple— she collects rocks. Her collection creates problems for two possible reasons: it takes up too much space and it is too heavy. In the Roxie story, her mother directs her to remove all her rocks from her room. She moves them to her tree house. The tree house collapses and creates an attractive rock garden around the trunk. Her mother thinks the result is very attractive.

Roger—Lesson 21

Roger loves hats, but he doesn't always remember where he leaves his hat. Sometimes he remembers, but someone or something has removed his hat from where Roger left it.

Bleep and Molly—Lessons 26, 31, 36, 46, 56, 61, 121, 126, 131, 136, 141

Bleep is an imperfect robot invented by Molly Mix-up, whose nickname comes from the fact that none of her inventions work exactly the way they should. Although Bleep is very talented, he has some unusual personality characteristics:

- He always says "bleep" at the beginning of his sentences.

- He often replies to directions such as, "Get the paint from the garage," by saying, "Bleep, okay baby."

- His verbal reports are sometimes unreliable (or confusing).

In the first episode, Bleep incorrectly relays a phone message. He had a phone conversation with a friend of Molly's, Mrs. Anderson, who thought she was talking to Molly, not Bleep. Mrs. Anderson asked where the two women should meet for lunch. Bleep indicated that there was a wonderful restaurant at the corner of 13th and Elm; however, the only thing on that corner was a wrecking yard. The women arrived at different times (Molly in a red van and Mrs. Anderson in a red sports car), parked their cars in front of the wrecking yard (in a drop-off zone) and searched for the restaurant. When they returned to their cars, they found that the cars had been dismantled and that the workers were ready to scrunch the remains of each vehicle. Molly gave the workers directions for reassembling the vehicles, but the results were two red vehicles—each half-sports-car and half-van. Nobody was very happy.

Sweetie and Honey— Lessons (21), 41, 51, 91, 101

Another character introduced is a nasty cat named Sweetie. His grammar is quite sophisticated because it always involves misunderstandings that are based on perspective.

Sweetie loves to chase things like little birds or helpless butterflies. His plans center around getting something to eat, and he says things like, "Yum, yum."

Sweetie is always foiled because he lacks information about what really takes place when he tries to execute his plan. Sweetie always thinks that he was foiled by his helpless prey and says something like, "From here those birds look pretty helpless, but let me tell you, they are mean and strong."

Andrea is a shy little mouse who is friends with a dog named Honey. Honey is a mean-looking bulldog who hates Sweetie.

Rolla—Lesson 66

Rolla's story grammar presents another type of "perspective" confusion. Rolla is a merry-go-round horse who wears the number 1. That number bothers her because there are eight horses, and horse number 8 is right in front of her. So one day she executes her plan. She thinks that if she could go slower, she could increase the distance between her and the horse in front of her.

When she attempts to go slow, the other horses go slow, the music slows down and sounds awful, and the merry-go-round turns so slowly that no one is sure it's moving.

Clarabelle—Lesson 71

Clarabelle is a big brown-and-white cow who loves to imitate other animals and even people. Her plans always fail in a humorous way.

Storytelling and Story Details

In some lessons, you read a story and ask the children specified questions. Here's an example from lesson 6.

EXERCISE 8

STORYTELLING

Paul Paints Plums

- Everybody, I'm going to read you a silly story. Listen to the things that happen in the story because you're going to fix up a picture that shows part of the story.
- This is a story about Paul. Listen:

PAUL PAINTS PLUMS

Everybody has favorite colors. Some people love red. Some people love yellow. Others love blue or green. Some like brown or black. Well, Paul had his favorite colors, too. But his favorite colors were not red or blue, or brown or black, or even white or yellow. His two favorite colors were pink and purple. It's hard to say which color Paul liked the most. Sometimes, he would prefer pink. At other times, he preferred purple.

Well, Paul also loved to paint. And whenever he painted, he'd use one of his favorite colors. One day, he was on his porch painting a picture of purple plums.

- Everybody, what was Paul's favorite color on that day? (Signal.) *Purple.*

Paul said, "Painting pictures of purple plums on the porch is perfect."

- That's hard to say. Listen again: Painting pictures of purple plums on the porch is perfect.
- Who can say that? (Call on a child. *Painting pictures of purple plums on the porch is perfect.*)

As Paul was painting, he dripped some purple paint on the floor of the porch. "Oh, pooh," he said. "Puddles of purple paint are on the porch, but I can fix it." So he got a great big brush and started to paint the whole floor of the porch purple.

- Everybody, is that the way **you** would fix up the purple puddles? (Signal.) *No.*
- How would you fix up the purple puddles? (Call on a child. Praise a reasonable response.)

But here's what Paul did: He got a great big brush and started to paint the whole porch purple. But just when he was almost finished, he backed into his painting and the painting fell against the window. It didn't break the window, but it got purple paint on the window pane.

- Listen: Why did the purple paint get on the window pane? (Call on a child. Idea: *The painting fell against the window.*)
- So now the floor of the porch is purple, and there is purple paint on the window pane.

"Whoa," Paul said. "Now there are patches of purple paint on the pane. But I can fix it."

He tried wiping the purple paint from the pane, but that didn't work. At last Paul said, "I fixed the floor of the porch, and I can fix that pane the same way."

- What do you think he'll do? (Call on a child. Idea: *paint the whole window pane purple.*)

> Paul said, "A purple pane may look perfectly pleasing." And he painted the whole window pane purple. But just as he was painting the last corner of the pane, some purple paint dripped on the wall.

- What do you think he'll do? (Call on a child. Idea: *paint the whole wall purple.*)
- Let's see.

> The purple paint dripped on the wall. "Wow," Paul said, "perhaps purple paint would look perfect on the wall." So you know what he did next. He painted the whole wall purple. And just as he was finishing up the last corner of the wall, his brother came out of the house. As his brother walked onto the porch, he rubbed against the wall and got a great smear of purple paint on his pants. Paul's brother tried to wipe the purple paint from his pants, but he just smeared the paint.
>
> "I'm a mess," his brother said.
>
> "So you are," Paul agreed. Then Paul smiled at his brother and said, "But brother, don't worry. I can fix it." And he did just that.

- What do you think he did? (Call on a child. Ideas: *Paul painted his brother purple* or *Paul painted his brother's pants purple.*)

Worksheet

EXERCISE 9

STORY DETAILS

a. (Hold up worksheet.) Everybody, find the picture of Paul. ✓
   This picture takes place after Paul had already painted some things.
- What did he start out painting? (Call on a child. Idea: *a picture of purple plums.*)

- What did he paint purple next? (Call on a child. Idea: *the floor of the porch.*)
- Why did he paint the floor of the porch purple? (Call on a child. Idea: *because he dripped purple paint on the porch.*)
- What did he paint after the floor of the porch? (Call on a child. Idea: *the whole window pane.*)
- Why did he paint the window pane purple? (Call on a child. Idea: *because he got purple paint on the window pane.*)
- What did he paint after he painted the window pane? (Call on a child. Idea: *the wall.*)
- Why did he paint the wall purple? (Call on a child. Idea: *because paint dripped on the wall.*)
- What's he doing in the picture? (Call on a child. Idea: *painting the wall.*)
- Who is that coming out the door? (Signal.) *His brother.* I can see that smear of paint on his brother's pants.
- What's Paul going to do after this picture? (Call on a child. Idea: *paint his brother's pants purple.*)

b. Listen: Get a purple crayon and put a little purple mark on everything that is **already** purple. Don't put a purple mark on anything that Paul hasn't painted purple yet. Raise your hand when you're finished.
   (Observe children and give feedback.)
- Name the things you marked with purple. (Call on several children. Praise children who name: *the plums, the floor of the porch, the window, the wall,* and *the smear on the pants.*)

c. Your turn: Fix up the picture so that all these things are purple—the plums, the floor of the porch, the window, the smear on Paul's brother's pants, and most of the wall. Later you can color the other parts of the picture any color you wish.

Extrapolation—What Characters Say

In some lessons, children identify the things that different characters would say. Character descriptions appear earlier in this section, pages 189–191. Here's the activity from lesson 76.

Worksheet 76

EXTRAPOLATION
What Characters Say

Note: A complete listing of character descriptions appears in the Teacher's Guide.

a. (Hold up worksheet. Point to top half.) Touch the pictures that have letters under them. ✓ These are pictures of characters from some stories you've heard. Each picture has a letter under it. The letter is the initial of the character in the picture.

b. Touch the first picture. ✓
Who is in that picture? (Signal.) *Honey.*
• What letter is under that picture? (Signal.) *H.*
H is the first letter in the word **Honey.**

c. Who is in the next picture? (Signal.) *Clarabelle.*
• What letter is under Clarabelle? (Signal.) *C.*
C is the first letter in her name.

d. Who is in the next picture? (Signal.) *Bleep.*
• What letter is under Bleep? (Signal.) *B.*
B is the first letter in Bleep's name.

e. Who is in the next picture? (Signal.) *Roger.*
• What letter is under Roger? (Signal.) *R.*
R is the first letter in Roger's name.

f. Who is in the last picture? (Signal.) *Sweetie.*
• What letter is under Sweetie? (Signal.) *S.*
S is the first letter in Sweetie's name.

g. Here's the game we'll play: I'll say five different things. For each thing I'll say, you're going to write the letter for the character who would say that. You're not going to say anything out loud. You'll just find the right picture and write the letter for that character.

h. Everybody, touch line 1 and keep touching it. ✓
• Listen and don't say anything. Here's the statement for line 1: "I'd love to go roller-skating just like those children are doing."
• Find the character who would say that. Write the letter for that character on line 1. Raise your hand when you're finished.
(Observe children and give feedback.)

i. Everybody, which character would love to go roller-skating just like the children? (Signal.) *Clarabelle.*
• So what letter did you write for number 1? (Signal.) *C.*
• (Write on the board:)

1. C

• Here's what you should have for number 1. Raise your hand if you got it right. ✓

j. Everybody, touch number 2. ✓
• Listen and don't say anything. Here's the statement for number 2: "That mouse can really bite hard."
• Find the character who would say that. Write the letter for that character on line 2. Raise your hand when you're finished.
(Observe children and give feedback.)

k. Everybody, which character would say, "That mouse can really bite hard"? (Signal.) *Sweetie.*
• So what letter did you write for number 2? (Signal.) *S.*
• (Write to show:)

1. C
2. S

• Here's what you should have for number 2. Raise your hand if you got it right. ✓

l. Everybody, touch number 3. ✓
• Listen and don't say anything. Here's the statement for number 3: "When I sat down, my hat was right over there; but now, I don't know where it is."
• Find the character who would say that. Write the letter for that character on line 3. Raise your hand when you're finished.
(Observe children and give feedback.)

m. Everybody, which character would have trouble finding a hat? (Signal.) *Roger.*
• So what letter did you write for number 3? (Signal.) *R.*
• (Write to show:)

1. C
2. S
3. R

- Here's what you should have for number 3. Raise your hand if you got it right. ✓
n. Everybody, touch number 4. ✓
- Listen and don't say anything. Here's the statement for number 4: "If that cat doesn't behave, I'll have to give him a little nip somewhere."
- Find the character who would say that. Write the letter for that character on line 4. Raise your hand when you're finished.
  (Observe children and give feedback.)
o. Everybody, which character would give a cat a little nip? (Signal.) *Honey.*
- So what letter did you write for number 4? (Signal.) *H.*
- (Write to show:)

> 1. C
> 2. S
> 3. R
> **4. H**

- Here's what you should have for number 4. Raise your hand if you got it right. ✓
p. Everybody, touch number 5. ✓
- Listen and don't say anything. Here's the statement for number 5: "Okay, baby."
- Find the character who would say that. Write the letter for that character on line 5. Raise your hand when you're finished.
  (Observe children and give feedback.)
q. Everybody, which character would say, "Okay, baby"? (Signal.) *Bleep.*
- So what letter did you write for number 5? (Signal.) *B.*
- (Write to show:)

> 1. C
> 2. S
> 3. R
> 4. M
> **5. B**

- Here's what you should have for number 5. Raise your hand if you got it right. ✓
r. Raise your hand if you got everything right. ✓
  Wow. You really know the characters we've read about.

Data Collection and Summary

In some lessons, children collect data. Here's part of the exercise from lesson 101.

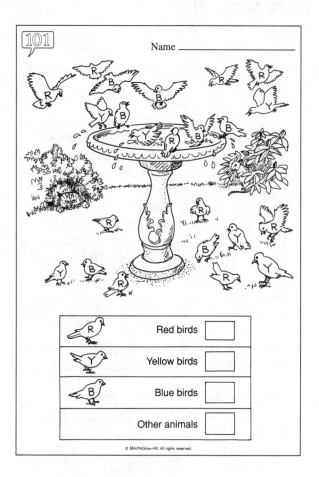

Worksheet 101

EXERCISE 7
DATA COLLECTION

a. (Hold up worksheet. Point to the picture.) This is a story about a woman named Bonnie who bought a birdbath for her yard.

> One day, Bonnie was talking to her neighbors. Bonnie said, "I always have red birds and yellow birds and blue birds in my yard. But there are always more **red** birds than any other color."
>
> One neighbor said, "No, that's not true. I've looked in your yard many times when I was trying to find Sweetie. And I know for a fact that there are always more **yellow** birds than any other color."
>
> "Not true," another neighbor said. "Every time I've looked in your yard while walking my wonderful dog, Honey, I've always seen more **blue** birds than birds of any other color."

- If the wise old rat heard this conversation, how do you think he'd go about finding the right answer? (Call on a child. Idea: *Count the birds.*)
- Yes, the smart way is to find out the answer by counting the birds. So **you** can be smart.
b. Look at the picture. The letters on the birds show what color they should be. The letter **R** on a bird shows that the bird should be **red.**
- Your turn: Take out your **red** crayon and put a **red** mark on all the birds that have the letter **R** on them. Don't miss any birds, but do it fast and don't color the whole bird. Just put a red mark on each bird inside the picture that has an **R** on it. Don't color the bird in the big box. Raise your hand when you're finished. (Observe children and give feedback.)
c. Now look at the box below the picture. You'll see a picture of a bird with an **R** on it.
- Touch that bird. ✓ Right after that bird are the words **red birds.** Then there's an empty box. Write the number of **red** birds in that box. Count all the red birds in the picture and write that number in the top box. Raise your hand when you're finished. (Observe children and give feedback.)
- Everybody, what number did you write for the **red** birds? (Signal.) *Ten.*
d. Now do the same thing for the **yellow** birds. Make a **yellow** mark on every bird in the

picture that has the letter **Y** on it. The **Y** is for **yellow.** After you make your yellow marks, count the **yellow** birds and write that number in the box for **yellow** birds. Raise your hand when you're finished. (Observe children and give feedback.)
- Everybody, what number did you write for the **yellow** birds? (Signal.) *Six.*
e. Now do the same thing for the **blue** birds. Make a **blue** mark on every bird in the picture that has the letter **B** on it. The **B** is for **blue.** After you make your blue marks, count the **blue** birds and write that number in the box for **blue** birds. Raise your hand when you're finished. (Observe children and give feedback.)
- Everybody, what number did you write? (Signal.) *Seven.*
- Get ready to read your numbers one more time.
- Listen: How many **red** birds are in the picture? (Signal.) *Ten.*
- How many **yellow** birds are in the picture? (Signal.) *Six.*
- How many **blue** birds are in the picture? *Seven.*
f. Let's see who was right about the birds in Bonnie's yard. Here's what Bonnie said: "There are always more **red** birds than any other color."
- Think about it. Is that statement true or false? (Signal.) *True.*
- One neighbor said, "There are always more **yellow** birds than any other color." Is that statement true or false? (Signal.) *False.*
- Another neighbor said that there are always more **blue** birds than any other color. Is that statement true or false? (Signal.) *False.*
- So who was right, Bonnie or one of her neighbors? (Signal.) *Bonnie.*
g. Before we leave this picture, there's one more box to fill out below the picture, but I really don't know what goes in there.
- Touch the last box below the picture. ✓ It says **other animals.** I guess they want you to write the number of other animals that are in the picture. But I really don't see any. Maybe you do. Look at the picture very

carefully. See if you can find any other animals in the picture. Count up any animals that are **not** birds and write that number in the last box. If you don't find any other animals, you can write **zero** in the box. Raise your hand when you have a number in the last box. (Observe children and give feedback.)

- Everybody, what number did you write for **other animals?** (Signal.) *Two.*
- I guess they were hiding in the picture. I didn't see them.

h. Later, you can color everything.

Sequencing Events

In some lessons children sequence events. For example, the story activity that appears in lesson 91 deals with Sweetie and a mouse named Andrea.

 Worksheet 91

EXERCISE 6

Note: If children do not have gray crayons, they may use their pencil.

SEQUENCE STORY

Sweetie and Andrea

a. (Hold up worksheet.)
Everybody, find the picture. ✓
This is a new kind of story. In this story, Andrea does some things and Sweetie does some things.

b. You're going to make a path for Andrea and a path for Sweetie. You'll make Andrea's path **gray** and Sweetie's path **yellow.**
- Listen.

> **SWEETIE AND ANDREA**
>
> Andrea the mouse was hungry. She looked out from her hole in the wall and saw that there were some peanuts on the table. Andrea loved peanuts. But she also saw that there was something else in the room. Something she didn't like very much.

- Everybody, who was that? (Signal.) *Sweetie.*

> As you know, that cat was named Sweetie and he was the meanest cat in town. Sweetie seemed to be sleeping on the rug, so Andrea crept into the room. Sweetie moved, so Andrea hid behind the scratching post.

c. Touch the place where Andrea went to first. ✓
Everybody, where was Andrea first? (Signal.) *Behind the scratching post.*
- Remember, Andrea's on the side of the scratching post where the cat can't see her. That's the side nearest her hole.
- Use your pencil and make a **1** in the circle to show that this is the first place Andrea went to. Make sure your **1** is on the side of the post that is **away** from Sweetie or your story may not have a happy ending at all. Raise your hand when you're finished. (Observe children and give feedback.)

d. That part of the story tells about **Andrea.** So you'll show the path with a **gray** crayon (or pencil). Draw a path from the picture of Andrea to the circle with a **1** in it. Raise your hand when you're finished. (Observe children and give feedback.)
- Here's the next thing that happened.

> Sweetie woke up and walked over to the scratching post. Sweetie stopped right across from where Andrea was hiding.

e. Touch the circle that shows where Sweetie is now. You should be touching the circle on the side of the scratching post closest to where Sweetie was. ✓

- Use your pencil to make a **2** in the circle to show that this is where Sweetie was. Raise your hand when you're finished.
  (Observe children and give feedback.)

f. This part of the story tells about **Sweetie.** So you'll show the path with a **yellow** crayon. Draw a yellow path from the picture of Sweetie to the circle with the **2** in it. Raise your hand when you're finished.
  (Observe children and give feedback.)

> **Andrea held her breath and waited. Sweetie scratched on the scratching post. Then Sweetie went in his bed and curled up with his eyes closed.**

g. Touch the circle that shows where Sweetie was after he scratched on the scratching post. ✓

- Everybody, where was Sweetie now? (Signal.) *In his bed.*
- Use your pencil and make a **3** in the circle to show that this is the next place Sweetie was. Raise your hand when you're finished.
  (Observe children and give feedback.)

h. Does this last part of the story tell what **Andrea** did or what **Sweetie** did? (Signal.) *What Sweetie did.*

- So what color will the path be? (Signal.) *Yellow.*
- Draw a yellow path from circle **2** to circle **3.**
  Raise your hand when you're finished.
  (Observe children and give feedback.)

> **While Sweetie was snoozing, Andrea climbed up the scratching post to the very top of it.**

i. Touch the circle that shows where Andrea went. ✓

- Where was Andrea now? (Call on a child. Idea: *at the top of the scratching post.*)
- Everybody, use your pencil and make a **4** in the circle to show that this is the next

thing that happened. Raise your hand when you're finished.
  (Observe children and give feedback.)

j. Does the last part of the story tell what **Andrea** did or what **Sweetie** did? (Signal.) *What Andrea did.*

- So what color will the path be? (Signal.) *Gray.*
- Draw a gray path from circle **1** to circle **4.** Raise your hand when you're finished.
  (Observe children and give feedback.)

> **Then Andrea jumped onto the table. She was pretty close to the peanuts.**

k. Touch the circle that shows where Andrea went this time. ✓

- Use your pencil and make a **5** in the circle to show that this is the next thing that happened. Raise your hand when you're finished.
  (Observe children and give feedback.)

l. Does this last part of the story tell what **Andrea** did or what **Sweetie** did? (Signal.) *What Andrea did.*

- So what color will the path be? (Signal.) *Gray.*
- Draw a gray path from circle **4** to circle **5.** Raise your hand when you're finished.
  (Observe children and give feedback.)

> **The last thing Andrea did was to eat the peanuts.**

m. Uh-oh, there's no circle to show where Andrea was when she ate the peanuts. Draw a path to the peanuts. Make sure the path is the right color. Raise your hand when you're finished.
  (Observe children and give feedback.)

- Later you can draw a picture of Andrea eating the peanuts.

n. Now you're going to help me retell the story. You'll do the numbers in order, starting with **1.** That's important. You first tell about **1.** Then you tell about **2.** Then you tell about **3** and so forth. At each number, you have to tell me **who** did something. You can tell by looking at the color of the path that goes **to** the number.

o. Touch number 1. ✓
  What's the color of the path that goes to that number? (Signal.) *Gray.*

- So you have to tell about **Andrea.** I'll show you how to do it: Andrea was by her mousehole. She was hungry. So she snuck from her hole over to the scratching post.

p. Everybody, touch number 2. ✓
  What's the color of the path that goes to number 2? (Signal.) *Yellow.*

- So who do you have to tell about? (Signal.) *Sweetie.*

- Sweetie went from someplace to another place.
  Tell where Sweetie started and what he went to. (Call on a child. Idea: *Sweetie went from the rug to the scratching post.*)

q. You just told about number 2. Everybody, what's the next number you'll touch? (Signal.) *Three.*

- Look at the path that leads to number 3.

- Who do you have to tell about for number 3? (Signal.) *Sweetie.*

- Tell where Sweetie was and what he did. (Call on a child. Idea: *After Sweetie scratched for a while, he went from the scratching post to his bed and went to sleep.*)

r. You just told about number 3. Everybody, what's the next number you'll touch? (Signal.) *Four.*

- Look at the path that leads to number 4. Who do you have to tell about for number 4? (Signal.) *Andrea.*

- Tell where Andrea was and what she did. (Call on a child. Idea: *Andrea climbed from the bottom to the top of the scratching post.*)

s. You just told about number 4. Everybody, what's the next number you'll touch? (Signal.) *Five.*

- Look at the path that leads to number 5. Who do you tell about for number 5? (Signal.) *Andrea.*

- Tell where Andrea was and what she did. (Call on a child. Idea: *Andrea jumped from the scratching post to the table.*)

t. Everybody, is that the end of the story? (Signal.) *No.*

- How does it end? (Call on a child. Idea: *Andrea goes to the peanuts and eats them.*)

u. Your turn: See if anybody can tell this hard, hard story. Remember, you have to tell about the numbers in order, starting with number 1. For each number, you look at the color of the path. If it's yellow, you tell what Sweetie did. If it's gray, you tell what Andrea did.

- Who can do it? (Call on a child.) Everybody else, follow along. If you hear a mistake, raise your hand.
  (Praise children who correctly describe the sequence.)

This type of activity is very important. The children's knowledge of the events is a good indicator of how they are able to reconstruct or retell the story. If they can't reenact the sequence, they probably can't retell it accurately. For them to reenact it, however, they must have a clear understanding of the order of the events.

Spelling Book Component

Spelling Lessons

Overview of Skills Taught

The spelling program is designed so that the children spell by sounds rather than by letter names. That is, they say the sounds in a word, then write the word.

(Teachers are sometimes concerned that the children will begin pausing between sounds in their reading if pausing is introduced in the spelling. This response does not usually occur. The work with spelling facilitates the children's performance in reading.)

Beginning with Spelling lesson 1, the children review saying the sounds in regularly spelled words. These words are presented orally. The children say the sounds in a word without pausing between the sounds. Next, the teacher demonstrates how to say the sounds the "hard way," which involves saying the sounds with pauses between them. Finally, the children write the word.

In Spelling lesson 12, the children are introduced to a review format. The words that appear in this format are words that have appeared frequently in the preceding lessons, or are new, easy, regular words. This format does not call for the children to say the sounds in a word before writing it. The children are instructed to "think about the sounds in _____ and write the word."

At Spelling lesson 24, the children start spelling words that are slightly irregular, such as **is** and **has.**

At Spelling lesson 70, the children begin spelling irregular words such as **was.** In the introductory format, the teacher presents a variation of the irregular format used in reading: When you write the word **was,** you write these sounds: **www aaa sss.** The children say the sounds. Then they write the word.

After an irregular word has appeared in the introductory format for one or two lessons, it appears in an abbreviated format in which the children say the sounds for the word (without a teacher demonstration) and then write the word.

At Spelling lesson 73, the children start writing an entire sentence from dictation. The children are responsible for remembering how to spell each of the words the right way. The children write one sentence during each lesson until lesson 118, at which time two sentences are introduced in each lesson. The children begin writing three sentences at lesson 154.

The words used in sentence writing have been presented frequently and must have appeared in the review format. The teacher says the sentence the children are to write. The children repeat the sentence. Then they say it the slow way (with a pause between the words). After that, they write the sentence.

Beginning with Spelling lesson 77, the children write sound combinations from dictation. The first sound combinations introduced are **ar** and **th.** Other combinations introduced in the program are **sh, ing, al, wh, er,** and **ck.**

Beginning at Spelling lesson 95, the children write words that contain the sound combination **th.** The teacher writes words containing the sound combination **th** on the board. The children first read these words and say the sounds for each of the words. After the teacher erases the board, the children write the words.

Time Requirements

There are 160 lessons in the *Reading Mastery Plus,* Level 1 Spelling Book. Each lesson takes approximately 5 to 10 minutes to teach. Begin Spelling lesson 1 after completing Reading lesson 1.

The children need the following skills to begin the spelling lessons:
1. identifying and writing the various sounds such as **m, t, s;**
2. "saying the sounds" in a word;
3. "saying a word fast."

Presenting the Lessons

General Procedures

Give each child lined paper and a pencil. Each lesson takes only a few lines; you may want to collect the papers and pass them out daily until the page is filled.

The children write dictated words in a column (one word below the next).

Depending on the performance of the group, you may be able to teach more than one spelling lesson per day. The criterion for accelerating is that the children achieve 100% mastery.

Important Information

1. The spelling program does not rely on joined letters or macrons (long lines over long vowels). Children are not to write either joined letters or macrons. Children also do not write capital letters.
2. If an **e** appears on the end of a word, call the sound $\bar{e}\bar{e}\bar{e}$ when sounding out the word (not **eee** as in **end**). Spelling by letter names comes easier to the children if they are used to referring to the **e**'s on the end of words by the letter name.
3. If a vowel in a word is long (the name of a vowel letter), say the long vowel sound when sounding out the word.

> Examples:
> The **o** in **over** would be $\bar{o}\bar{o}\bar{o}$ (since it is pronounced long in the word).
> The first **e** in **ever** would be **eee** (since it is not pronounced long in the word).
> The **o** in **not** would be short: **ooo.**
> The **o** in **no** would be long: $\bar{o}\bar{o}\bar{o}$.

General Correction Procedures

If the children make mistakes, follow the correction procedure of (1) model and (2) test.

If you ask the children to say the sounds in the word **man,** and they make mistakes:

1. (Model) Here are the sounds in **man.** Listen. **Mmm (pause) aaa (pause) nnn.**

2. (Test) Your turn. Say the sounds in **man.** (Signal for each sound as children say) *mmm* (pause) *aaa* (pause) *nnn.*

If a child makes a mistake when you ask the children to think about the sounds in the word **stop** and write the word:

1. (Model) Here are the sounds in the word **stop.** Listen, **Sss** (pause) **t** (pause) **ooo** (pause) **p.**

2. (Test) Your turn. Say the sounds in **stop.** (Signal for each sound as the children say) *sss* (pause) *t* (pause) *ooo* (pause) *p.*

3. (Delayed test) Think about the sounds in (pause) **stop** and write the word. ✓

Note: When signaling children to respond to a sound out series, use audible signals: (Tap) *sss* (Pause. Tap.) *t* (Pause. Tap.) *ooo* (Pause. Tap.) *p.*

Summary of Skills Taught

At the end of the spelling program, the children can spell regular words and some irregular words by sounds, and they can write the words accurately. They can spell by sounds words that contain common sound combinations, such as **ar, al, sh, th,** and **wh.** They can accurately spell the words in a variety of simple sentence forms, including questions and some fairly long statements.

Literature Book Component

Literature Lessons

Reading Mastery Plus, Level 1 has a Literature component that consists of the Literature Guide and 15 trade books that are used in the literature lessons. The Literature Guide has 16 complete literature lessons and blackline masters that are to be reproduced for student material.

Time Requirements

Literature lessons are scheduled every ten lessons, starting with lesson 10. The Literature lesson should be scheduled as part of the regular Language lesson. Allow about 30 minutes for each Literature lesson. Schedule additional time if needed. Ideally that time should not come from the time allotted for the regular Reading lessons.

Materials

In addition to the blackline masters for each literature lesson, children need specific materials for each activity. The major supplies that they need are crayons, scissors, construction paper, a stapler, tape, and paste. Some activities also call for other materials.

Preparation

Before presenting each Literature lesson, read the scheduled activity, secure the materials, and run off the appropriate blackline masters.

Presenting the Lessons

Each Literature lesson is based on a theme from the selection. The following chart lists the lesson themes and gives a brief summary of the activities for each lesson.

Themes and Activities

Title	Presented with lesson*	Theme	Activities**
Here Are My Hands	10	Self-Awareness and Learning about Others	Each child makes two pages for a group book.
The Velveteen Rabbit	20	The Importance of Love	Children sequence the rabbit's progression. Each child creates a velveteen rabbit booklet.
Pumpkin Pumpkin	30	Plant Growth	Children sequence pumpkin growth pictures. Each child creates a pumpkin growth booklet.
Maxie's Cat	40	Cats	Each child creates a chart showing what Maxie's cat Smokey likes and hates.
Fish Eyes	50	Counting	Each child makes a page for a group counting book.
I See Circles	60	Shapes, Shapes, Shapes!	Each child creates pictures from simple shapes for a classroom display or group book.
Goodnight Moon	70	Objects That Rhyme	Each child creates a stick puppet and pairs up rhyming objects.

*Note that selections may be resequenced to take advantage of "teachable moments." On a rainy day, you could present the literature selection for lesson 90, *Listen to the Rain,* instead of presenting the next scheduled literature lesson.

**Note that there are large-group and individual activities. The activities for each selection may be presented to the entire class or to reading groups.

Title	Presented with lesson*	Theme	Activities**
The Lion and the Mouse	80	Big and Small Need and Help Each Other	Children create lion paws and mouse ears and act out the story.
Listen to the Rain*	90	A Rainy Day	Each child completes a rainy-day picture as part of a group book.
Blue Cat	100	Colors	Each child completes a page for a class rainbow book.
Eating the Alphabet	110	The Alphabet	Each child creates one page of a class alphabet book.
How to Pick a Person	120	Pets	Each child creates pictures and descriptions of a favorite pet for a classroom display or group book.
The Perfects	130	Perfect Isn't Always the Best	Each child makes paper dolls with perfect and messy clothes, then makes up a story about how the dolls got messy.
The Lazy Donkey	140	Sometimes Jobs Become Harder When You Try to Make Them Easier	Each child participates in and records results of a weight-and-water experiment.
Potatoes on Tuesday	150	Simple Poetry Reflecting the Days of the Week	Each child makes two pages for a group poem.
Independent Reader Selections	160	Sharing Books	Children read their favorite books to other children.

Time Requirements

Most activities will take about 30 minutes; however, if you choose to present the optional activities that are listed for each selection, the activity could require considerably more time. Ideally, this time would not come from the regular reading lessons, but would be scheduled at a different time of the school day.

Materials

Children need blackline masters and crayons for each literature lesson. In addition, most lessons require construction paper, scissors, a stapler, tape, and paste. Specific activities sometimes call for other materials, such as wallpaper samples, colored tissue paper, craft sticks or tongue depressors, small sacks, sand, salt, sponges or cotton balls, and water.

Note that some books listed under Materials for Optional Activities are available through SRA.

Lesson 160 requires an Independent Reader for every three children.

Preparation

Before presenting each literature lesson, read the scheduled literature activity, secure the necessary materials, and run off the appropriate blackline masters.

Bibliography of Correlated Trade Literature

At the back of this guide, you will find a bibliography of correlated trade literature that includes an Independent Reading List and a Themed Literature List. The selections in these lists are generally found in school and public libraries. *Reading Mastery Plus* teachers can work closely with their school and public librarians to coordinate the acquisition of selections which are not already a part of a library's current collection. Most of the titles listed are still in print and many are available as paperbacks that can be purchased relatively inexpensively from various student book clubs.

Independent Reading List selections, located on page 95 of the Literature Guide, are suggested for independent reading. Present the books to your children at any time after they have completed the specified lessons in *Reading Mastery Plus,* Level 1.

Themed Literature List selections, starting on page 96 of the Literature Guide, are to be read aloud. This list has been structured for easy reference and use. This list:

• indicates every *Reading Mastery Plus,* Level 1 story selection,

• notes the lessons in which the story is presented,

• identifies a theme suggested by the story,

- recommends books which relate to the suggested theme,

- denotes the genre of the selection.

Read aloud to the students from selections suggested in this list either as a lead-in or a follow-up to a *Reading Mastery Plus* text selection. Reading aloud to students is an excellent way of promoting literature as well as expanding student vocabulary and knowledge of story structure. Discuss with the students the ways the correlated literature relates to the *Reading Mastery Plus* text selections.

Using *Reading Mastery Plus* as core instruction, you can consult the list for books related to specific themes and as a starting point for developing theme-based activities that integrate reading, language arts, and content instruction. By organizing instruction around a theme, you can demonstrate to students how knowledge and skills are interrelated and foster a holistic approach to learning.

Seatwork Component

Seatwork Lessons

The *Reading Mastery Plus,* Level 1 component, Seatwork, has blackline masters for 160 lessons. These lessons are in the Seatwork book. The activities are correlated with the reading lessons in orthography, vocabulary, and skill requirements.

Time Requirements

Schedule one seatwork activity per day. Allow 5–10 minutes for each activity. The activities should not be presented as a part of the regular reading lesson. One group of children may do their seatwork while you are working with another group.

Materials

Each child will need a copy of the seatwork activity.

Procedure

The directions at the top of each page are to be read to the children. Most children will be able to work the activities without further help, but some children will need more guidance. You may want to expand on the directions and perhaps even "walk through" each new type of activity with your children the first time it appears. If your children have difficulty with a particular activity, just skip it for a while. You may want to try it again later, when you think your children are ready for it.

Skills

Each activity focuses on a major reading skill covered in the previous reading lessons. Children complete activities in sound discrimination, word recognition, sentence structure, literal comprehension, following directions, sequencing, inferential comprehension, and paraphrasing.

Language Arts Component

Language Arts Extensions

The Language Arts Guide presents 50 lessons. The lessons are correlated with Reading lessons 101–150 in vocabulary and skill development.

Time Requirements and Scheduling

Allow 10–30 minutes for each language arts extension lesson. The earlier lessons are not as time-consuming as the later lessons. Present the first language arts extension lessons after the children have completed Reading lesson 100. Activities continue through extension lesson 150. If children are not able to write words at the rate of about four words per minute, delay the introduction of the extension material until children have completed Level 1,

Language lesson 145. Then present extensions at the rate of one or two per day.

Materials

You will need the teacher presentation script and a copy of any needed blackline master for each child. Each lesson may also require lined paper, pencils, crayons, or colored pencils.

Procedure

The script conventions for the extension lessons are the same as those for the language and reading lessons. The teaching practices are also the same. For information about these practices, refer to Teaching the Program, page 20 of this guide.

Skills

Children will work on the following skills in the Level 1 Language Arts extension lessons.

- Writing "main-idea" sentences from pictures

- Using a "∧" to insert revised text

- Writing notes and lists

- Reporting and writing directions based on a single picture or picture sequences

Independent Readers Component

Independent Reader Lessons

Reading Mastery Plus, Level 1 has a collection of eight stories to be presented after children have completed specific lesson ranges in the reading program. The text of each story consists only of words that children have learned by the lesson at which the book is introduced to and mastered by the children. See Appendix F for a list of the story titles and corresponding lesson ranges.

Time Requirements

Each activity requires time for the child to read the story and complete the worksheet. The children may also participate in extended activities.

Materials

Each child will need a copy of the story to read. Each child will also need a pencil and the specific worksheet from the reproducible blackline masters.

Procedure

Give each child a copy of the book they are to read. Remind the children that after they read the book they will answer questions about it.

After each child has completed the reading, give the child a copy of the worksheet to complete for that book. The child should complete the questions by writing the correct responses in the blanks and circling the yes/no answers.

Extended Activities

The children may reenact parts of the story or illustrate part of the story on the back of the worksheet.

List of Independent Readers

After Lesson	
15	**Sit**
45	**A Little Fish and His Mom**
70	**The Goat That Rolled**
85	**Pat and the Corn**
105	**The Car**
115	**The Big Gold Ring**
135	**The Boy Who Yelled "Wolf"**
155	**The Bad Wind and the 3 Clouds**

Placement

Placement Procedures

Placement at the Beginning of the School Year

Children who have completed *Reading Mastery Plus,* Level K may be placed in *Reading Mastery Plus,* Level 1 without taking the placement test; however, it's a good idea to test the children so they can be grouped homogeneously. To place new children in *Reading Mastery Plus,* Level 1, individually administer the placement test. A blackline master of that test appears on page 212. Reproduce a copy for each child to be tested. Follow the test-administration procedures specified on page 211.

Fast Start Program

If children did not go through *Reading Mastery Plus,* Level K or if they do not pass the placement test, place them in the *Fast Start* program. This is a 25-lesson program that teaches children the basic word-reading skills that are taught in *Reading Mastery Plus,* Level K. The *Fast Start* program teaches letter sounds and phonological skills.

• Group children according to their performance on the placement test. No group should have more than 12 children. Ideally, the lowest-performing group would be the smallest group.

• Recognize that you should probably regroup children again after about 15–20 teaching days. Regroup on the basis of in-class and test performance.

Placement for Mid-Year Students

To find the best placement for a child entering the program mid-year, administer in-program tests until the child fails a test. Start with Mastery Test 1 (lesson 6) and present the tests in sequence until the child fails the passing criterion. Place the child in the lesson following the last passed test. If the child passes Mastery Test 4 (lesson 21) but fails Mastery Test 5 (lesson 26), place the child at lesson 22. If the child fails Mastery Test 7, place the child just after Mastery Test 6 at lesson 32.

Note: If the only options for placement of the incoming child are your reading groups, use a simplified version of the placement procedure. Present the tests that are closest to where your groups are. If your groups are at lessons 96, 88, and 62, present Mastery Test 12 (lesson 61) first. If the child fails Mastery Test 6, place the child in your lowest group at lesson 62, and do what you can to prepare the child. If the child passes Test 12, present Test 18 (lesson 91). If the child fails Test 18, place the child at lesson 62. If the child passes Test 18, present Test 19 (lesson 96). If the child fails Test 19, place the child at lesson 88. If the child passes the test, place the child at lesson 96.

Regrouping Throughout the Year

One of the simpler ways to determine whether children are grouped appropriately is to refer to the in-program tests that occur throughout the program. If a child fails Mastery Test 1 (lesson 6) and fails Mastery Test 2 (lesson 11), the child is probably not appropriately placed in the program. Performance on the tests discloses which skills the child does not have. If the skill deficiency is extensive, the child should be placed in a different group.

If a child consistently performs better than the others in the group and already has reading behaviors that are being taught in *Reading Mastery Plus,* Level 1, place the child in a more advanced group.

Plan to regroup the children several times during the school year. See Scheduling and Grouping for Reading Lessons, page 17 of this guide.

Placement for Language

The grouping requirements are the same for both the language and the reading component of *Reading Mastery Plus,* Level 1. Children should be assigned to the same instructional group for both components.

Administering the Placement Test

Before You Begin

Before you begin teaching the program, administer the placement test printed on the next two pages to each child. Use the test to determine whether a child enters *Reading Mastery Plus,* Level 1 or whether the child should enter *Reading Mastery Plus,* Fast Start. The test is scored on the Placement Test Scoring Sheet, which appears on page 215 of this book.

Make a copy of the blackline master of the *Reading Mastery Plus,* Level 1 Placement Test (page 212) for each child. Use the child's copy to mark errors that the child makes. The simplest procedure is to give the child your copy of the placement test. Mark errors on the child's copy.

Administer the test individually to each child, circling the number of points earned for each task on a Placement Test Scoring Sheet. Then circle the appropriate entry point for the child. Testing each child requires about two to four minutes. You should be able to complete the testing of all the children within one hour on the first day of school. Instruction should begin on the second day.

Reading Mastery Plus, Level 1 Placement Test

Student's Name _____

t

th   n

c

a   d   o   s

                                  ē
i   r

m   f

it ∙ is ∙ fat.

Placement Test Directions

Note: If a child makes 5 or more errors, do not present part 2.

Part 1

You're going to tell me the sound of each letter, not the name but the sound that it makes.

(Touch under each letter. Child says sounds:)

a. (test item 1) (Touch under **th**.) What sound? (Signal.) *thththth.*
b. (test item 2) (Touch under **t**.) What sound? (Signal.) *t.*
c. (test item 3) (Touch under **c**.) What sound? (Signal.) *k.*
d. (test item 4) (Touch under **n**.) What sound? (Signal.) *nnn.*
e. (test item 5) (Touch under **a**.) What sound? (Signal.) *aaa.*
 f. (test item 6) (Touch under **d**.) What sound? (Signal.) *d.*
g. (test item 7) (Touch under **o**.) What sound? (Signal.) *ooo.*
h. (test item 8) (Touch under **s**.) What sound? (Signal.) *sss.*
 i. (test item 9) (Touch under **i**.) What sound? (Signal.) *iii.*
 j. (test item 10) (Touch under **r**.) What sound? (Signal.) *rrr.*
k. (test item 11) (Touch under **ē**.) What sound? (Signal.) *ēēē.*
 l. (test item 12) (Touch under **m**.) What sound? (Signal.) *mmm.*
m. (test item 13) (Touch under **f**.) What sound? (Signal.) *fff.*

Total number of test items: **13**

Part 2

a. (test item 1) Put your finger on the ball of the arrow. (The child responds.)
b. (test item 2) Touch the first word. (The child is to touch under **it**.)
c. (test item 3) Sound it out. Get ready. (Tap for each sound.) *iiit.*
d. (test item 4) Say it fast. (Signal.) *It.*
   (test item 5) What word? (Signal.) *It.*
e. Touch the next word. (The child responds.)
   (test item 6) Sound it out. Get ready. (Tap for each sound.) *iiisss.*
 f. (test item 7) Say it fast. (Signal.) *Is. (Iz.)*
   (test item 8) What word? (Signal.) *Is.*
g. Touch the next word. (The child responds.)
   (test item 9) Sound it out. Get ready. (Tap for each sound.) *Fffaaat.*
h. (test item 10) Say it fast. (Signal.) *Fat.*
   (test item 11) What word? (Signal.) *Fat.*

Total number of test items: **11**

What to Do (Summary of Placement Information)

If child makes 5 or more errors, do not present part 2. (0–8 points in Part 1)

If child makes 4 or fewer errors, present part 2. (9–13 points in Part 1)

Placement:

Place children in either the *Reading Mastery Plus,* Fast Start program, lesson 1, or at lesson 1 in the *Reading Mastery Plus,* Level 1 program.

Children who made 5 or more errors in part 1 are to begin at Fast Start lesson 1.

Children who took both parts 1 and 2 and made 9 or more errors are to begin at Fast Start lesson 1. (0–15 points)

Children who took both parts 1 and 2 and who made between 0–8 errors are to begin at *Reading Mastery Plus,* Level 1, lesson 1. (16–24 points)

Placement in Fast Start

Place children in *Reading Mastery Plus,* Fast Start if they are first graders who don't pass the *Reading Mastery Plus,* Level 1 placement test.

Placement Test Scoring Sheet for *Reading Mastery Plus*, Level 1

Student's Name _____ Date _____

Circle 1 point if the student answers or responds (touches) correctly.

PART 1: SOUNDS				PART 2: SENTENCE			
th	item 1	0	1 point	(Touch.)	item 1	0	1 point
t	item 2	0	1 point		item 2	0	1 point
c	item 3	0	1 point	it	item 3	0	1 point
n	item 4	0	1 point		item 4	0	1 point
a	item 5	0	1 point		item 5	0	1 point
d	item 6	0	1 point	is	item 6	0	1 point
o	item 7	0	1 point		item 7	0	1 point
s	item 8	0	1 point		item 8	0	1 point
i	item 9	0	1 point	fat	item 9	0	1 point
r	item 10	0	1 point		item 10	0	1 point
ē	item 11	0	1 point		item 11	0	1 point
m	item 12	0	1 point		Total Points ☐		
f	item 13	0	1 point				

Total Points ☐

Number of Points

9–13   Continue testing in part 2. (Check box) ☐

0–8   Start at *Reading Mastery Plus,* Fast Start, lesson 1. (Check box) ☐

Combined Number of Points (Parts 1 & 2)

16–24   Start at *Reading Mastery Plus,* Level 1, lesson 1.

0–15   Start at *Reading Mastery Plus,* Fast Start, lesson 1.

In-Program Mastery Tests

In-program tests give you feedback on the effectiveness of your teaching, serve as a backup for your daily evaluation of the children's performance, and provide information for regrouping the children.

Four Types of Tests in Level 1 Reading

Reading Mastery Plus, Level 1 contains four types of in-program tests: Individual Mastery Tests; Individual Reading Checkouts for Rate and Accuracy; Reading Hard Words; and Group Reading Accuracy Tests.

A list of the in-program tests appears below. Note that early in the program there are 20 mastery tests and that, from lesson 135 until the end of the program (lesson 160), the only type of test presented is the individual reading checkout for rate and accuracy. Checkouts start at lesson 54 and occur in every fifth lesson in the program.

Lesson 6 Mastery Test 1

Lesson 11 Mastery Test 2

Lesson 16 Mastery Test 3

Lesson 21 Mastery Test 4

Lesson 26 Mastery Test 5

Lesson 31 Mastery Test 6

Lesson 36 Mastery Test 7

Lesson 41 Mastery Test 8

Lesson 46 Mastery Test 9

Lesson 51 Mastery Test 10

Lesson 54 Reading Checkout

Lesson 55 Reading Checkout

Lesson 56 Reading Checkout
Mastery Test 11

Lesson 61 Reading Checkout
Mastery Test 12

Lesson 66 Reading Checkout
Mastery Test 13

Lesson 71 Reading Checkout
Mastery Test 14

Lesson 76 Reading Checkout
Mastery Test 15

Lesson 81 Reading Checkout
Mastery Test 16

Lesson 86 Reading Checkout
Mastery Test 17

Lesson 91 Reading Checkout
Mastery Test 18

Lesson 95 Reading Checkout
Mastery Test 19

Lesson 100 Reading Checkout
Mastery Test 20

Lesson 105 Reading Checkout

Lesson 108 Reading Hard Words

Lesson 110 Reading Checkout

Lesson 115 Group Reading Accuracy Test
and Reading Checkout

Lesson 120 Reading Checkout

Lesson 121 Group Reading Accuracy Test

Lesson 125 Reading Checkout

Lesson 130 Reading Checkout

Lesson 131 Group Reading Accuracy Test

Lesson 135 Reading Checkout

Lesson 140 Reading Checkout

Lesson 145 Reading Checkout

Lesson 150 Reading Checkout

Lesson 155 Reading Checkout

Lesson 160 Reading Checkout

Administering Mastery Tests 1–20 (Lessons 6–100)

Use the following procedures when administering the mastery tests 1–20:

1. Test each child individually.

2. No child should see or hear another child being tested before he or she has taken the test.

3. Test the children at a time other than the regularly scheduled reading lesson. Your most capable children may be tested a day or two early, so that only the children you are doubtful about will have to be tested on the day indicated in the Presentation Book.

4. Before presenting a test, write the names of the children in the group on a sheet of paper. After presenting each test item, record a pass (P) or a fail (F) next to the child's name. At the end of the test, record the total number of items missed by the child.

5. When presenting the test, have the child sit next to you so that both of you can see and work from the test page.

6. Use the acetate page protector when doing the story-reading tests.

The children's performance on a test determines whether the group should proceed to the next lesson or repeat exercises from previous lessons in order to firm up a critical skill. The criterion for a weak group is specified at the end of each test. Procedures for firming critical skills are also provided. These firming procedures may take longer than a single reading period.

If a group is weak, present the firming procedures to the entire group, but readminister the test only to those children who failed it initially. If the group is still weak, review and practice the critical teaching behaviors that are discussed in the Teacher's Guide for the skill being tested. Then repeat the firming procedures and retest the group. If the group is considered firm but more than one child was weak on the test items, present the firming procedures to the children who were weak. Do the firming at a time other than the regularly scheduled reading lesson. Do not prevent the entire group from moving ahead to the next lesson.

Below is Mastery Test 1. This test is presented after lesson 6, before lesson 7.

Mastery Test 1 (after lesson 6, before lesson 7)

Mastery Tests—General Instructions

All children are to be given each test individually.

The test is NOT to be administered during the period allotted for reading.

A child should neither see nor hear another child working on the test.

a. When I touch the letter, you say the sound.
b. **(test item)** (Point to **o.**) Get ready. (Touch **o.**) *ooo.*
c. **(test item)** (Point to **n.**) Get ready. (Touch **n.**) *nnn.*
d. **(test item)** (Point to **c.**) Get ready. (Touch **c.**) *c.*

o   n   c

e. (Point to **ēat, mēat, nēat.**) These words rhyme.
f. **(test item)** (Touch the ball for **ēat.**) Sound it out. Get ready. (Touch **ē, t.**) *Eēēt.*
g. **(test item)** What word? (Signal.) *Eat.*
h. **(test item)** (Quickly touch the ball for **mēat.**) This word rhymes with (pause) *ēēt.* Get ready. (Touch **m.** Move your finger quickly along the arrow.) *Mmmēat.*
i. **(test item)** What word? (Signal.) *Meat.*
j. **(test item)** (Quickly touch the ball for **nēat.**) This word rhymes with (pause) *ēēt.* Get ready. (Touch **n.** Move your finger quickly along the arrow.) *Nnnēat.*
k. **(test item)** What word? (Signal.) *Neat.*

Total number of test items: **9**

A group is weak if more than one-third of the children missed any of the items on the test.

What to Do

If the group is firm on Mastery Test 1:
Present lesson 7 to the group during the next reading period. If more than one child missed any of the items on the test, present the firming procedures specified below to those children. Present these firming procedures as soon as possible but do not prevent the entire group from moving ahead to the next lesson.

If the group is weak on Mastery Test 1:

A. Present these firming procedures to the group during the next reading period.
   1. Lesson 3, Reading Vocabulary, exercises 12, 13.
   2. Lesson 4, Sounds, exercises 3, 4.
   3. Lesson 4, Reading Vocabulary, exercises 12, 13.
   4. Lesson 5, Sounds, exercises 4, 5.
   5. Lesson 6, Reading Vocabulary, exercises 15, 16.
B. After presenting the above exercises, again give Mastery Test 1 individually to members of the group who failed the test.
C. If the group is firm (less than one-third of the total group missed any of the items on the retest), present lesson 7 to the group during the next reading period.
D. If the group is still weak (more than one-third of the total group missed any items on the retest), repeat A and B during the next reading period.

Individual Reading Checkouts for Rate and Accuracy (Lessons 54–160)

Individual reading checkouts begin after the children have learned to read stories the fast way on the first reading. Checkouts appear in lessons 54, 55, 56, and in every fifth lesson until the end of the program. The checkouts are presented to the children individually. They are very important for both the children and for you. For the children, they provide practice in reading a long passage the fast way. The checkouts also demonstrate to the children that they are to use the strategy of reading the fast way and are not to continue sounding out words.

For you, the checkouts provide information about the children's progress. This information is not a duplication of the mastery-test information. The checkouts show you in detail whether the children are progressing acceptably, whether additional firming is needed, whether children tend to make particular mistakes you hadn't observed, and whether individuals should be placed in a different part of the program.

To pass a checkout, a child must read a selection within a specified period of time and must make no more than three errors. The length of the selections and the time vary from checkout to checkout, but these details are specified in the checkout instructions.

Make a permanent chart with children's names and lesson numbers for recording the results of individual checkouts. A sample chart is shown below.

An Individual Checkout Chart appears on page 246 of this guide. The chart may be reproduced for use in your classroom.

Sample Individual Checkout Chart

Name	Lessons

(Chart showing lessons 54, 55, 56, 61, 66, 71, 76, 81, 86, 91, 95, 100, 105 with entries for Carol, David, Joan, Kim, Raúl)

Below is a format from lesson 54. It describes the checkout procedure.

Lesson 54

Reading Checkout

(Make a permanent chart for recording results of individual checkouts. See Teacher's Guide for sample chart.)

EXERCISE 25

2½-minute individual checkout: rate and accuracy

a. As you are doing your worksheet, I'll call on children one at a time to read the **whole story.** If you can read the whole story the fast way in less than two and a half minutes and if you make no more than three errors, I'll put two stars after your name on the chart for lesson 54.

b. If you make too many errors or don't read the story in less than two and a half minutes, you'll have to practice it and do it again. When you do read it in under two and a half minutes with no more than three errors, you'll get one star. Remember, two stars if you can do it the first time, one star if you do it the second or third time you try.

c. (Call on a child. Tell the child:) Read the whole story very carefully the fast way. Go. (Time the child. If the child makes a mistake, quickly tell the child the correct word and permit the child to continue reading. As soon as the child makes more than three errors or exceeds the time limit, tell the child to stop.) You'll have to read the story to yourself and try again later. (Plan to monitor the child's practice.)

d. (Record two stars for each child who reads appropriately. Congratulate those children.)

e. (Give children who do not earn two stars a chance to read the story again before the next lesson is presented. Award one star to each of those children who meet the rate and accuracy criterion.)

END OF LESSON 54

If more than one-third of the children in the group fail to pass the third checkout (lesson 56), you should carefully examine your teaching procedures because the children are not performing acceptably. Pay particular attention to the way you present all reading-vocabulary tasks, and make sure that you are presenting a sufficient number of individual turns to the lower performers in the group. Also, consider placing the children who do not pass the checkouts on the first trial in a group that is at an earlier lesson in the program.

If children make more than three errors and do not complete the checkout selection in the specified time, do not work on reading rate. Work on accuracy, and do not hurry the children to try to read fast. Simply give them a lot more practice at reading accurately. As their accuracy improves, praise them when they read faster, but make it very clear that they are to read accurately.

If children make errors because they are trying to read fast, tell them to slow down. The rates that are specified for checkouts should be easily attained by the children without rushing. Remember, the first priority is accuracy; rate will follow with practice and reinforcement.

Reading Hard Words
(Lessons 108, 113, 127, 142)

Lessons that present a reading-hard-words exercise have no story and no additional reading-vocabulary exercises. In the reading-hard-words task, the children individually read a column of words. In lesson 108, a scoring key tells the teacher whether to firm the children or to proceed to the next lesson in the program (lesson 109). (See page 72 for firming procedures.)

Although lessons 113, 127, and 142 do not have scoring keys, they can also be used for testing and firming children.

Below are the student and teacher materials for the reading-hard-words exercise that appears in lesson 108. The scoring key appears at the bottom.

līked	barkiñg	when
swim	that	therₑ
fōr	hērₑ	other
get	shē	funny
got	they	hōrsₑ
end	wherₑ	cāmₑ
and	how	giveₑ
at	whȳ	trȳiñg
āte	dōn't	rīdiñg
ēat	didn't	hard

Lesson 108 Textbook

READING HARD WORDS
EXERCISE 4

Hard words in reader

a. You're going to read hard words today. Look at page 5. ✓

b. If you can read all of the words in a column without making a mistake, you'll get_____. (Reward the children with stars, points, and so on.)

c. (Call on a child.) Read the words in the first column. Start at the top and go down the column. Everybody, touch the words that are being read. Raise your hand if you hear a mistake.

d. (Call on a different child to read the second column.)

e. (Give each child a turn at reading one column of words. Praise the children who read each word in the column without making a mistake. Children who make a mistake must repeat the word until firm.)

> **To correct**
> 1. (Immediately say the correct word.)
> 2. (Tell the child who made the mistake:) Touch that word. (Pause.) What word?
> 3. (Then tell the child:) Now go back to the top of the column and read the words again.

If the children average more than one mistake, repeat exercise 4 before presenting lesson 109.

Lesson 108 Presentation Book

Note that rewards are mentioned in step b. These could be stars or points.

Group Reading Accuracy Tests (Lessons 115, 121, 131)

The group reading accuracy tests are presented as part of the story reading for specified lessons. The teacher tallies all first-reading errors (whether they are made by the group or by individual children). The performance criteria for each test appear in the presentation materials for the lesson. These criteria indicate whether the children are to repeat lessons or proceed to the next lesson. The criteria from lesson 115 are shown below.

Group Accuracy Test

Place the group on the basis of story reading accuracy for the first reading of story 115, exercise 11.

1. If the group scored 8 or fewer errors, proceed to lesson 116 as the next reading lesson.
2. If the group scored more than 8 errors, repeat lesson 114 as the next reading lesson. On the following day present lesson 115. The test for reading accuracy in lesson 115 is to be repeated as part of lesson 115.

Lesson 115

Purposes for In-Program Tests

The in-program tests have these purposes:

1. They make sure that children are firm on critical skills before they proceed in the program.

2. They give you feedback about your presentations—to let you know if you are actually firming the children when you present lessons or if you are not repeating examples enough to make sure the children know exactly what to do.

3. They give you information about children who do not belong in a particular small group.

The information about the children's performance is particularly important for regrouping the children. The placement test gives you information about how each child performs at the beginning of the year, but it does not tell you how fast the child will progress. Some children start low and progress rapidly. Others start with more skills but proceed more slowly. (See Scheduling and Grouping for Reading Lessons.)

Appendix A

SAMPLE READING LESSONS

Teacher scripts for Reading lessons 54 and 106 and the corresponding student materials (Worksheets 54 and 106, Storybook 54 and Textbook 106) are reproduced here in their entirety so that you can practice the skills discussed in this guide before presenting Reading lessons to your students.

Lesson 54

SOUNDS

EXERCISE 1

Teaching p as in pat

a. (Point to **p**.) My turn to say the sound for the letter **p**. It's a quick sound.

b. My turn. (Pause. Touch **p** for an instant, saying:) **p**. (Do not say **puuh**.)

c. Again. (Touch **p** and say:) **p**.

d. (Point to **p**.) Your turn. When I touch the letter, you say the sound. (Pause.) Get ready. (Touch **p**.) *p*.

e. Again. (Touch **p**.) *p*.

f. (Repeat e until firm.)

EXERCISE 2

Individual test

(Call on different children to identify **p**.)

EXERCISE 3

Sounds firm-up

a. Get ready to say the sounds when I touch them.

b. (Alternate touching **p** and **d**. Point to the sound. Pause one second. Say:) Get ready. (Touch the sound.) *The children respond.*

c. (When **p** and **d** are firm, alternate touching **p, g, d,** and **t** until all four sounds are firm.)

EXERCISE 4

Individual test

(Call on different children to identify **p, g, d,** or **t.**)

EXERCISE 5

Sounds firm-up

a. (Point to **p**.) When I touch the sound, you say it.

b. (Pause.) Get ready. (Touch **p**.) *p*.

c. Again. (Repeat *b* until firm.)

d. Get ready to say all the sounds when I touch them.

e. (Alternate touching **k, v, u, ō, p, sh, h,** and **n** three or four times. Point to the sound.) (Pause one second. Say:) Get ready. (Touch the sound.) *The children respond.*

EXERCISE 6

Individual test

(Call on different children to identify one or more sounds in exercise 5.)

22   Lesson 54

mop

cop

top

was

ōld

READING VOCABULARY

EXERCISE 7

Children rhyme with mop

a. (Touch the ball for **mop.**) You're going to read this word the fast way. (Pause three seconds.) Get ready. (Move your finger quickly along the arrow.) *Mop.*

b. (Touch the ball for **cop.**) This word rhymes with (pause) **mop.** (Move to **c,** then quickly along the arrow.) *Cop.* Yes, What word? (Signal.) *Cop.*

c. (Touch the ball for **top.**) This word rhymes with (pause) **mop.** (Move to **t,** then quickly along the arrow.) *Top.* Yes, What word? (Signal.) *Top.*

EXERCISE 8

Children identify, then sound out an irregular word (was)

a. (Touch the ball for **was.**) Everybody, you're going to read this word the fast way. (Pause three seconds.) Get ready. (Move your finger quickly along the arrow.) *Was.* Yes, **was.**

b. Now you're going to sound out the word. Get ready. (Quickly touch **w, a, s** as the children say *wwwaaasss.*)

c. Again. (Repeat *b.*)

d. How do we say the word? (Signal.) *Was.* Yes, **was.**

e. (Repeat *b* and *d* until firm.)

EXERCISE 9

Individual test

(Call on different children to do *b* and *d* in exercise 8.)

EXERCISE 10

Children read the fast way

(Touch the ball for **ōld.**) Get ready to read this word the fast way. (Pause three seconds.) Get ready. (Signal.) *Old.*

EXERCISE 11

Children read the words the fast way

(Have the children read the words on this page the fast way.)

EXERCISE 12

Individual test

(Call on different children to read one word the fast way.)

23   Lesson 54

Do not touch any small letters.

of

to

that

cōat

gōat

EXERCISE 13

Children identify, then sound out an irregular word (of)

a. (Touch the ball for **of.**) Everybody, you're going to read this word the fast way. (Pause three seconds.) Get ready. (Move your finger quickly along the arrow.) *Of.* Yes, **of.**

b. Now you're going to sound out the word. Get ready. (Quickly touch **o, f** as the children say oooff.)

c. Again. (Repeat b.)

d. How do we say the word? (Signal.) *Of.* Yes, **of.**

e. (Repeat b and d until firm.)

f. (Call on different children to do b and d.)

EXERCISE 14

Children identify, then sound out an irregular word (to)

(Repeat the procedures in exercise 13 for **to.**)

EXERCISE 15

Children read the fast way

(Touch the ball for **that.**) Get ready to read this word the fast way. (Pause three seconds.) Get ready. (Signal.) *That.*

EXERCISE 16

Children sound out the word and tell what word

a. (Touch the ball for **cōat.**) Sound it out.

b. Get ready. (Touch **c, ō, t** as the children say cōōt.)

• (If sounding out is not firm, repeat b.)

c. What word? (Signal.) *Coat.* Yes, **coat.**

EXERCISE 17

Children sound out the word and tell what word

a. (Touch the ball for **gōat.**) Sound it out.

b. Get ready. (Touch **g, ō, t** as the children say gōōt.)

• (If sounding out is not firm, repeat b.)

c. What word? (Signal.) *Goat.* Yes, **goat.**

EXERCISE 18

Children read the words the fast way

(Have the children read the words on this page the fast way.)

EXERCISE 19

Individual test

(Call on different children to read one word the fast way.)

Storybook

STORY 54

EXERCISE 20

First reading—children read the story the fast way

(Have the children reread any sentences containing words that give them trouble. Keep a list of these words.)

a. (Pass out Storybook.)

b. Open your book to page 37 and get ready to read. ✔

c. We're going to read this story the fast way.

d. Touch the first word. ✔

e. Reading the fast way. First word. (Pause three seconds.) Get ready. (Tap.) *Thē.*

f. Next word. ✔
(Pause three seconds.) Get ready. (Tap.) *Old.*

g. (Repeat f for the remaining words in the first sentence. Pause at least three seconds between taps. The children are to identify each word without sounding it out.)

h. (Repeat d through g for the next two sentences. Have the children reread the first three sentences until firm.)

i. (The children are to read the remainder of the story the fast way, stopping at the end of each sentence.)

j. (After the first reading of the story, print on the board the words that the children missed more than one time. Have the children sound out each word one time and tell what word.)

k. (After the group's responses are firm, call on individual children to read the words.)

EXERCISE 21

Individual test

a. I'm going to call on different children to read a whole sentence the fast way.

b. (Call on different children to read a sentence. Do not tap for each word.)

EXERCISE 22

Second reading—children read the story the fast way and answer questions

a. You're going to read the story again the fast way and I'll ask questions.

b. First word. ✔
Get ready. (Tap.) *Thē.*

c. (Tap for each remaining word. Pause at least three seconds between taps. Pause longer before words that gave the children trouble during the first reading.)

d. (Ask the comprehension questions below as the children read.)

After the children read:	You ask:
The old goat had an old coat.	What did she have? (Signal.) *An old coat.*
The old goat said, "I will eat this old coat."	What did she say? (Signal.) *I will eat this old coat.*
So she did.	What did she do? (Signal.) *She ate the old coat.*
"That was fun," she said.	What did she say? (Signal.) *That was fun.*
"I ate the old coat."	What did the goat say? (Signal.) *I ate the old coat.*
"And now I am cold."	What did she say? (Signal.) *And now I am cold.*
Now the old goat is sad.	How does she feel? (Signal.) *Sad.* Why? (Signal.) *The children respond.*

EXERCISE 23

Picture comprehension

a. What do you think you'll see in the picture? (Call on a child. Accept appropriate responses.)

b. Turn the page and look at the picture. ✔

c. (Ask these questions:)

1. How does that goat feel? (Call on a child. Idea: *Cold and sad.*)
2. Why is she out in the cold without a coat? (Call on a child. Idea: *Because she ate her coat.*)
3. Did you ever go outside without a coat when it was cold? (Call on a child. Accept appropriate responses.)

Worksheet 54

SUMMARY OF INDEPENDENT WORK

EXERCISE 24

Introduction to independent activity

a. (Hold up worksheet 54.)

b. Everybody, you're going to do this worksheet on your own. (Tell the children when they will work the items.) Let's go over the things you're going to do.

Sentence copying

a. (Hold up side 1 of your worksheet and point to the first line in the sentence-copying exercise.)

b. Everybody, here's the sentence you're going to write on the lines below.

c. Get ready to read the words in this sentence the fast way. First word. ✓

Get ready. (Tap.) *Thē.*

d. Next word. ✓

Get ready. (Tap.) *Goat.*

e. (Repeat *d* for the remaining words.)

f. After you finish your worksheet, you get to draw a picture about the sentence, **thē gōat āte thē cōat.**

Sound writing

a. (Point to the sound-writing exercise.) Here are the sounds you're going to write today. I'll touch the sounds. You say them.

b. (Touch each sound.) *The children respond.*

c. (Repeat the series until firm.)

Matching

a. (Point to the column of words in the Matching Game.)

b. Everybody, you're going to follow the lines and write these words.

c. Reading the fast way.

d. (Point to the first word. Pause.) Get ready. (Signal.) *The children respond.*

e. (Repeat *d* for the remaining words.)

f. (Repeat *d* and *e* until firm.)

Cross-out game

(Point to the boxed word in the Cross-out Game.) Everybody, here's the word you're going to cross out today. What word? (Signal.) *Not.* Yes, **not.**

Pair relations

a. (Point to the pair-relations exercise on side 2.) You're going to circle the picture in each box that shows what the words say.

b. (Point to the space at the top of the page.) After you finish, remember to draw a picture that shows **thē gōat āte thē cōat.**

Reading Checkout

(Make a permanent chart for recording results of individual checkouts. See Teacher's Guide for sample chart.)

EXERCISE 25

2½-minute individual checkout: rate and accuracy

a. As you are doing your worksheet, I'll call on children one at a time to read the **whole story.** If you can read the whole story the fast way in less than two and a half minutes and if you make no more than three errors, I'll put two stars after your name on the chart for lesson 54.

b. If you make too many errors or don't read the story in less than two and a half minutes, you'll have to practice it and do it again. When you do read it in under two and a half minutes with no more than three errors, you'll get one star. Remember, two stars if you can do it the first time, one star if you do it the second or third time you try.

c. (Call on a child. Tell the child:) Read the whole story very carefully the fast way. Go. (Time the child. If the child makes a mistake, quickly tell the child the correct word and permit the child to continue reading. As soon as the child makes more than three errors or exceeds the time limit, tell the child to stop.) You'll have to read the story to yourself and try again later. (Plan to monitor the child's practice.)

d. (Record two stars for each child who reads appropriately. Congratulate those children.)

e. (Give children who do not earn two stars a chance to read the story again before the next lesson is presented. Award one star to each of those children who meet the rate and accuracy criterion.)

END OF LESSON 54

Present Language lesson 54 and Spelling lesson 54 before presenting lesson 55.

54

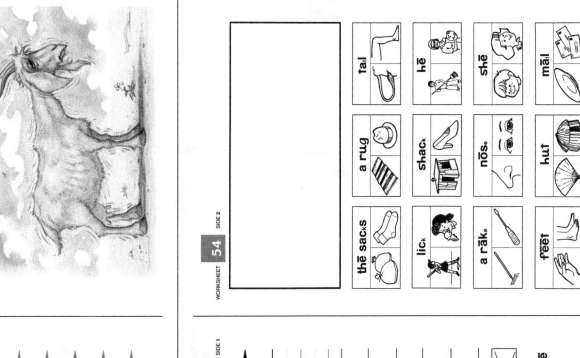

54

thē ōld gōₐt had an ōld cōₐt.

thē ōld gōₐt said, "I will ēₐt this

ōld cōₐt." sō shē did.

"that was fun," shē said. "I āteₑ

thē ōld cōₐt. and now I am cōld."

now thē ōld gōₐt is sad.

Name _____

thē gōₐt āteₑ thē cōₐt.

the goat ate the coat

g ____ hit

c ____ ōld

k ____ sāve

d ____ how

t ____ I

not

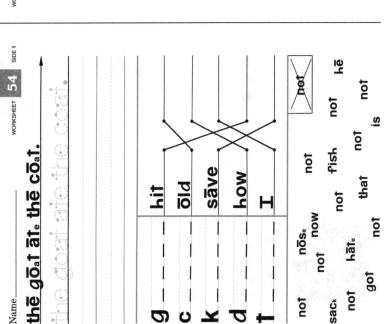

Lesson 106

SOUNDS

EXERCISE 1

Sounds firm-up

a. (Point to the sounds.) Tell me these sounds.

b. (Point to each sound.) Get ready. (Touch the sound.) *The children say the sound.*

c. (Repeat problem sounds until the children can correctly identify all sounds in order.)

Individual test

(Call on several children to identify one or more sounds.)

er   ē   ch   g

ā   e   th   sh   h

wh   y   p

READING VOCABULARY

Do not touch small letters.

Get ready to read all the words on this page without making a mistake.

To correct

(Have the children sound out and tell what word.)

where

EXERCISE 2

Sound out first

a. (Touch the ball for **where**.) Sound it out. Get ready. (Quickly touch under **wh, e, r** as the children say *whwhwheeerrr*.)

b. What word? (Signal.) *Where*. Yes, **where**.

c. (Repeat exercise until firm.)

EXERCISE 3

there

Sound out first

a. (Touch the ball for **there**.) Sound it out. Get ready. (Quickly touch under **th, e, r** as the children say *thththeeerrr*.)

b. What word? (Signal.) *There*. Yes, **there**.

c. (Repeat exercise until firm.)

EXERCISE 4

Introduce ar as in shark

ar

a. (Point to **ar**.) When these letters are together, they usually say (pause) **are**. What do these letters say? (Signal.) *Are*. Yes, **are**.

b. (Repeat *a* until firm.)

EXERCISE 5

arf

ar words

a. (Point to **ar** in **arf**.) What do these letters say? (Signal.) *Are*. Yes, **are**.

b. (Touch the ball for **arf**.) Read this word the fast way. Get ready. (Signal.) *Arf*. Yes, **arf**.

c. (Repeat *a* and *b* for **barking**.)

barking

EXERCISE 6

Read ar word the fast way

shark

a. (Touch the ball for **shark**.) Read this word the fast way. (Pause two seconds.) Get ready. (Signal.) *Shark*. Yes, **shark**.

b. (Point to **ar** in **shark**.) Everybody, what do these letters say? (Signal.) *Are*. Yes, **are**.

c. (Touch the ball for **shark**.) Sound it out. Get ready. (Quickly touch under **sh, ar, k** as the children say *shshshark*.)

d. What word? (Signal.) *Shark*. Yes, **shark**.

e. (Repeat *c* and *d* until firm.)

EXERCISE 7

other

Sound out first

a. (Touch the ball for **other**.) Sound it out. Get ready. (Quickly touch under **o, th, er** as the children say *ooothththurrr*.)

b. What word? (Signal.) *Other*. Yes, **other**.

c. (Repeat exercise until firm.)

(Repeat any troublesome words.)

Individual test

(Call on different children. Each child reads a different word.)

līked

help

Do not touch small letters.

Get ready to read all the words on this page without making a mistake.

To correct

(Have the children sound out and tell what word.)

swam

EXERCISE 9

Read the fast way first

a. (Touch the ball for **help**.) Read this word the fast way. (Pause two seconds.) Get ready. (Signal.) *Help.* Yes, **help**.

b. (Return to the ball.) Sound it out. Get ready. (Quickly touch under **h**, **e**, **l**, **p** as the children say *heeelllp*.)

c. What word? (Signal.) *Help.* Yes, **help**.

d. (Repeat *b* and *c* until firm.)

e. (Repeat the task for **helped**, **after**, **līked**, **yelled**, **awāy**, and **swimming**.)

EXERCISE 8

Last part, first part

a. (Cover **s**. Point to **wam**.) Read this part of the word the fast way. (Pause two seconds.) Get ready. (Signal.) *Wam.* Yes, **wam**.

b. (Uncover **s**. Point to **s**.) First you say sss. (Move your finger quickly under **wam**.) Then you say (pause) **wam**.

c. (Touch the ball for **swam**.) Get ready. (Move to **s**, then quickly along the arrow.) *Ssswam.*

d. Say it fast. (Signal.) *Swam.* Yes, what word? (Signal.) *Swam.* Yes, **swam**. Good reading.

e. (Repeat *c* and *d* until firm.)

yelled

awāy

helped

after

swimming

(Repeat any troublesome words.)

Individual test

(Call on different children. Each child reads a different word.)

4   Lesson 106

Do not touch small letters.

Get ready to read all the words on this page without making a mistake.

To correct

(Have the children sound out and tell what word.)

EXERCISE 10

Read the fast way

a. Read these words the fast way.
b. (Touch the ball for **another.** Pause two seconds.) Get ready. (Signal.) *Another.* Yes, **another.**
c. (Repeat *b* for **whȳ, when,** and **funny.**)

another

whȳ

when

funny

---

book

EXERCISE 11

Read the fast way first

a. (Touch the ball for **book.**) Read this word the fast way. (Pause two seconds.) Get ready. (Signal.) *Book.* Yes, **book.**
b. (Return to the ball.) Sound it out. Get ready. (Quickly touch under **b, oo, k** as the children say *booook*.)
c. What word? (Signal.) *Book.* Yes, **book.**
d. (Repeat *b* and *c* until firm.)

took

EXERCISE 12

Read the fast way first

a. (Touch the ball for **took.**) Read this word the fast way. (Pause two seconds.) Get ready. (Signal.) *Took.* Yes, **took.**
b. (Return to the ball.) Sound it out. Get ready. (Quickly touch under **t, oo, k** as the children say *tooook*.)
c. What word? (Signal.) *Took.* Yes, **took.**
d. (Repeat *b* and *c* until firm.)

Read the fast way

a. Read these words the fast way.
b. (Touch the ball for **looked.** Pause two seconds.) Get ready. (Signal.) *Looked.* Yes, **looked.**
c. (Repeat *b* for **cooked.**)

looked

cooked

Individual test

(Call on individual children to read a column of words from this lesson. If the column contains only one or two words, direct the child to read additional words from an adjacent column. Praise children who read all words with no errors.)

STORY

EXERCISE 14

First reading—title and three sentences

a. (Pass out Textbook.)

b. Everybody, open your reader to page 1.

c. Everybody, touch the title.

d. I'll tap and you read each word in the title the fast way.

e. First word. ✓
(Pause two seconds.)
Get ready. (Tap.) *Arf.*

f. Next word. ✓
(Pause two seconds.)
Get ready. (Tap.) *The.*

g. (Repeat f for the remaining word in the title.)

h. Everybody, say the title. (Signal.) *Arf the shark.* Yes, **Arf the shark.**

i. Everybody, get ready to read this story the fast way.

j. First word. ✓
(Pause two seconds.) Get ready. (Tap.) *Arf.*

k. Next word. ✓
(Pause two seconds.) Get ready. (Tap.) *Was.*

l. (Repeat k for the remaining words in the first three sentences. Have the children reread the first three sentences until firm.)

EXERCISE 15

Remaining sentences

a. I'm going to call on different children to read a sentence. Everybody, follow along and point to the words. If you hear a mistake, raise your hand.

b. (Call on a child.) Read the next sentence.

> **To correct** word-identification errors
> (**from,** for example)
>
> 1. That word is **from.** What word?
>   *From.*
> 2. Go back to the beginning of the sentence and read the sentence again.

c. (Call on a different child.) Read the next sentence.

d. (Repeat c for most of the remaining sentences in the story.)

e. (Occasionally have the group read a sentence. When the group is to read, say:) Everybody, read the next sentence. (Pause two seconds. Tap for each word in the sentence. Pause at least two seconds between taps.)

arf the shark[1]

arf was a barking shark. arf was a little shark, but she had a big bark that made the other fish swim away.[2]

a shark swam up to arf and said, "you are a shark. let's play." arf was happy. "arf, arf," she said.[3] and the other shark swam far, far away. arf was not happy now.[4]

another shark swam up to arf. "you are a shark," he said. "let's play."

arf was happy. "arf, arf," she said. and the other shark swam far, far away. arf was not happy now.

then a big, big fish, that liked to eat sharks swam up to the other sharks.[5]

"help, help," they yelled.[6]

but the big fish was swimming after them very fast. stop[7]

EXERCISE 16
Second reading—sentences and questions

a. You're going to read the story again. This time I'm going to ask questions.

b. Starting with the first word of the title. ✓ Get ready. (Tap as the children read the title.)

c. (Call on a child.) Read the first sentence.

To correct word-identification errors (**from**, for example)

1. That word is **from.** What word? *From.*

2. Go back to the beginning of the sentence and read the sentence again.

---

d. (Call on a different child.) Read the next sentence.

e. (Repeat *d* for most of the remaining sentences in the story.)

f. (Occasionally have the group read a sentence.)

g. (After each underlined sentence has been read, present each comprehension question specified below to the entire group.)

[1] What's this story about? (Signal.) *Arf the shark.*
[2] Who was Arf? (Signal.) *A little shark.*
[3] What did Arf say? Let's hear you say it like Arf said it. (Signal.) *Arf, arf.*
[4] Why wasn't she happy? (Call on a child. Accept appropriate responses.)
[5] What did the big fish like to eat? (Signal.) *Sharks.* Let's see if the big fish eats any.
[6] Why did the sharks yell? (Call on a child. Idea: *They were scared; a big fish that liked to eat sharks was swimming toward them.*)
[7] Is this the end of the story? (Signal.) *No.* Right. We stop now. What do you think will happen? (Call on a child. Accept reasonable responses.) We'll find out next time.

EXERCISE 17
Picture comprehension

a. Look at the picture. ✓

b. (Ask these questions:)
1. Show me the shark you think is Arf. ✓
2. What does it look like Arf is doing? (Call on a child. Accept reasonable responses.)
3. What is that big fish doing? (Call on a child. Accept appropriate responses.)
4. What would you do if you were Arf? (Let the children comment for ten seconds. Then comment briefly.)

STORY ITEMS

EXERCISE 18

Read the story items

a. (Hold up Worksheet 106.)

b. (Point to the story-items exercise.) Everybody, you're going to read the items for the story you just read. You're going to circle the answers later.

c. (Touch the blank in item 1.) Here's where something is missing. When you get to this blank, say "**blank.**"

d. Get ready to read item 1 the fast way. First word. ✓
Get ready. (Tap.) *Arf.*

e. Next word. ✓
Get ready. (Tap.) *Was.*

f. (Repeat e for the remaining words in item 1.)

g. Tell me the answer. Arf was a barking. . . . . (Signal.) *Shark.* What word goes in the blank? (Signal.) *Shark.* (The children are not to circle the answers now.)

h. (Repeat d through g for item 2.)

i. You're going to do these items later. Remember to circle the right answer for each item.

SENTENCE COPYING

EXERCISE 19

Read sentence to copy

a. (Point to the sentence shē is in a car.)

b. Here's the sentence you're going to write on the lines below. Everybody, touch this sentence on your worksheet. ✓

c. Get ready to read the words in this sentence the fast way. First word. Get ready. (Tap for each word as the children read:) *She is in a car.*

d. (Have the children reread the sentence the fast way.)

e. (Point to the dotted words on the first line.) Later, you're going to trace the dotted words in this sentence. Then you're going to write these words on the other lines.

SOUND WRITING

EXERCISE 20

Identify sounds to be written

a. (Point to the sound-writing exercise.) Everybody, here are the sounds you're going to write today. I'll touch the sounds. You say them.

b. (Touch each sound.) *The children respond.*

c. (Repeat b until firm.)

d. You're going to write a sound on each bar. You'll write the sounds later.

READING COMPREHENSION

The children will need pencils.

EXERCISE 21

Read story, answer items

a. (Hold up side 2 of your worksheet and point to the word **reading.**) Everybody, touch this story on your worksheet. ✓

b. Reading the fast way. First word. ✓
Get ready. (Tap.) *A.*

c. Next word. ✓
Get ready. (Tap.) *Boy.*

d. (Repeat c for the remaining words in the story.)

e. (Hold up your worksheet. Touch the blank in item 1.) Everybody, here's where something is missing. When you get to this blank, say "**blank.**"

f. Reading item 1 the fast way. First word. ✓
Get ready. (Tap.) *A.*

g. Next word. ✓
Get ready. (Tap.) *Blank.*

h. (Repeat g for the remaining words in item 1.) *Ate cake.*

i. Everybody, what word goes in the blank? (Signal.) *Boy.*

j. (Repeat i until firm.)

k. Look at the words under item 1 and get ready to touch the word that goes in the blank. (Pause.) Get ready. (Signal.) ✓

l. Circle the word **boy.** ✓

m. (Repeat f through l for item 2.)

PICTURE COMPREHENSION
EXERCISE 22
Write words for picture

Refer to sounds, not letter names, in missing words.

a. (Hold up side 2 of your worksheet and point to the first picture.) Look at this picture. Tell me what you see. (Accept reasonable responses.)

b. Everybody, who looks old? (Signal.) *The man.* Yes, this man is old.

c. Everybody, what is the man holding? (Signal.) *A rug.* Yes, he has a . . . . (Signal.) *Rug.*

d. (Repeat *b* and *c* until firm.)

e. (Point to the sound in the blank in item 1.) Something is missing. When you get to this, say "**blank.**" What will you say? (Signal.) *Blank.*

f. Everybody, touch item 1 next to the picture. ✓

g. Get ready to read item 1 the fast way. First word. ✓

Get ready. (Tap.) *This.*

h. Next word. ✓

Get ready. (Tap.) *Blank.*

i. (Repeat *h* for the remaining words in item 1.)

j. (Repeat *g* through *i* until firm.)

k. What word goes in the blank? (Signal.) *Man.*

l. I'll say the sounds in the word **man.** mmm (pause) aaa (pause) nnn. Again. mmm (pause) aaa (pause) nnn.

m. Your turn. Say the sounds in **man.** Get ready. (Signal for each sound as the children say:) *mmm* (pause) *aaa* (pause) *nnn.*

n. (Repeat *l* and *m* until firm.)

o. Look at the blank in item 1. The **mmm** is already written in the blank. So what sounds are you going to write next? (Signal for each sound as the children say:) *aaa* (pause) *nnn.* (Repeat until firm.)

p. Everybody, write the missing sounds for man. ✓

q. (Repeat *g* through *p* for item 2.)

r. You'll do the items for the other picture later.

SUMMARY OF INDEPENDENT WORK
EXERCISE 23
Introduction to independent activity

a. (Hold up side 1 of Worksheet 106.)

b. Everybody, you're going to finish this worksheet on your own. (Tell the children when they will work the remaining items.) Let's go over the things you're going to do.

Story items

(Point to the story-items exercise.) Remember to read the items and circle the answers that tell what happened in the story.

Sentence copying

(Point to the first line in the sentence-copying exercise.) Remember—you're going to trace the words in this sentence. Then you're going to write the sentence on the other lines.

Sound writing

(Point to the sound-writing exercise.) Remember to write a sound on each bar.

Picture comprehension

a. (Point to the second picture in the picture-comprehension exercise.) Everybody, you're going to look at this picture. Then you're going to read each item and write the missing words.

b. Remember—the first sound of each missing word is already written in the blank.

END OF LESSON 106

Present Language lesson 106 and Spelling lesson 106 before presenting lesson 107.

arf the shark

arf was a barking shark. arf
was a little shark, but shē had a
big bark that mādₑ the other fish
swim awāy.

a shark swam up to arf and
said, "you arₑ a shark. let's plāy."

arf was happy. "arf, arf,"
shē said. and the other shark
swam far, far awāy. arf was
not happy now.

another shark swam up to
arf. "you arₑ a shark," hē said.
"let's plāy."

arf was happy. "arf, arf,"
shē said. and the other shark

swam far, far awāy. arf was
not happy now.

then a big, big fish that līked
to ēₐt sharks swam up to the
other sharks.

"help, help," they yelled.
but the big fish was
swimming after them very fast.

stop

Name ____________

WORKSHEET **106** SIDE 1

stōry Items

1. arf was a barking ____.
    - card
    - shark
    - farm

2. a big ____ swam up to the other sharks.
    - fish
    - fin
    - fan

---

shē is in a car.

she is in a car.

---

n ___ ___ ___

u ___ ___ ___

m ___ ___ ___

h ___ ___ ___

w ___ ___ ___

v ___ ___ ___

WORKSHEET **106** SIDE 2

rēading

a boy āte cāke.

hē got sick.

1. a ____ āte cāke.
    - man
    - boy
    - girl

2. hē got ____.
    - sick
    - sad
    - wet

1. this **m**______ is ōld.
2. hē has a **r**______.

1. the **b**______ is in the trēē
2. the **p**______ is in the trēē.

Level 1, Letter 1

To the family of _____

This school year your child is enrolled in the *Reading Mastery Plus* program. *Reading Mastery Plus,* Level 1 will help your child learn how to sound out words and letters and how to read words the fast way without first sounding them out. Your child will practice by reading word lists and stories. Your child will answer questions and get practice completing activities and reading independently. And best of all, your child will find that reading is enjoyable.

In *Reading Mastery Plus,* Level 1, your child will read stories written with a special alphabet. The letters in this special alphabet are almost like the letters in the regular alphabet. The only difference is that they will help your child figure out how to pronounce words. Once your child learns to read well, the special alphabet will no longer be used.

And in *Reading Mastery Plus,* Level 1, your child will learn to read well. Children who complete *Reading Mastery Plus,* Level 1 will be able to read more than 1500 words.

The best thing you can do this year is to let your child know that the work done in *Reading Mastery Plus,* Level 1 is very important. This is the year that your child will learn the skills that will be needed every year in school and beyond.

If you have any questions or want more ideas about how to help your child with reading this year, please call me at the school. I'll be happy to talk with you.

Thank you,

_____

Para la familia de _____

Este año escolar su hijo está inscrito en el programa *Reading Mastery Plus*. *Reading Mastery Plus*, Nivel 1 ayudará a su hijo a aprender cómo pronunciar palabras y letras y cómo leer las palabras de forma rápida sin primero pronunciarlas. Su hijo practicará leyendo listas de palabras e historias. Responderá preguntas y practicará completando actividades y leyendo independientemente. Y lo mejor de todo es que su hijo descubrirá que leer es divertido.

En *Reading Mastery Plus*, Nivel 1, su hijo leerá historias escritas con un alfabeto especial. Las letras en este alfabeto especial son casi iguales a las letras en el alfabeto regular. La única diferencia es que ayudarán a su hijo a entender cómo deben pronunciarse las palabras. Una vez que su hijo aprenda a leer bien, el alfabeto especial no se utilizará más.

Y, en *Reading Mastery Plus*, Nivel 1 su hijo aprenderá a leer bien. Los niños que completen *Reading Mastery Plus*, Nivel 1 podrán leer más de 1500 palabras.

Lo mejor que usted puede hacer este año es dejar que su hijo sepa que el trabajo que hace en *Reading Mastery Plus*, Nivel 1 es muy importante. Este es el año en el que su hijo aprenderá las destrezas que se necesitarán cada año en la escuela y más allá.

Si tiene alguna pregunta o quiere más ideas acerca de cómo ayudar a su hijo con la lectura este año, por favor llámeme a la escuela. Me encantará hablar con usted.

Gracias,

_____

To the family of _____

Your child has completed _____ lessons of *Reading Mastery Plus,* Level 1. During this school term, your child has learned the sounds of the letters and how to put those sounds together to read words the fast way. Every day, your child has read lists of words and stories. Your child has learned how to read to find answers to questions and to get information. These are important skills that will lead to success next year in school and in all the years to come.

During this break in the school year, encourage your child to continue to read something every day. Children who read more become better, faster readers. You should be proud of the progress your child is making.

If you have any questions or want more ideas about how to help your child with reading during this break in the school year, please call me at the school. I'll be happy to talk with you.

Thank you,

_____

Para la familia de _____

Su hijo ha terminado _____ lecciones de *Reading Mastery Plus,* Nivel 1. Durante este período escolar su hijo ha aprendido los sonidos de las letras y cómo ponerlos juntos para leer palabras de forma rápida. Cada día su hijo ha leído historias y listas de palabras. Su hijo ha aprendido a leer para encontrar las respuestas a las preguntas y a obtener información. Éstas son destrezas importantes que conducirán al éxito en el próximo año escolar y en los años venideros.

Durante este receso del año escolar, anime a su hijo a que continúe leyendo algo diariamente. Los niños que leen más se convierten en lectores mejores y más rápidos. Debe estar orgulloso del progreso que su hijo está mostrando.

Si usted tiene preguntas o quiere más ideas acerca de cómo ayudar a su hijo con la lectura durante este receso del año escolar, por favor llámeme a la escuela. Me encantará hablar con usted.

Gracias,

_____

APPENDIX C   REPRODUCIBLE CALENDAR

This reproducible Calendar is for Language lessons with Calendar activities.
Note: Fill in your monthly calendar in two stages. First fill in the current month.

(sample Month)   _September_

Sunday	Monday	Tuesday	Wednesday	Thursday	Friday	Saturday
					1	2
3	4	5	6	7	8	9
10	11	12	13	14	15	16
17	18	19	20	21	22	23
24	25	26	27	28	29	30

From Lesson 33 until the end of the program, children are asked to say the date that is one week from today. Fill in the first part of the upcoming month when this information is called for in the lesson.

September

Sunday	Monday	Tuesday	Wednesday	Thursday	Friday	Saturday
					1	2
3	4	5	6	7	8	9
10	11	12	13	14	15	16
17	18	19	20	21	22	23
24	25	26	27	28	29	30
October						
1	2	3	4	5	6	7

Sunday	Monday	Tuesday	Wednesday	Thursday	Friday	Saturday	

Source: Fast A-B Lit Guide BLM 2D

Individual Reading Checkout Chart

Name	54	55	56	61	66	71	76	81	86	91	95	100	105	110	115	120	125	130	135	140	145	150	155	160

APPENDIX E
Duplicate Stories

Mastery Test Supplement

DUPLICATE STORIES

The following pages contain duplicate stories to be used for reteaching children who do not pass

Mastery Test 4 (Stories 9, 10, and 11),

Mastery Test 6 (Stories 19, 20, and 21), and

Mastery Test 8 (Stories 29, 30, and 31).
The pages may be reproduced for use by your students.

this■sack

is■fat.

is■this

a■mitt?

thē■man■is

not■sad.

hē ▪ is ▪ an ▪ ant.

hē ▪ has ▪ a ▪ socₖ

on ▪ his ▪ fēēt.

hē ▪ has ▪ an ▪ ant.

that ▪ ant ▪ ātₑ

a ▪ fat ▪ sēēd.

hē ▪ ātₑ ▪ a ▪ fig.

and ▪ hē

is ▪ sicₖ.

this·is·a·cat.

this·cat·has·fat

fēēt.·this·cat·can

run·in·thē·mud.

shē·has·a·cat.

that·cat·is

not·littlₑ.·that·cat

is·fat.

hē·has·a·shacₖ.

thē·shacₖ·is·in·thē

sand.·thē·man·is

in·thē·shacₖ.

APPENDIX F
List of Independent Readers
and
Independent Reading List

Independent Reading

The Level 1 program includes 8 Independent Readers. Each story is keyed to a particular part of the program and presents only words that children are able to read. In addition to reading the Independent Readers, children should be encouraged to supplement their classroom reading with their self-selected independent reading materials. An annotated list of suitable outside reading books appears on the following page of this guide. You might use the list to stock your own classroom library or ask your librarian to have the titles available for your students.

List of Independent Readers

After Lesson	
15	**Sit**
45	**A Little Fish and His Mom**
70	**The Goat That Rolled**
85	**Pat and the Corn**
105	**The Car**
115	**The Big Gold Ring**
135	**The Boy Who Yelled "Wolf"**
155	**The Bad Wind and the 3 Clouds**

Independent Reading List

Note: You may schedule these selections for your children at any time during *Reading Mastery Plus,* Level 1.

Lesson	Title and Description
101	**Have You Seen My Cat?** Eric Carle. When a boy's cat disappears, his search leads him to many other cats, but none are his cat. In the end, a man and woman tell him where his cat is. (94 words)
116	**We Hide, You Seek.** Jose Aruego and Ariane Dewey. A nearsighted rhino who is playing a game of hide-and-seek accidentally finds the other animals who are hiding by stepping on them or startling them. Then the rhino hides in a unique hiding place. The other animals cannot find the rhino because the rhino hides in a group of other rhinos. (29 words)
131	**I Love You, Dear Dragon.** Margaret Hillert. A dragon accompanies a boy to school, makes valentines with him, and sits with him when the boy's father reads stories. The boy loves dear dragon. (275 words)
136	**If All the Seas Were One Sea.** Janina Domanska. The story suggests what would happen if all trees became one tree, if all axes were made into one ax, and if all people were combined to make one person. If all the seas were one sea, what a great sea that would be. (89 words)
141	**Blue Sea.** Robert Kalan. Bigger fish chase smaller fish through holes. The only fish that gets through the smallest hole is the littlest fish. (75 words)
153	**Green Eggs and Ham.** Dr. Seuss. Sam-I-Am repeatedly offers a character wearing a black hat green eggs and ham, but the character refuses to eat them until the end of the story. The character then discovers that green eggs and ham are good. (812 words)
156	**Go, Dog, Go!** Philip D. Eastman. Dogs of various shapes, colors, and sizes have a series of adventures in cars, on boats, and in trees. (518 words)
156	**The Farmer in the Dell** (Story length varies.)
157	**Mine's the Best.** Crosby N. Bonsall. Two boys have balloons at the beach. Each boy argues that his balloon is the best. As the boys argue, the balloons deflate. Then somebody comes along the beach with bundles of fully inflated ballons. (107 words)

APPENDIX G

Reading Vocabulary Word List

The number following each word refers to the lesson in which the word first appears as a reading vocabulary word. HW indicates that a word first appears in a "Hard Word" list in the Textbook.

a 2	bed 72	bus 74	clouds 145	dog 56
about 143	been 150	but 73	coat 54	doing 78
afraid 145	before 147	buttons 123	coats 53	don's 121
after 101	began 159	buy 124	cold 53	don't 108HW
again 158	behind 148	cake 116	come 86	door 148
all 126	bending 156	cakes 45	coming 147	dot 14
almost 140	bent 104	call 127HW	cooked 106	down 55
also 133	best 111	called 131	cop 54	dream 130
always 133	bet 132	calling 127HW	cops 59	dreaming 130
and 17	better 91	cam 151	corn 65	drop 121
another 106	big 72	came 19	could 133	dropped 121
answered 120	bigger 149	can't 131	couldn't 136	dropping 122
ant 15	bike 87	candy 132	cow 39	drops 122
any 135	bikes 114	cane 150	cows 63	duck 69
anyone 148	bill 96	cannot 123	creek 109	dug 80
are 58	bird 122	cap 149	cried 114	each 61
arf 106	bit 72	cape 149	cross 149	eagle 88
arm 61	bite 75	car 58	cry 105	ears 32
around 145	blow 121	card 84	crying 109	eat 4
art 59	blowing 159	careful 149	cut 13	eating 71
ask 115	bones 117	carmen 143	dad 81	either 93
asked 116	book 97	cars 61	dark 79	elephant 134
ate 5	books 107	cart 134	darker 159	elf 149
back 74	bottom 150	cats 63	day 92	even 102
bag 124	bout 141	caves 62	deer 83	ever 85
bags 122	box 87	charm 147	did 31	eyes 146
bake 116	boy 79	cheer 137	didn't 108HW	fade 16
baked 117	boys 85	cheered 137	dig 80	fall 126
bakes 116	bring 95	cheering 137	digging 79	falling 138
ball 125	bringing 95	chicks 69	digs 38	falls 134
balls 138	broke 94	children 143	dim 126	far 60
bank 111	broom 90	chip 91	dime 90	farm 60
bark 111	brother 83	chips 60	dinner 136	farmer 113HW
barked 107	brothers 123	chops 59	dip 55	farms 125
barking 106	brush 92	chore 90	dirty 151	fast 102
barn 98	brushed 92	chunks 132	dish 34	faster 105
be 72	brushing 99	circle 112	dive 76	fate 157
beans 85	bug 69	clean 151	do 63	father 146
because 122	bugs 72	cloud 140	does 151	fatter 101

feel 41	got 29	hot 9	let 66	mom 39
feet 2	grabbed 123	hound 145	let's 73	money 122
fell 104	grass 144	hounds 147	lick 21	moo 143
felt 136	ground 146	house 143	licks 37	mooing 144
fig 19	grow 159	how 39	lid 25	moon 91
fill 95	gum 33	hug 44	lie 150	mop 54
filled 97	had 11	hugged 156	life 103	more 65
fin 14	hall 126	hugs 51	lift 68	mother 83
find 81	ham 11	hunt 82	lifted 158	mountain 145
fine 96	hand 22	hunting 82	like 76	mouse 143
fire 160	hanging 147	I'll 129	liked 96	much 132
fishing 73	happened 159	I'm 150	likes 115	mud 15
fit 2	happy 112	ick 116	line 80	must 92
five 158	hard 108HW	ill 25	little 28	my 97
fix 154	has 14	inside 131	lived 80	nail 24
float 160	hat 14	into 79	lock 22	name 5
floor 129	hate 21	is 2	log 56	named 114
fly 97	hates 117	jane 112	look 98	names 38
flying 112	hats 35	jill 114	looked 101	near 82
fog 56	have 48	jump 93	looking 132	need 52
football 132	having 78	jumped 94	looks 107	needed 140
for 45	he 9	jumping 112	lots 50	never 85
forest 160	head 103	jumps 94	loud 140	next 110
found 148	hear 117	just 140	love 83	nine 96
fox 87	hears 32	keep 153	loved 91	no 44
from 101	held 122	kept 125	mack 8	nod 43
full 149	help 106	kicked 135	made 16	nose 46
fun 12	helped 106	kicks 43	magic 146	note pad 119
funny 106	her 84	kind 116	mail 23	now 37
game 23	here 65	kiss 44	main 126	nut 13
games 38	herself 146	kissed 70	make 160	nuts 48
gate 41	hid 151	kit 155	maker 159	oats 53
gates 41	hide 151	kite 155	making 159	of 47
gave 50	him 43	kites 157	mall 129	off 124
get 66	himself 136	kitten 47	many 149	oh 130
getting 72	his 9	know 158	mark 156	old 46
girl 62	hit 9	lady 125	meal 118	on 1
give 50	hits 43	lake 65	mean 19	once 145
glad 144	hitting 88	land 22	meat 20	one 118
glasses 134	hold 49	landed 158	meets 130	only 147
go 45	holding 152	last 129	men 68	open 147
goat 52	hole 80	late 20	met 66	opened 148
goats 53	home 64	leaf 73	miles 126	or 45
goes 130	hop 86	leave 118	mill 25	other 83
going 70	hope 130	led 79	miss 29	ouch 147
gold 97	horn 121	left 128	mitt 10	our 143
good 115	horse 107	legs 121	mole 129	out 140

tiger 101	tree 101	was 40	wind 157	**FAST START WORDS**
tim 159	tried 114	water 112	wins 34	ad . . . . FS 16
time 78	trip 125	waves 62	wipe 104	am . . . . FS 10
times 99	try 109	we 24	wish 35	an . . . . FS 21
tired 150	trying 108HW	we'll 157	with 36	at . . . . FS 22
to 51	tub 75	week 133	woke 150	can . . . . FS 23
today 160	tug 96	well 118	won't 158	cat . . . . FS 22
told 80	two 159	went 66	wood 157	dan . . . . FS 21
took 99	under 101	were 127HW	word 134	dear . . . . FS 19
toot 122	up 68	wet 66	work 153	ear . . . . FS 12
tooth 99	us 15	what 111	would 131	fan . . . . FS 23
top 54	very 110	when 99	wouldn't 136	fat . . . . FS 22
topper 87	walk 74	where 99	yard 80	fear . . . . FS 18
tops 64	walked 91	while 160	years 112	feed . . . . . . FS 14
tore 93	wall 140	white 99	yelled 101	if . . . . FS 15
touch 98	walter 136	who 120	yellow 125	in . . . . FS 21
touched 148	walter's 138	why 100	yes 80	is . . . . FS 18
touching 133	want 123	wife 103	you 79	it . . . . FS 19
toy 86	wanted 125	will 25	you'll 157	mad . . . . FS 16
toys 85	wants 141	win 37	your 96	man . . . . FS 25
trapped 160				me . . . . FS 11
				neat . . . . . . FS 24
				not . . . . FS 24
				ram . . . . FS 11
				ran . . . . FS 21
				rat . . . . FS 23
				read . . . . . . FS 14
				rock . . . . FS 23
				sad . . . . FS 12
				see . . . . FS 10
				seed . . . . . . FS 12
				seem . . . . . . FS 13
				sit . . . . FS 19
				tear . . . . FS 20
				that . . . . FS 21
				the . . . . FS 17
				tin . . . . FS 25